IMAGES
of America

BASEBALL IN NORTH CAROLINA'S PIEDMONT

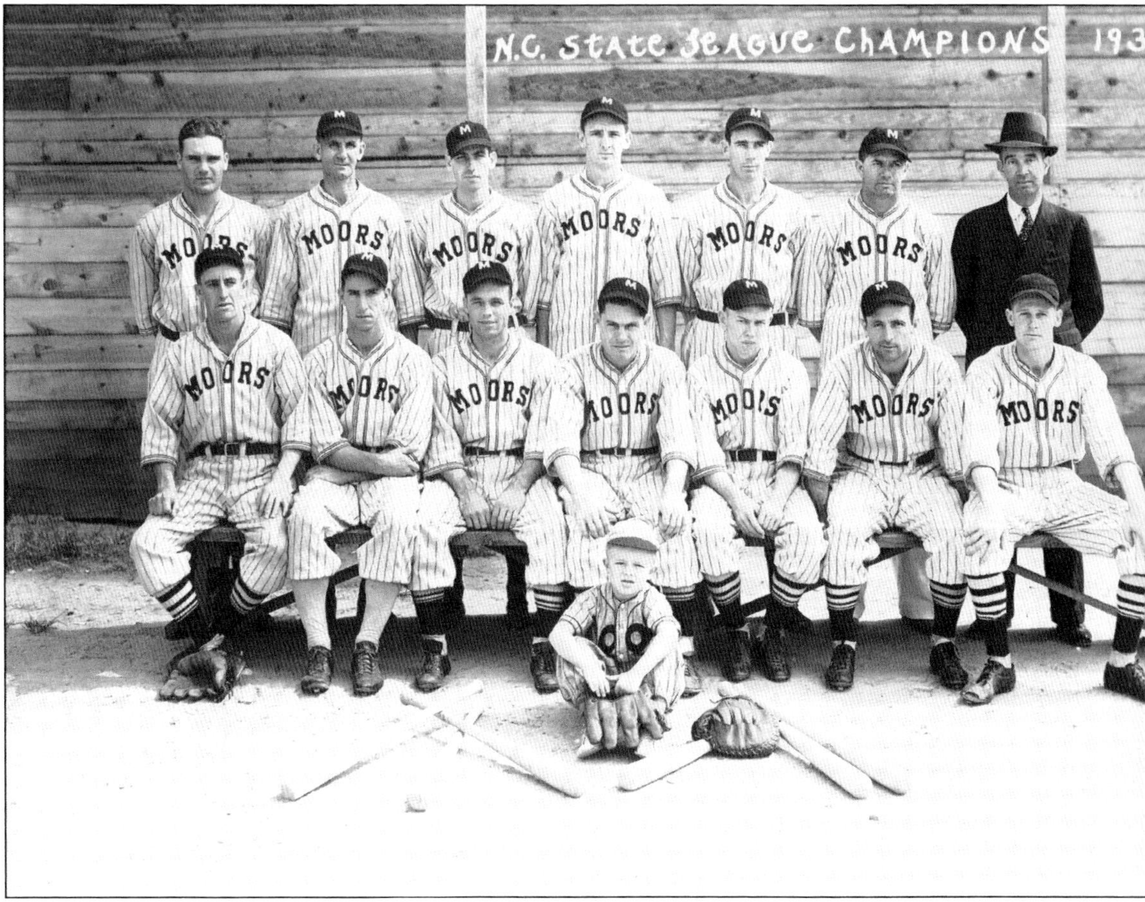

The 1937 Mooresville Moors are one of the hundreds of professional minor league teams that have called North Carolina home. Former big leaguer Jim Poole was the playing manager for the Moors that season and led his team to the North Carolina State League title with a 74-35 record. In this photo the batboy is Freddie Clark. From left to right are the following: (front row) Wallace Godwin, Charlie Robinson, Johnny Hicks, Luther Whitlock, Paul Blair, Selby Keller, and Charlie Frye; (back row) Richard Robinson, Jim Poole (manager), Leonard White, Joe Rucido, Clyde Teague, Tripp Sigmon, and C.F. Clark (president). (Courtesy of Norman Small.)

(*on the cover*) The 1939 Durham Bulls, a farm club of the Cincinnati Reds, competed in the Piedmont League. Pictured from left to right are (front row) Everett Hill, Van Harrington, Wayne Blackburn, Don Bird, and Tom Oliver; (middle row) three unidentified players, Oscar Roettger, Allen Hunt, Elmer Riddle, and Pudge Powers; (back row) Charles Aleno, Barney DeForge, Charles Hawley, Edwin Ignasiak, Harry Wolfe, and two unidentified players. (Courtesy of Miles Wolff.)

IMAGES
of America

Baseball in North Carolina's Piedmont

Chris Holaday

ARCADIA
PUBLISHING

ISBN 978-0-7385-1413-0

Published by Arcadia Publishing
Charleston, South Carolina

Printed in the United States of America

Library of Congress Catalog Card Number: 2001096800

For all general information contact Arcadia Publishing at:
Telephone 843-853-2070
Fax 843-853-0044
E-mail sales@arcadiapublishing.com
For customer service and orders:
Toll-Free 1-888-313-2665

Visit us on the Internet at www.arcadiapublishing.com

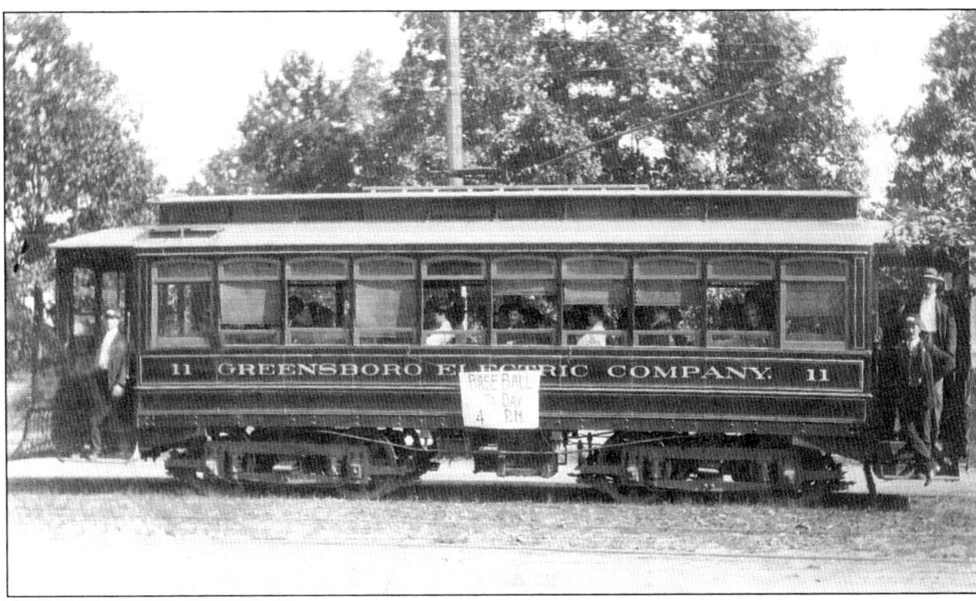

In the days before television and even movie theaters, baseball games were the primary source of entertainment in most towns. In this *c.* 1910 photo, a Greensboro trolley travels the city's rails with a sign announcing that day's game. (Courtesy of Greensboro Historical Museum Archives.)

CONTENTS

ACKNOWLEDGMENTS

There are many people who have helped in the creation of this book and deserve my thanks. Dozens of former baseball players took the time to dig through closets and attics to find old photos for me. Hopefully the credit line after each photo will serve as an appropriate acknowledgement of these individuals. Several museums were of great assistance in this project, including the Greensboro Historical Museum and the High Point Museum. I would also like to thank Steve Massengill with the North Carolina Department of Archives and History and Lynn and Jim Rumley with the Cooleemee Textile Heritage Center. Bitsy McKee was an immense help with the technical aspects of putting this book together and Laura Daniels at Arcadia Publishing deserves many thanks for her guidance and patience.

Many of the images in this book have been collected over the course of several years and some of the former players who were kind enough to share their scrapbooks with me have passed away. They may be gone, but I hope that players like Norman Small, Crash Davis, Cecil "Turkey" Tyson, Gaither Riley, and others will live on in these pages.

INTRODUCTION

In French, the name means "foot of the mountains," but the Piedmont is the geographical area of several southeastern states that actually fall between the elevations of 300 and 1,500 feet. The Piedmont's eastern border is traditionally the Fall Line, the point at which rivers fall from the rocky Piedmont onto the flat and sandy Coastal Plain. For the purpose of this book, the eastern boundary of the region was roughly chosen as one that follows the path of Interstate 95. On the other side of the state, a line was drawn that runs (starting in the south) just west of the towns of Forest City, Hickory, and Mount Airy.

In North Carolina, most of the state's manufacturing industry has historically been centered in the Piedmont. Most of the state's population, more than the other two regions combined, resides in this area as well. Because of this, it has also been home to a rich heritage in the game of baseball, a sport popular in the Piedmont for more than a century.

In the early years of the 20th century, most little boys growing up in the Piedmont learned to play baseball. Whether it was on a rural farm field or a vacant lot in the city, boys could be found playing baseball and dreaming of big league stardom. Today, with the growth of sports like soccer, there are more choices for youngsters who want to get involved in athletics, but baseball continues to flourish and the game is extremely popular from tee ball to Little League and beyond.

North Carolina has an abundance of colleges and universities, and baseball at that level has always been popular as well. From the big Division I universities like the University of North Carolina at Chapel Hill and Duke University right down to small colleges like Guilford and Catawba, baseball has always been an important part of campus life. In the years before World War II, some collegiate baseball rivalries were among the biggest sporting events in the state. One example of this was the annual Easter Monday game between Wake Forest and North Carolina State that took place for more than 50 years. In an area now more famous for its top-level collegiate basketball, baseball isn't quite what it used to be, but area colleges and universities continue to field great teams and produce players that go on to the major leagues.

Up until the 1950s, nearly every town and crossroads in the Piedmont had some sort of baseball team. Groups of men and boys would get together to represent their community for Saturday games. Sometimes their uniforms didn't match and their ball fields were a bit overgrown, but many of these teams had surprisingly large followings.

The next step up from the town teams were the industrial league teams, with the workers of the textile mills as the most prominent participants. These baseball teams provided entertainment to company employees and helped develop an important sense of community. Mill workers would turn out by the hundreds—and sometimes thousands—to watch their company's team take on the mill from a nearby town. The level of competition in the textile leagues could be fierce. Companies would hire new employees solely based on their baseball abilities. Often they were given jobs in the mill that involved very little work, but once it was time for baseball they were supposed to earn their real pay on the diamond.

Though North Carolina has never had its own major league team, it has nonetheless been the home of dozens of professional minor league teams. As the population of the state grew in the early years of the 20th century, professional baseball as entertainment became economically feasible. Beginning in cities like Charlotte, Durham, and Greensboro, the pro game soon spread and by the 1930s it was being played even in small towns like Mayodan and Landis. Many of these teams were affiliated with major league clubs that served to develop young talent by bringing players along one step at a time. If a club thought a player had made progress, they might promote him to a higher level. Eventually the best players would make it to the big leagues. Other minor league clubs in the Piedmont were independent and made their money by selling promising young players to the big league clubs. The minor leagues died out in many small towns by the early 1950s (primarily because of the growth of television), but they are still going strong in many of the larger cities. Area teams including the Durham Bulls, who had an attendance total of more than 500,000 fans in 2001, and the Carolina Mudcats, who play in the Wake County town of Zebulon, are among the most successful in the country.

All of the levels at which the game has been played in the region combine to make the history of baseball in the North Carolina Piedmont unique. Hopefully the photos in this book have captured some of the special qualities of the game and will help preserve the memories.

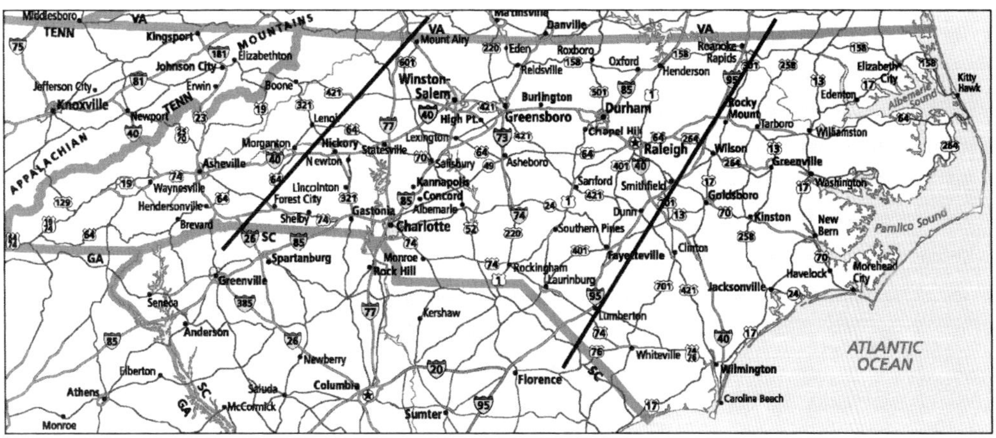

The two lines on this map roughly define the Piedmont, the section of North Carolina covered in this book. Encompassing most of the states larger cities including Charlotte, Durham, Greensboro, Winston-Salem, and Raleigh, this area has a tremendously rich history in the game of baseball.

One

The Youth Game

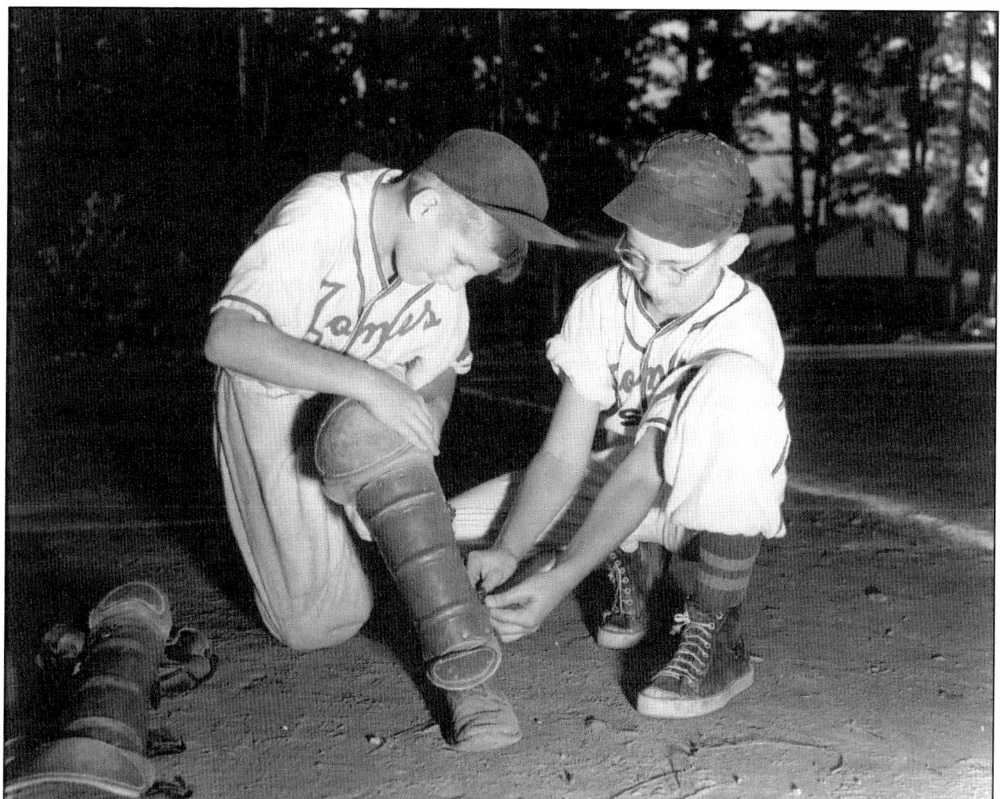

Two unidentified young boys prepare for a game of baseball in the Raleigh area c. 1950. (Courtesy of the North Carolina Department of Archives and History.)

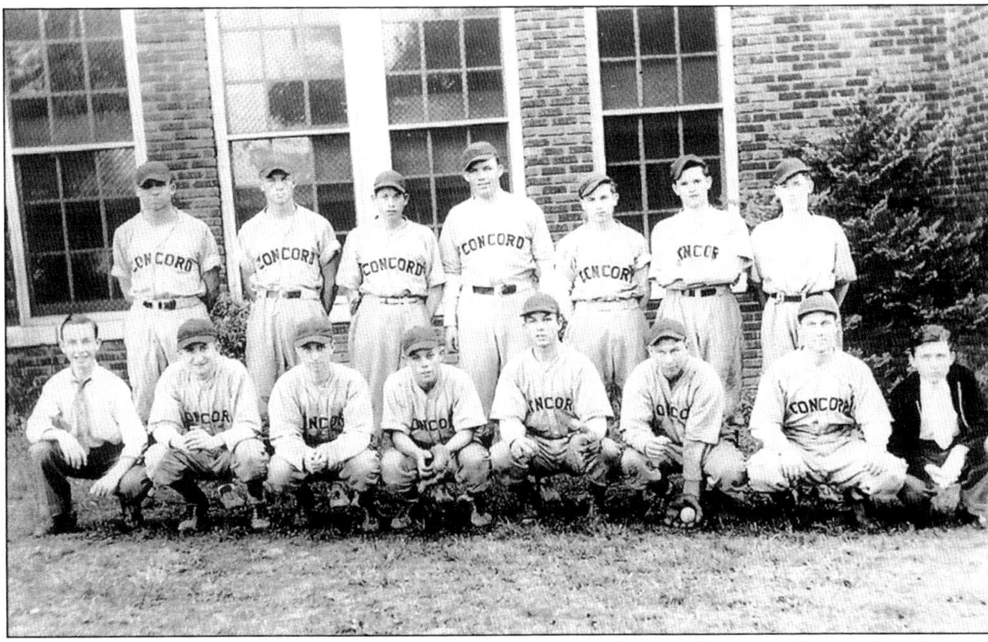

This 1936 Concord High School team was champion of the Southern Piedmont Conference. The team members pictured here, from left to right, are (front row) Jimmy Alexander, L.C. Harmon, Bill Morrison, Fred Walters, Earl Walters, "Boney" Greene, "Lefty" Bratton, and Hoy Lippard; (back row) Jim Beaver, "Shorty" Allred, Marshall Goldston, Jim Faulkenberry, Johnny Jones, Earl Williams, and Bedford Biles. (Courtesy of George Patterson.)

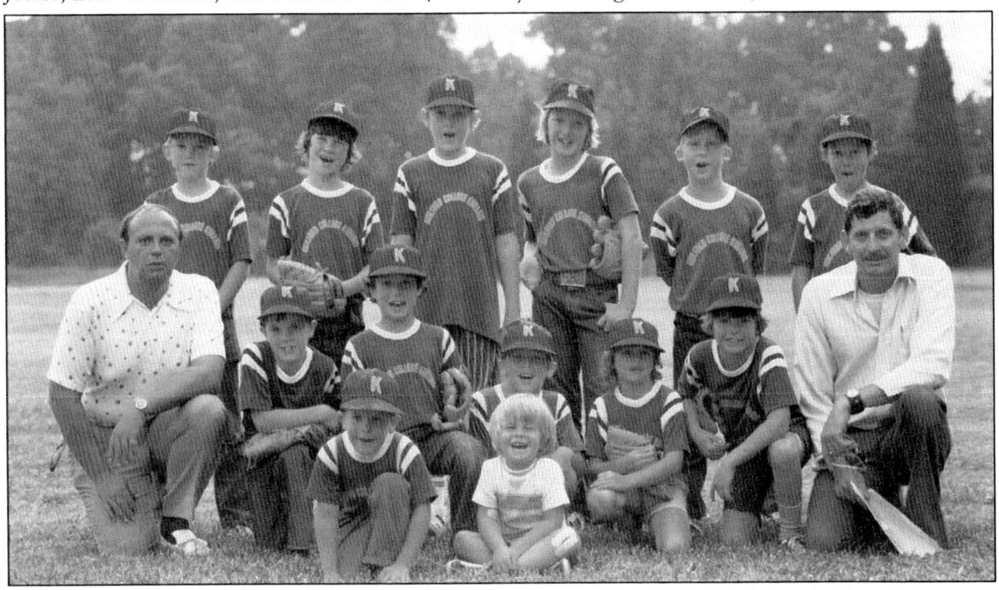

Young players just learning the game of baseball often play tee ball, where the batter hits the ball off a tee instead of being pitched to. This is the 1975 Guilford College Kiwanis, a tee ball team from Greensboro. From left to right are the following: (front row) Coach Holland, Chad Blake, unidentified, Daren Chilton, Derrick Holland, Robbie Mazoli, and Coach Mazoli; (back row) Robert Schenk, Grant Burns, Scott Gollar, Kevin Wood, Allan Boyd, and Marty Fowler. The batboys are Justin Holland and Chuck Mazoli. (Courtesy of Allan Boyd.)

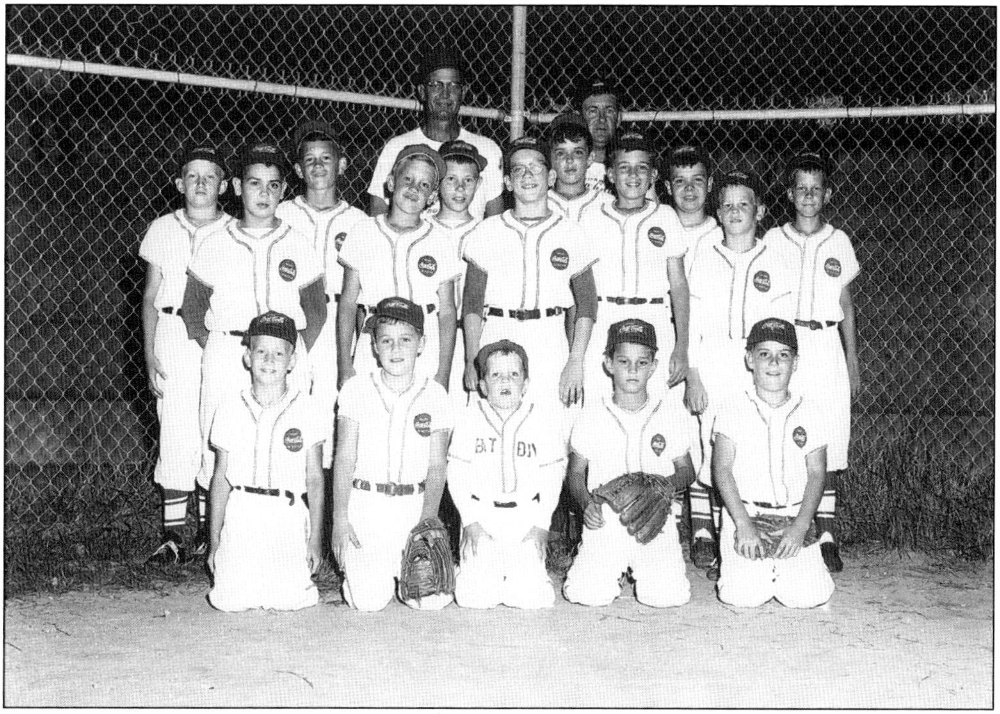

The two youth teams shown on this page competed in Raleigh's Western Boulevard Little League in 1964. Founded in 1939, Little League has helped thousands of boys and girls learn and enjoy the game of baseball. (Courtesy of the North Carolina Department of Archives and History.)

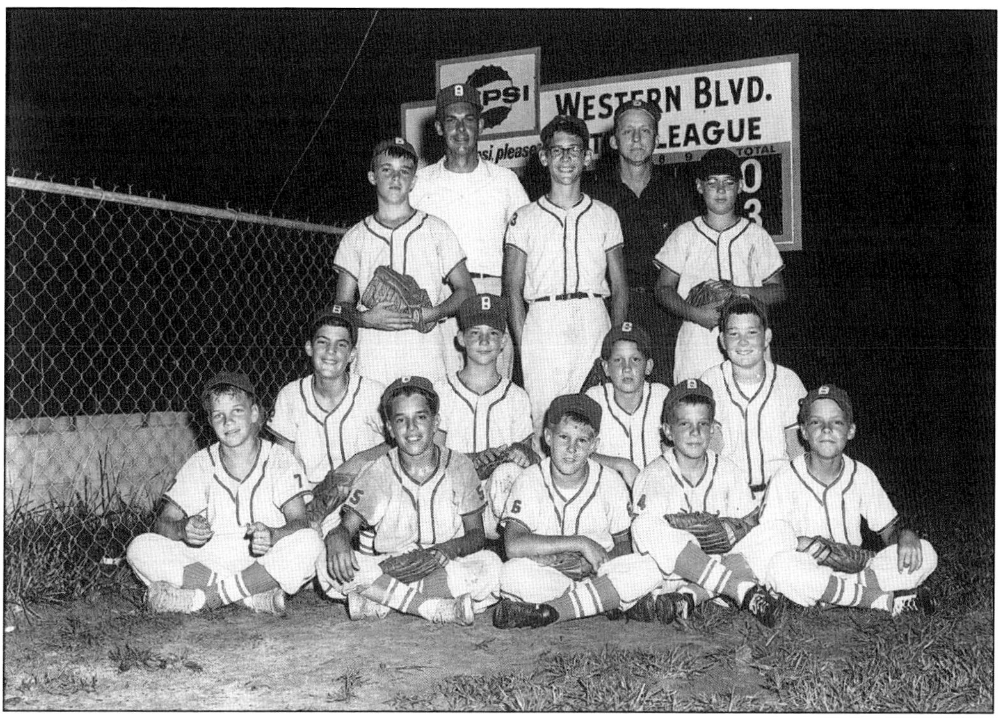

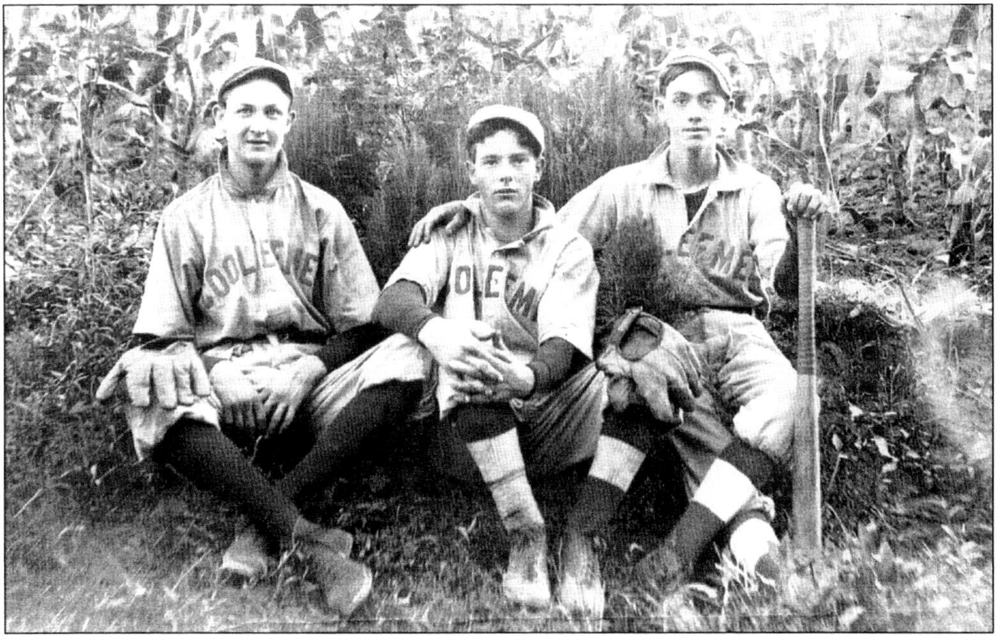

This photo of high school players from Cooleemee was taken *c.* 1915. The players, from left to right, are Noah Grimes, Oscar "Red" Vogler and Ray Barnhart. (Courtesy of Cooleemee Textile Heritage Center Archives.)

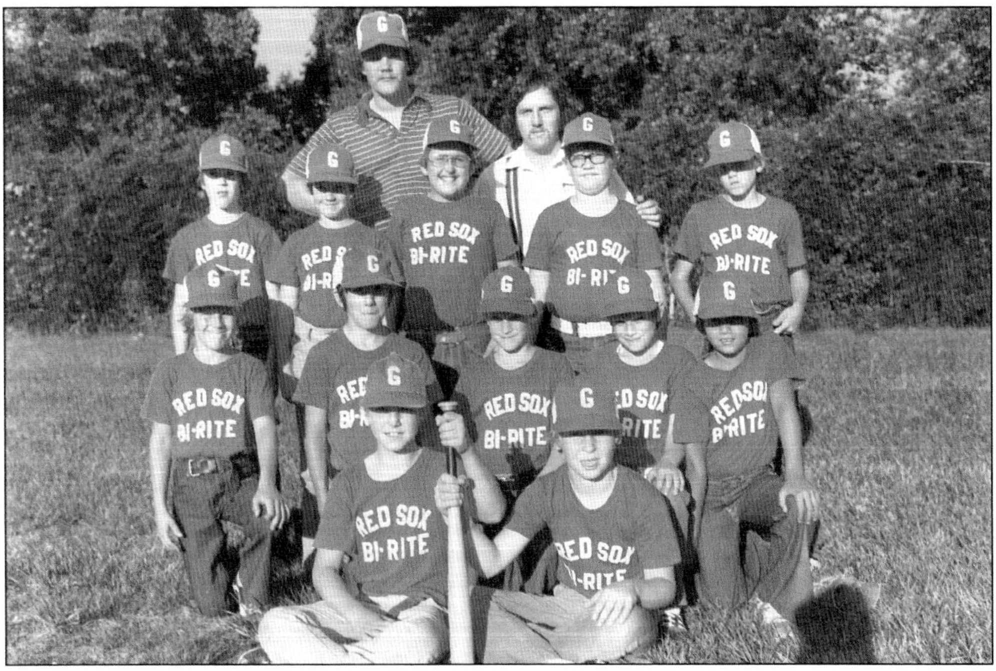

The 1976 Bi-Rite Red Sox were a Greensboro-area Little League team. In this photograph are, from left to right, as follows: (first row) Keith Houck and Allan Boyd; (second row) Mike ?, Jeff Campbell, Daniel Wilhoit, David Wilhoit, and Amy ?; (third row) Ken Smith, Martha Hogan, Rusty ?, Bill Courtney, and David Detheridge; (fourth row) Coach Steve Wyrick and Coach Tim Smith. (Courtesy of Allan Boyd.)

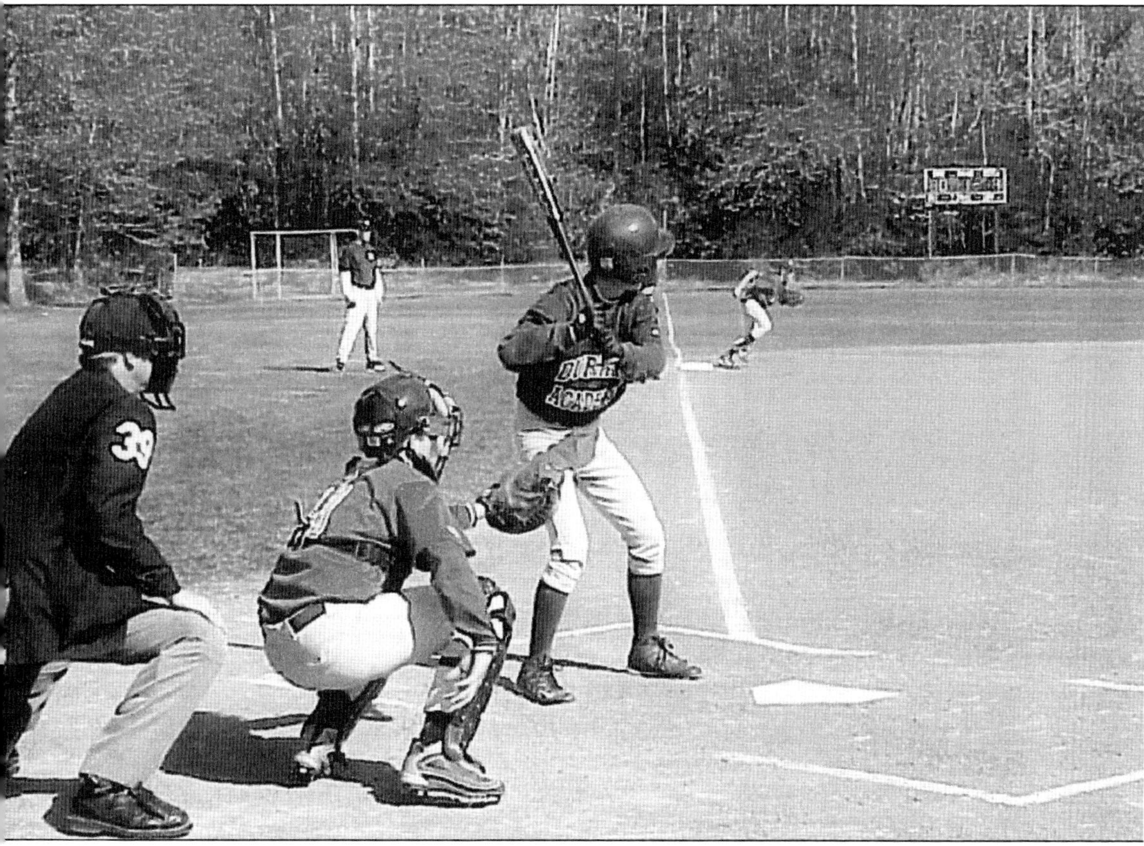

Jeff Speir, a member of the Durham Academy junior varsity team, waits for the pitch in a 2001 game against Cary Academy while coach Rich Nowalk watches from the third base box. The Cavaliers, led by head coach Torsie Judkins, finished the season with a 7-4 record. High school baseball in North Carolina has always been highly competitive and most players hone their skills at the junior varsity level before moving up to the varsity. (Courtesy of Rich Nowalk.)

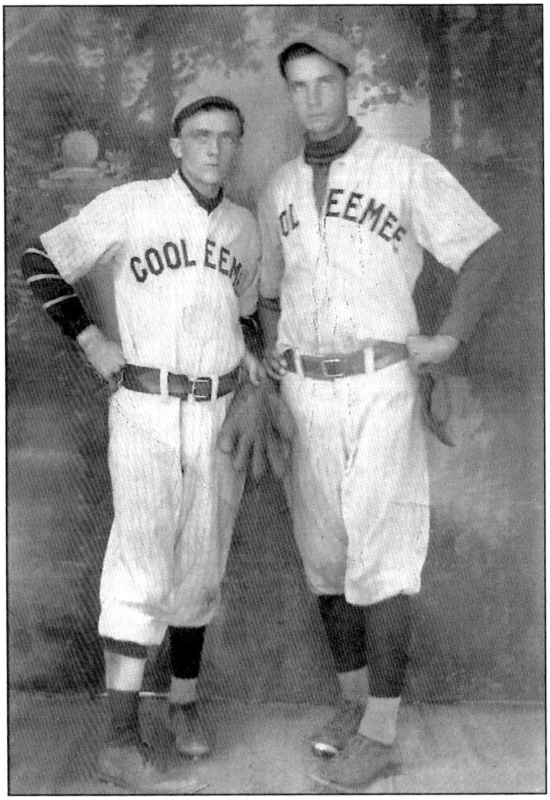

Clay Alexander and Ralph Poole pose for a studio portrait in their Cooleemee baseball uniforms, sometime around 1920. (Courtesy of Cooleemee Textile Heritage Center Archives.)

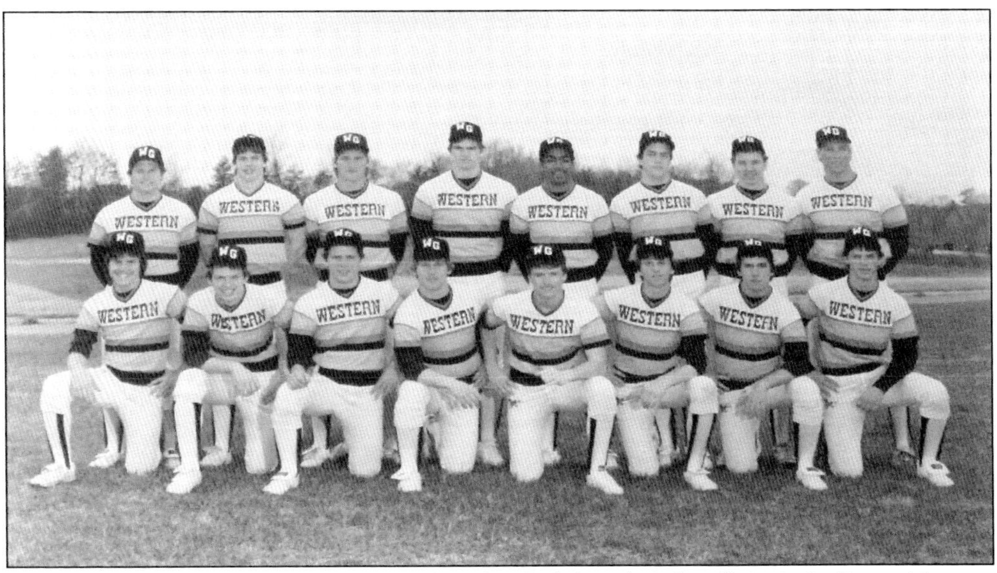

This team from Western Guilford High School defeated Asheville's A.C. Reynolds, two games to none, to win the 1984 AAA State Championship. From left to right are the following: (front row) Beau Mann, Jeff Leonard, Bryan Causey, Allan Boyd, Jimmy Duncan, Matt Bowman, Jeff Campbell, and Jason Stewart; (back row) Coach Brett Stell, Scott Muscat, Eddie Eudy, Jerry Russell, Tony Chavis, David Page, Craig Lett, and Coach Mark Maudhouse. (Courtesy of Allan Boyd.)

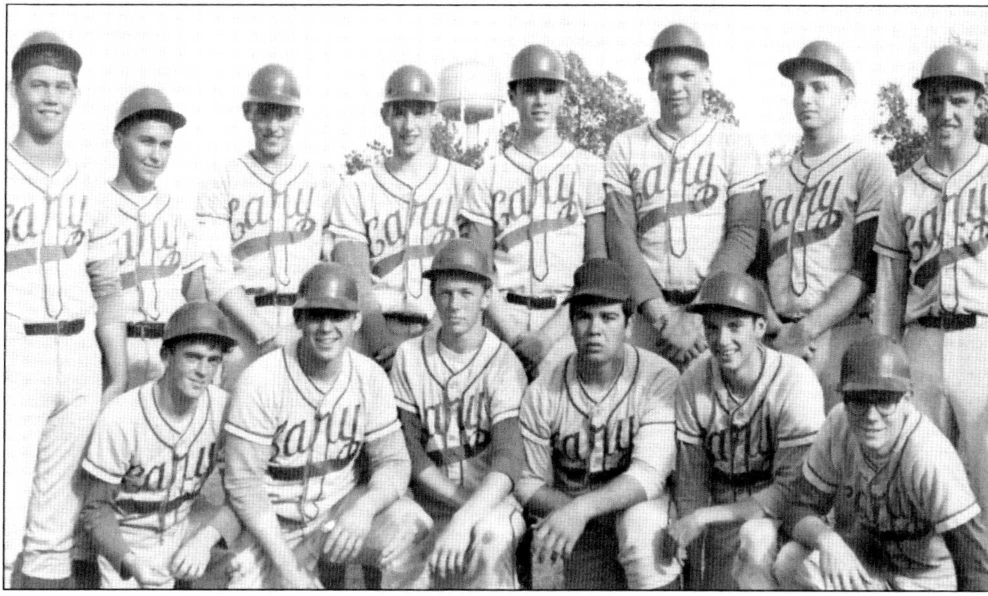

Over the years, Cary High School has fielded some great baseball teams. The members of the 1969 squad, from left to right, are (front row) Yates Horton, Charlie Prince, Dennis Eason, Tommy Holderfield, Craig Jones, and Don Hendricks; (back row) Bobby Mitchell, Rex Frazier, Dan Stewart, Bill Briggs, Tom Beebe, Mike Thomas, Johnny McMillan, and Gerald Pollard. (From the collection of the author.)

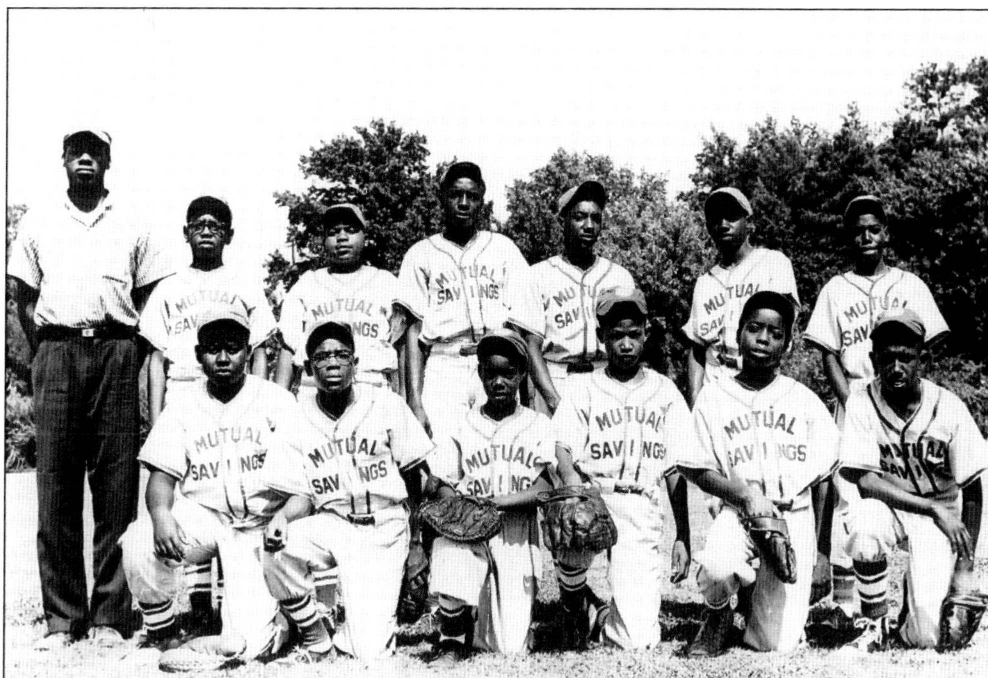

This 1957 photo shows the Mutual Savings and Loan Bank of Durham's youth baseball team, which was sponsored by John Stewart at John Avery's Boy's Club in Durham. (Courtesy of the North Carolina Department of Archives and History.)

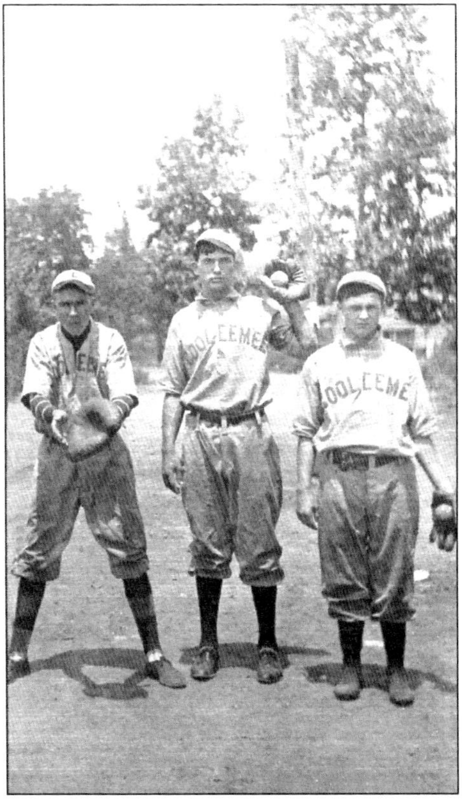

A trio of serious-looking high school players from the Davie County town of Cooleemee are pictured here in this c. 1920 photo. (Courtesy of Cooleemee Textile Heritage Center Archives.)

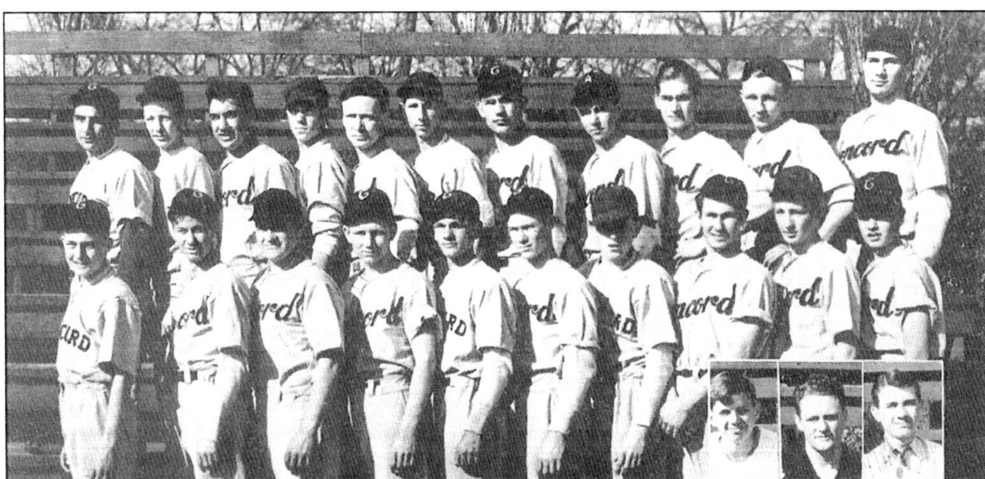

Many members of the 1942 Concord High School Spiders were off to the military as soon as the school year ended. From left to right are the following: (front row) Joe Dorton, "Jeep" Montooth, Bill Cook, Johnny Cranford, Jack Bratton, Bob Harvey, George Fisher, Junior Farrington, Gerald "Hank" Utley, and Gice Allen; (back row) Paul Boulus, Ed Utley, Taffy Williams, John Robinson, Jim Goodman, Harry Winecoff, "Doc" Mullis, Jimmy Shaffer, Ted Pinner, "Footsie" Bost, and Clyde Biggers; (inset) Coach Harry Hollingsworth, Turk Pharr (manager), and Coy McDaniel (assistant manager). (Courtesy of Hank Utley.)

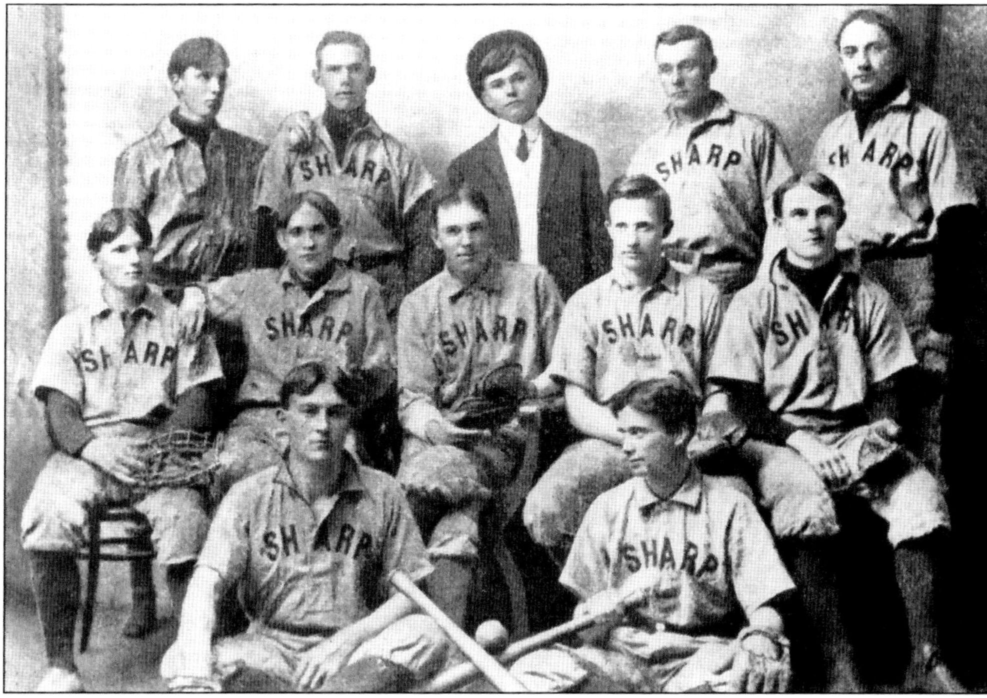

In 1900, J.M. Sharp established Sharp Institute, a co-educational day and boarding school in Rockingham County. It opened with 50 students, but enrollment climbed to 225 by 1906 as the school's reputation as one of the area's best preparatory institutions grew. Unfortunately, Sharp Institute burned in 1907 and was not reopened. This photo is of the school's 1903 baseball team. (Courtesy of the North Carolina Department of Archives and History.)

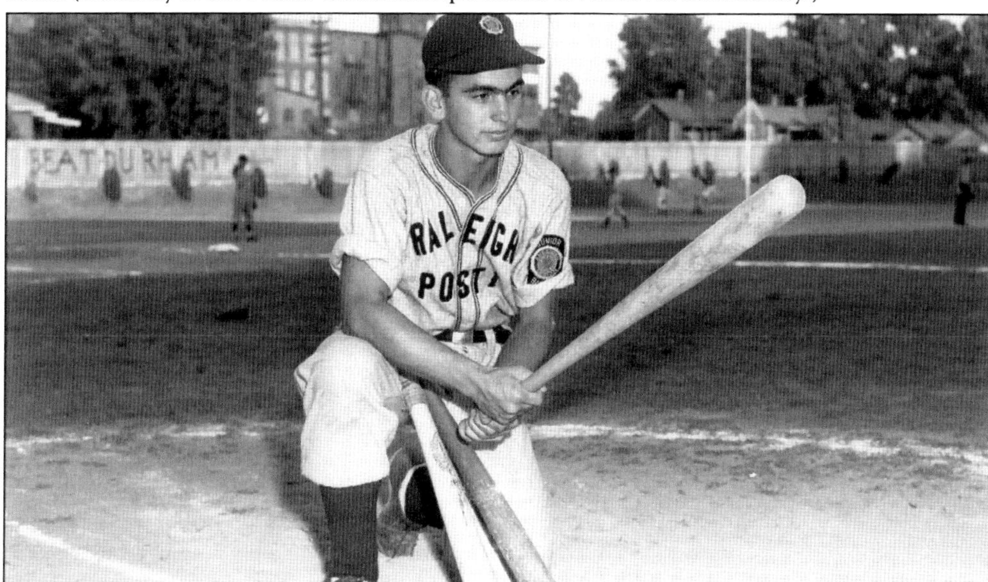

Many high school players take part in summer baseball sponsored by the American Legion. This photo of an unidentified player from an American Legion post team in Raleigh was taken in the late 1940s. (Courtesy of the North Carolina Department of Archives and History.)

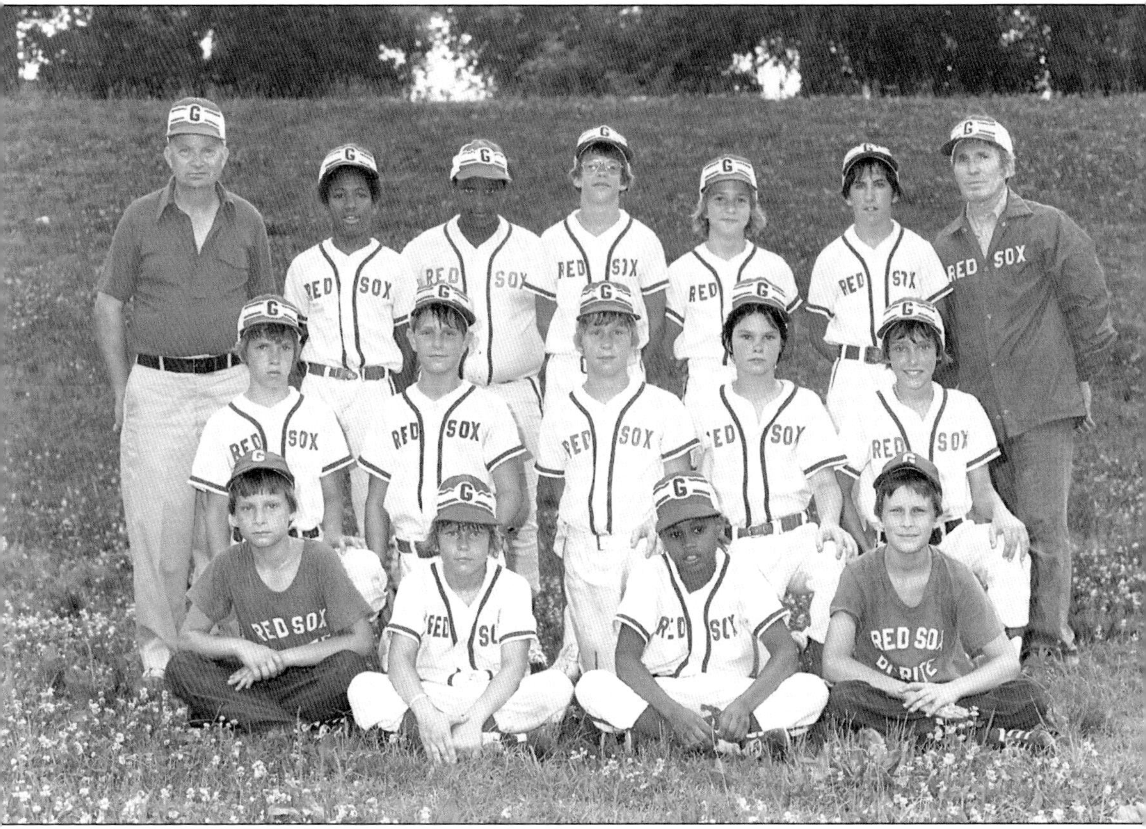

The 1977 Guilford Red Sox were a select Little League team composed of the better players from the Guilford College area of Greensboro. From left to right are the following: (front row) David Wilhoit, Mike Fidishun, Pat Byrd, and Daniel Wilhoit; (middle row) Brent Fewell, Keith Houck, Allan Boyd, Farron Welborn, and Ronnie Hamilton; (back row) Coach Wilhoit, Carlos Greer, Lacy Morehead, Todd Chadwick, Jeff Campbell, and Coach Stumpy Brown. (Courtesy of Allan Boyd.)

Two

THE COLLEGIANS

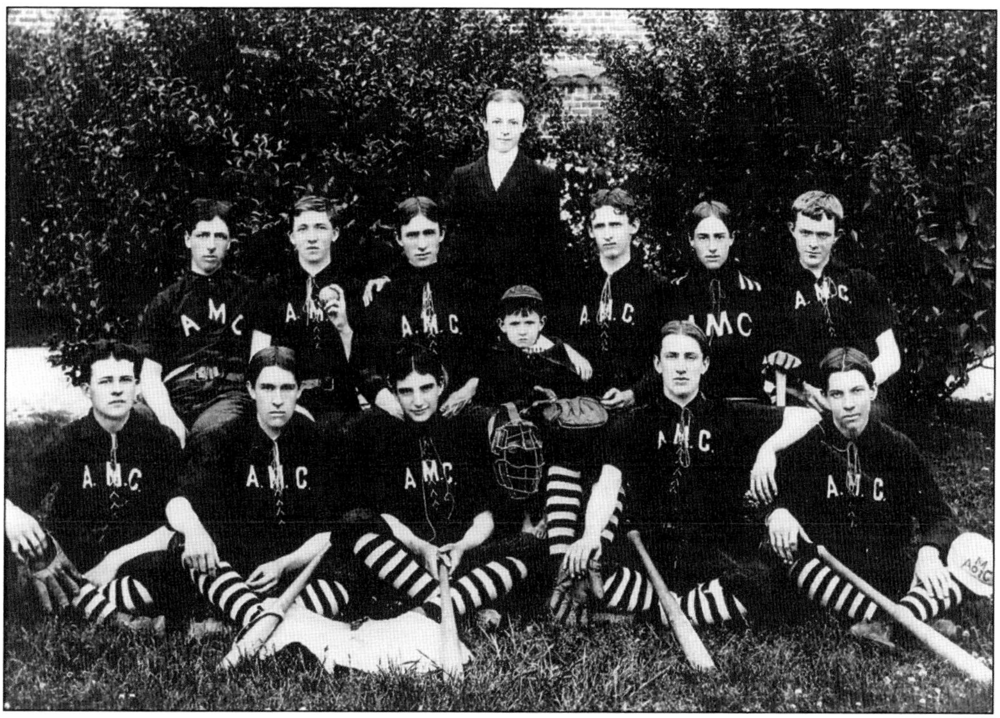

One of the early baseball teams to represent North Carolina A&M College, the school now known as North Carolina State University, was this one from 1899. The players, from left to right, are (front row) Henry Dorsette, F.D. Ross, Paul Faison, William Caserly, and F.W. Bonitz; (back row) W.H. Person, Ed Person, Bill Fenner, Ned Wood (manager), J.W. Shore, Leslie Norman, and Colon Love. The mascot is Wallace Riddick. (Courtesy of the University Archives, North Carolina State University Libraries.)

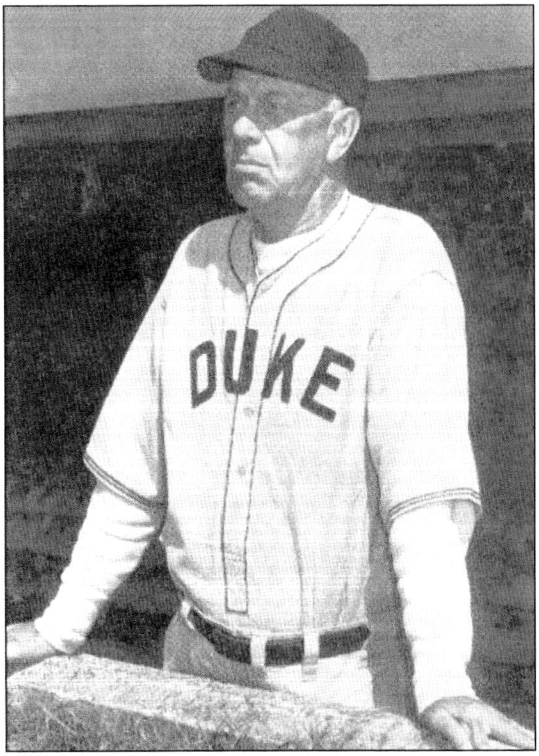

Former big league pitcher Jack Coombs coached the Duke Blue Devils from 1929 through 1952. A former star pitcher who won 31 games in the 1909 season for the Philadelphia Athletics and had a 5-0 record in World Series play, Coombs had great success at Duke. During his 24 seasons at the helm his teams had a combined record of 381-171-3, won six Southern Conference championships, and produced 47 major league players. (From the collection of the author.)

Members of the Wake Forest College baseball team posed for this photo c. 1900. Just a few years earlier, in May of 1891, Wake Forest had defeated the University of North Carolina by the score of 10-7 in 11 innings in the first official intercollegiate baseball game ever played in the state of North Carolina. (Courtesy of the North Carolina Department of Archives and History.)

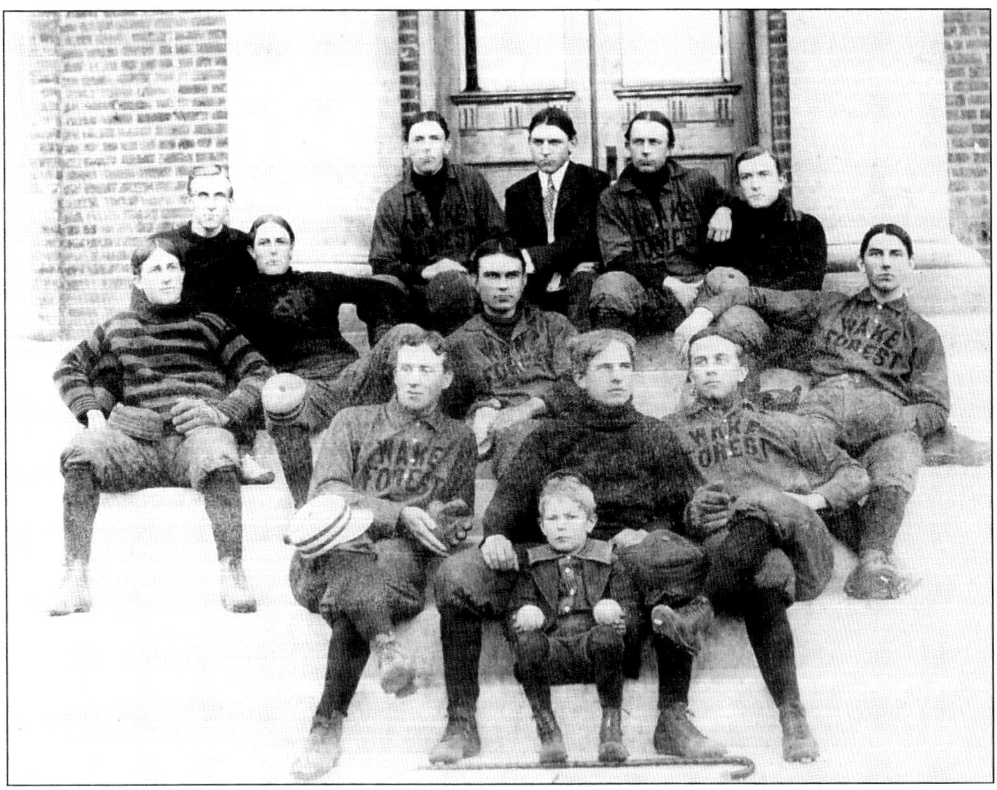

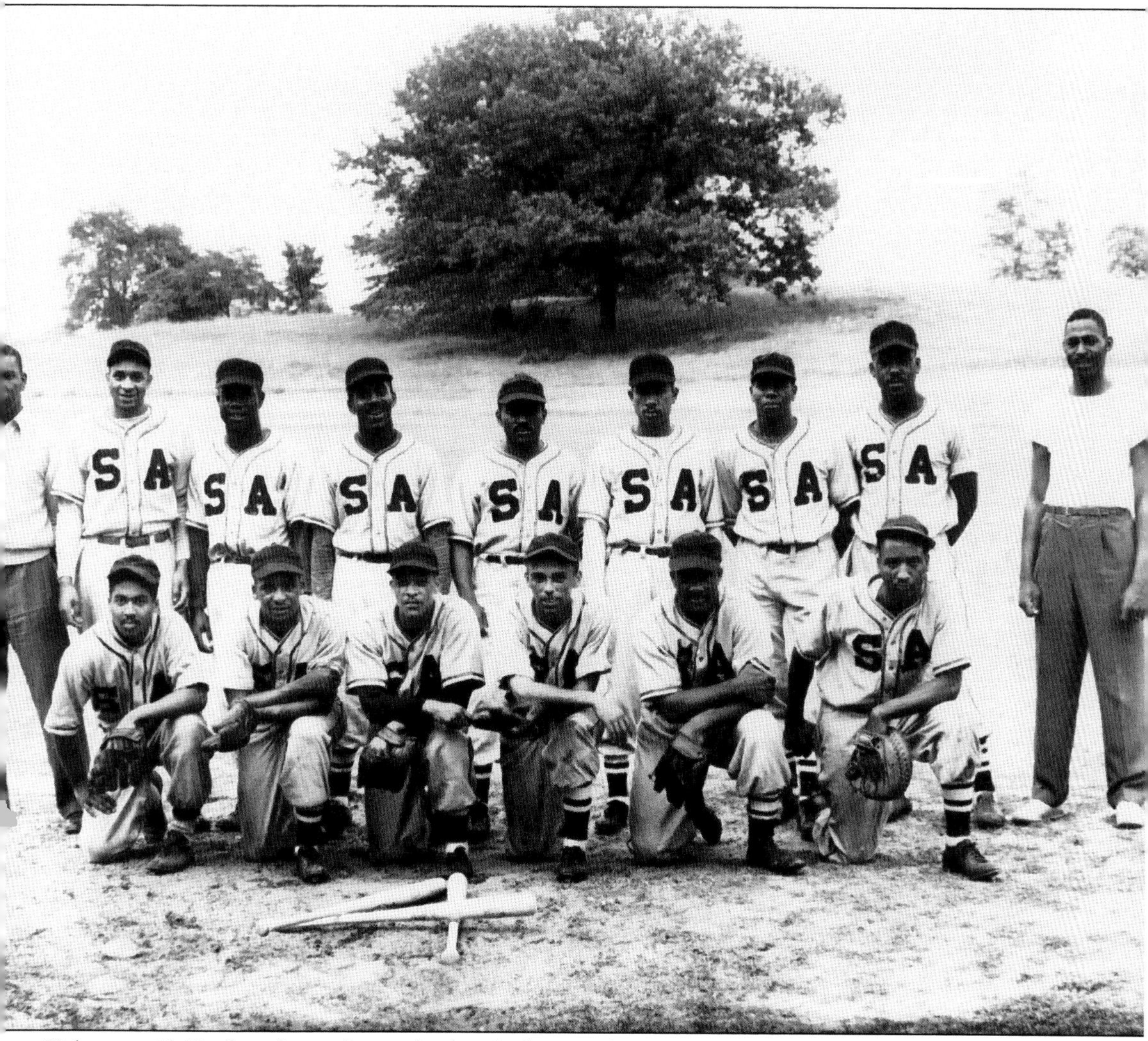

Taken in 1949, this photo shows the baseball team from St. Augustine's College in Raleigh. Founded in 1867 by the Episcopal Church for the education of freed slaves, St. Augustine's has become one of the country's most highly respected private, historically black institutions of higher learning. Currently the school's baseball teams compete in the Central Intercollegiate Athletic Association (NCAA Division II), a conference that also includes inter-city rival Shaw University. (Courtesy of the North Carolina Department of Archives and History.)

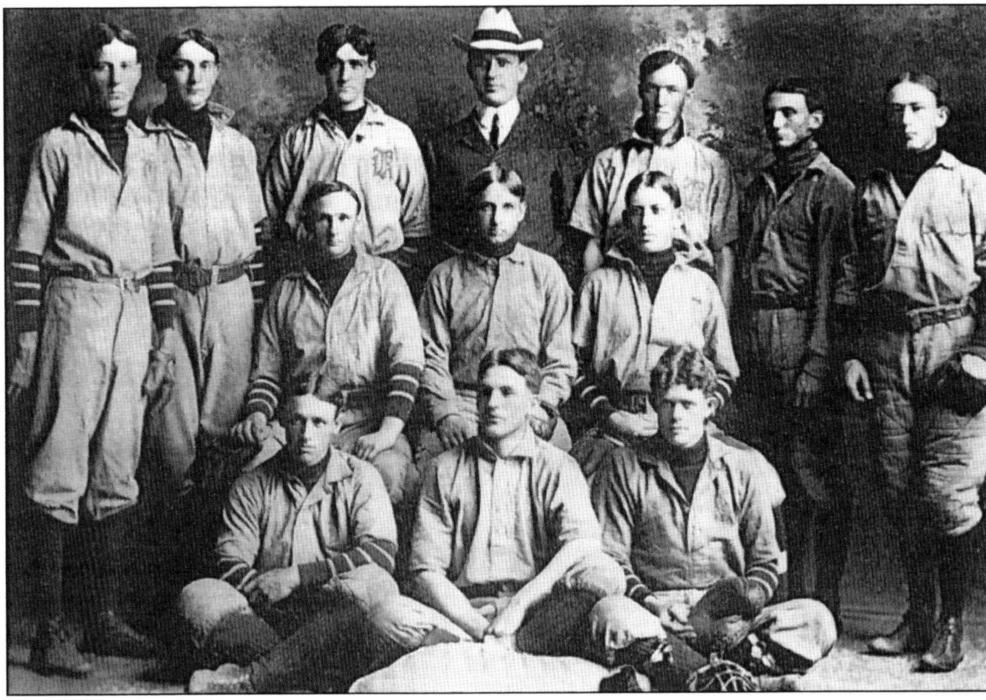

Though the players on this 1903 North Carolina A&M baseball team are unidentified, the team manager was O. Max Gardner (back row, center), who would serve as governor of North Carolina from 1929 to 1933. (Courtesy of the University Archives, North Carolina State University Libraries.)

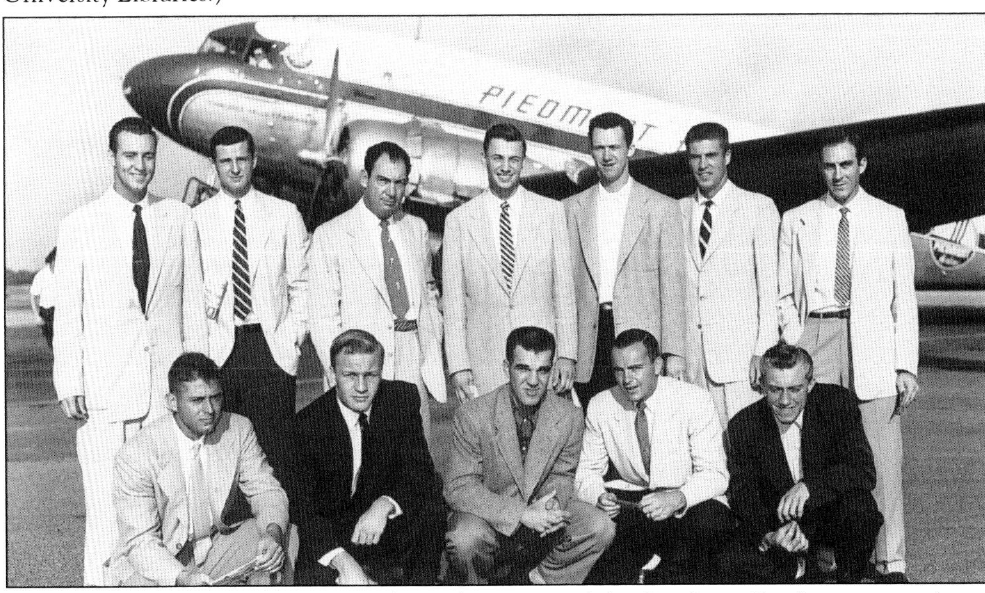

Duke University baseball team members, champions of the Southern Conference, are shown here at the Raleigh-Durham Airport preparing to leave for the NCAA baseball tournament on June 14, 1953. Duke played well at the Omaha, Nebraska tournament and defeated Northern Colorado, but lost each of their games to Texas and Boston College by one run. (Courtesy of the North Carolina Department of Archives and History.)

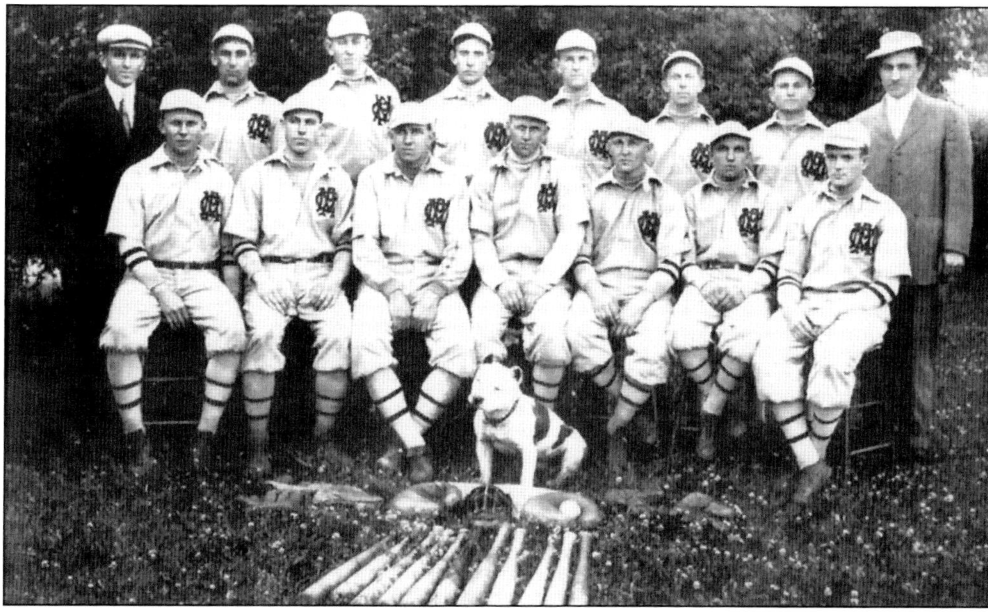

The 1910 North Carolina A&M team finished the season as "Champions of the South" with a 16-1-3 record. The star of the team was first baseman Dave Robertson, who would go on to enjoy several good seasons in the major leagues, primarily with the New York Giants. From left to right are the following: (front row) ? Black, ? Hartsell, Dave Robertson, ? Sexton, D.W. Seifert, ? Brown, and ? Speer; (back row) J.L. Springs (manager), ? Bost, ? Riddick, ? Stafford, ? Council, ? Freeman, ? Ross, and Coach Frank Thompson. (Courtesy of the University Archives, North Carolina State University Libraries.)

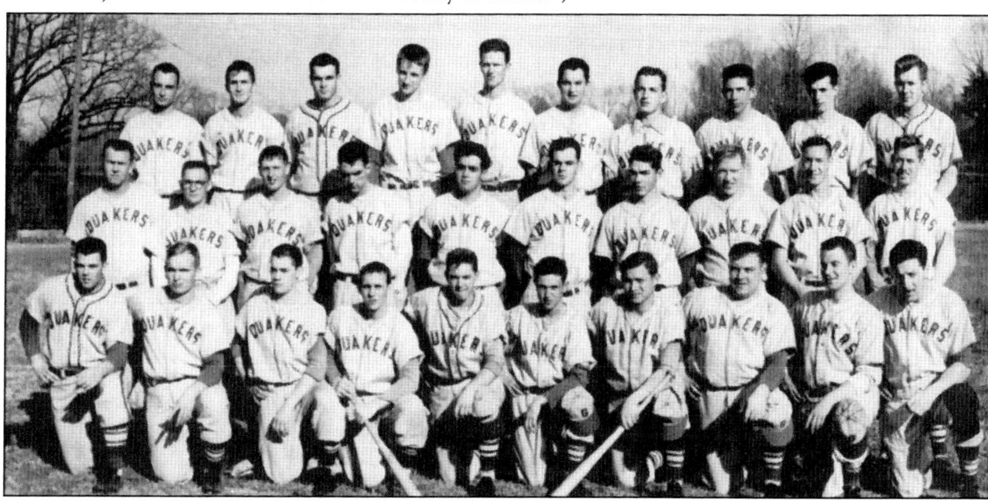

The 1956 Guilford College Quakers competed in the North State Conference, which also included such schools as High Point College and Elon College. The team members, from left to right, are (front row) Bob Alligood, Don Van Benschoten, Joe Pegram, George Helton, Tommy Dillon, Ronald O'Neill, ? Moble, Bob Allred, Eldon Parks, and Daniel Marcone; (middle row) George Petty, Newton Greiner, Charlie Atkinson, Richard Welborn, William Gilmore, Billy West, ? Payle, Ralph Nelson, Chick Trafford, and Warren Nichols; (back row) Robert Driver, Robert Patton, Roy Boyles, Roger Roan, Bob Cornish, Bill Barnette, Charles Benedetto, L.S. Bell, Vincent Breitenburger, and Os Schmidt. (Courtesy of Betty Jane Holaday.)

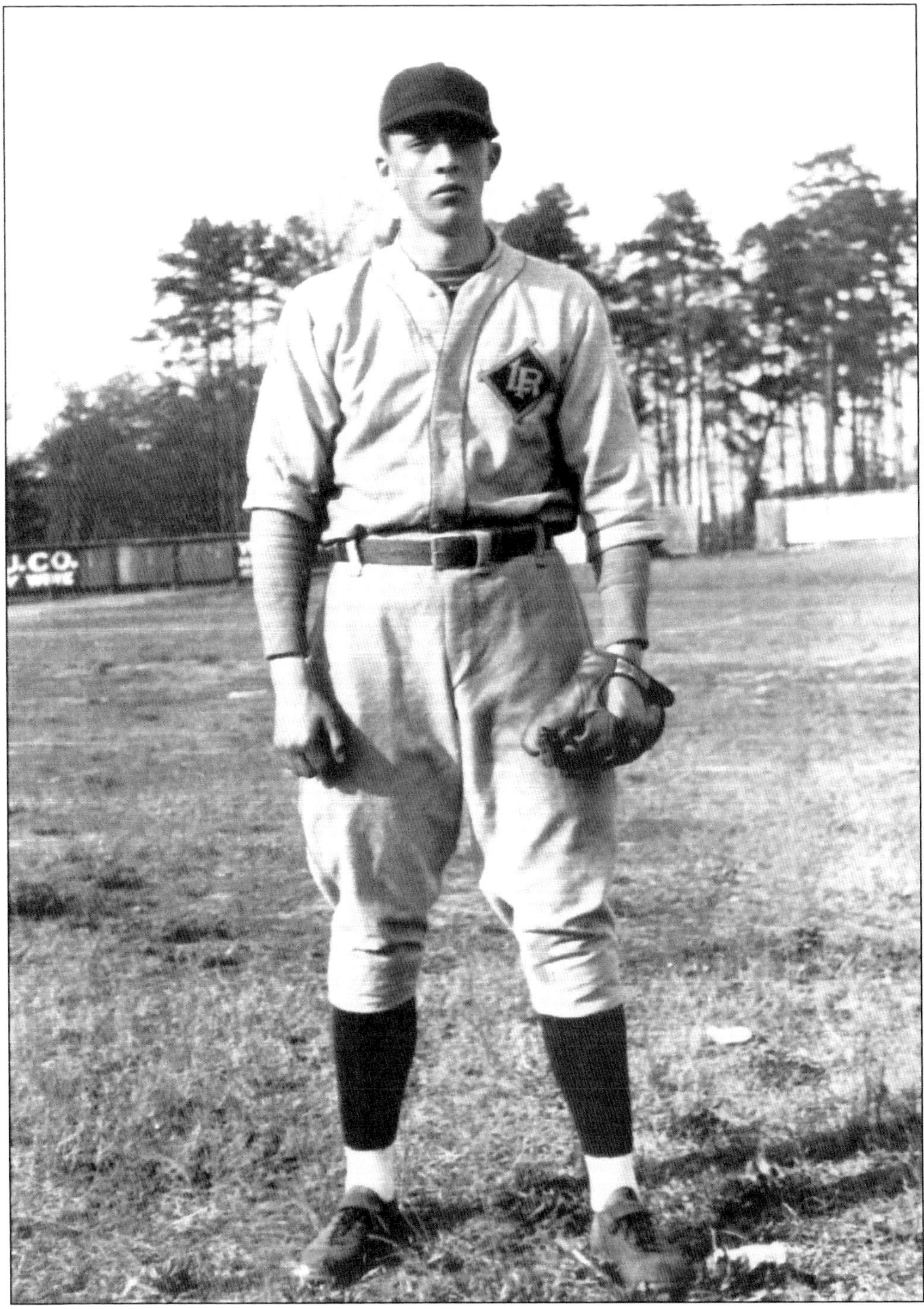

Glenn "Razz" Miller was a star outfielder for Hickory's Lenoir-Rhyne College in the early 1930s. Also an ordained Lutheran minister, Miller stopped preaching in order to play professional baseball. After spending several successful seasons playing for teams in towns including Landis, he decided to return to the ministry. (Courtesy of Hank Utley.)

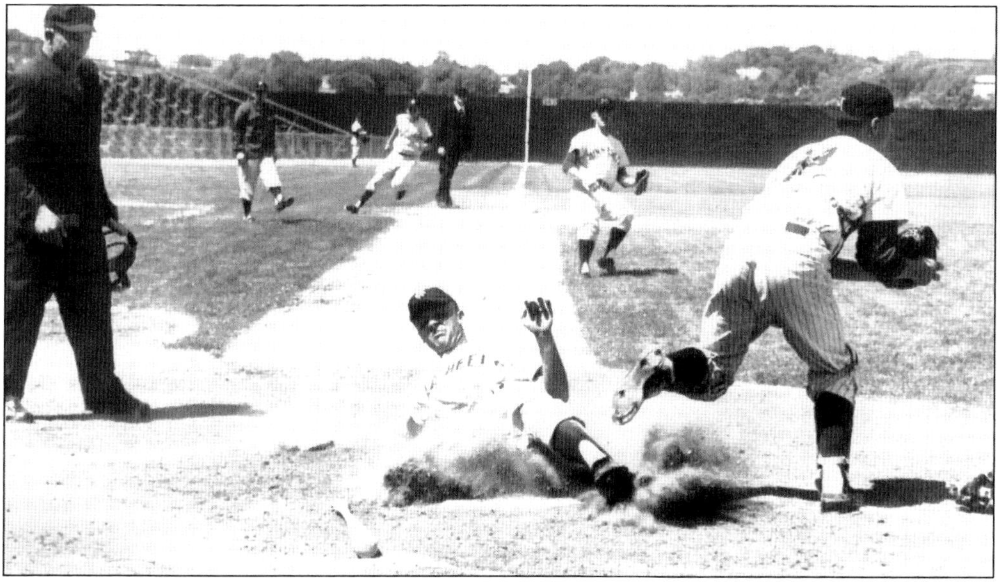

University of North Carolina outfielder John Burgwyn safely slides home during a 1960 NCAA College World Series game in Omaha, Nebraska against the University of Minnesota. Carolina scored three runs in the first inning but Minnesota recovered to take the game 8-3. After finishing with a record of 22-7, the Tar Heels earned their first-ever trip to the College World Series that season. (From the collection of the author.)

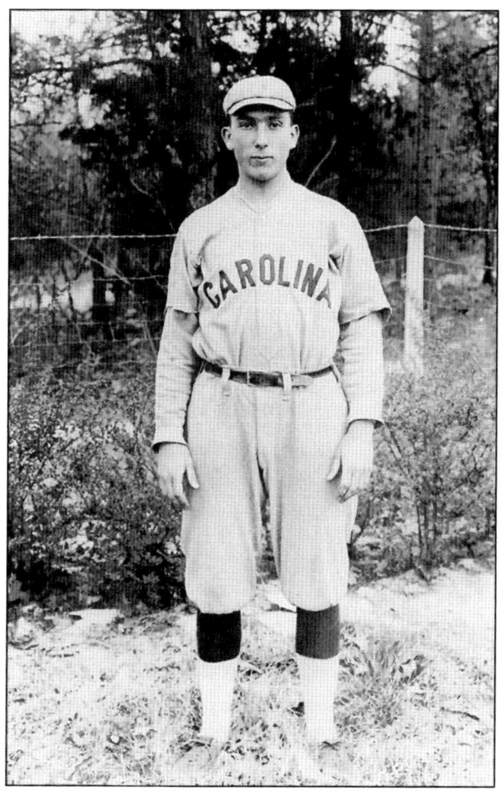

Pitcher Jack Powell was captain of the University of North Carolina's baseball team in 1918 and 1919. (Courtesy of the North Carolina Department of Archives and History.)

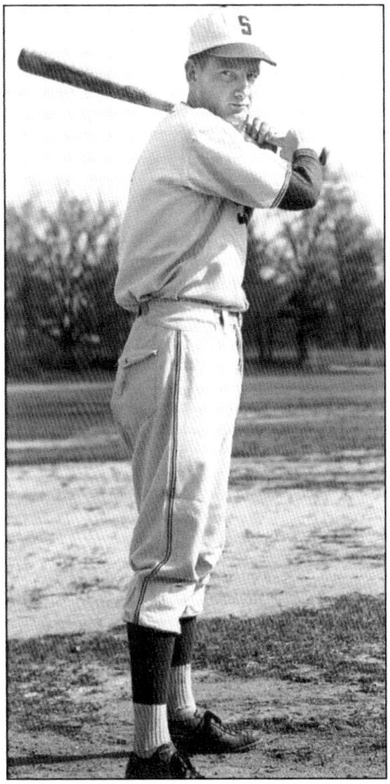

Hank Utley was the starting third baseman for North Carolina State University in the late 1940s. He continued to contribute to baseball long after his playing career was over by becoming one of the game's prominent historians. (Courtesy of Hank Utley.)

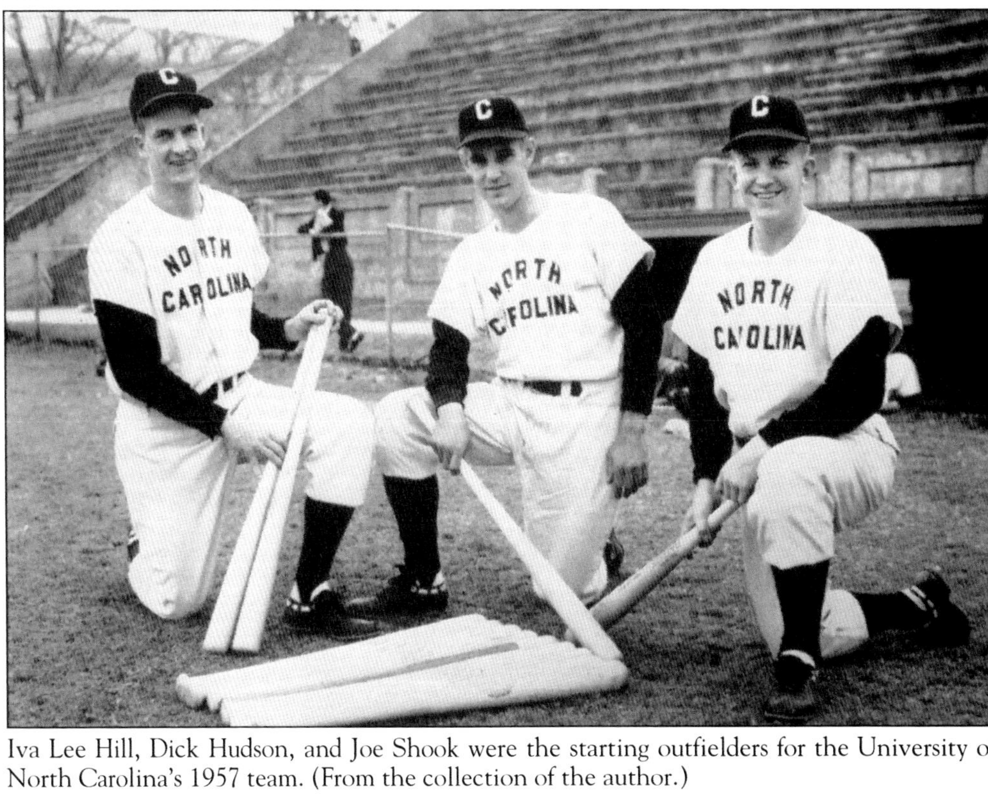

Iva Lee Hill, Dick Hudson, and Joe Shook were the starting outfielders for the University of North Carolina's 1957 team. (From the collection of the author.)

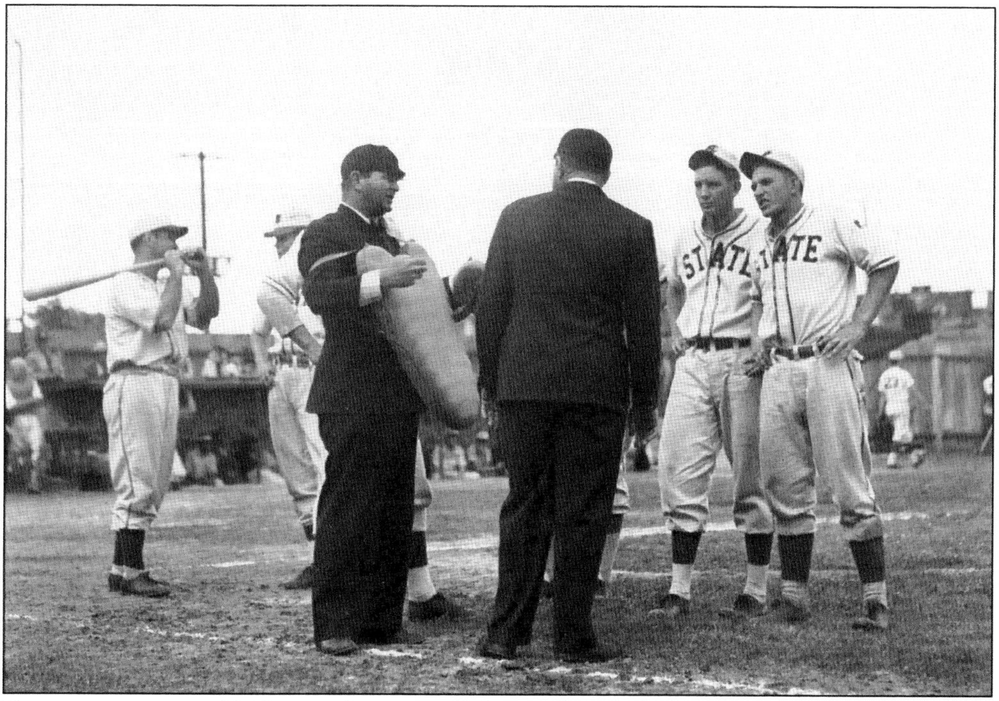

During action in a 1946 game between rivals North Carolina State and the University of North Carolina, State's Chick Doak was ruled out for not reporting to the umpire as a pinch hitter. Doak and Jim Edwards are seen at left while their teammates Hank Utley and Charley Richkus argue with the umpire at right. In 18 innings Carolina won the game by the score of 8-5. (Courtesy of Hank Utley.)

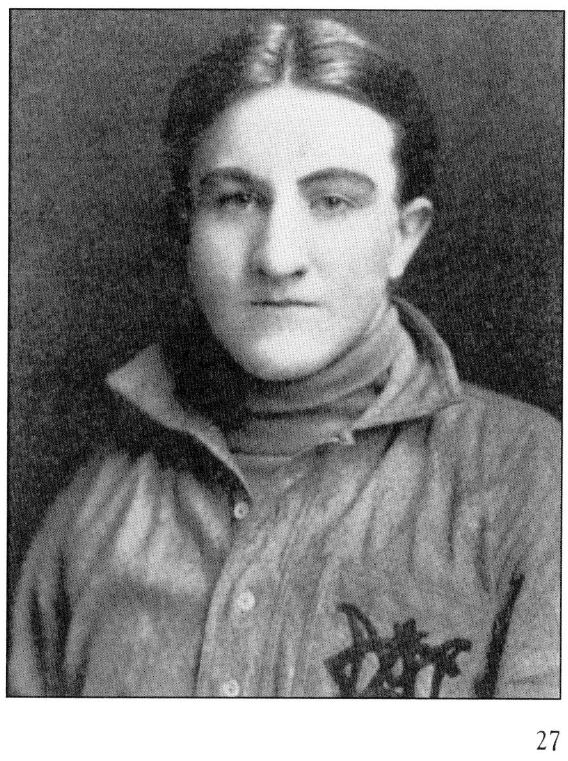

Frank Thompson was one of the early baseball stars for North Carolina State University. Captain of both the varsity baseball and football teams, he was voted the best all-around athlete of the Class of 1909. The Raleigh native even served as coach of the baseball team his senior year. When the United States entered World War I, Thompson joined the Army and was given the rank of lieutenant with the 15th Machine Gun Battalion. He was killed in action on September 13, 1918. (Courtesy of the University Archives, North Carolina State University Libraries.)

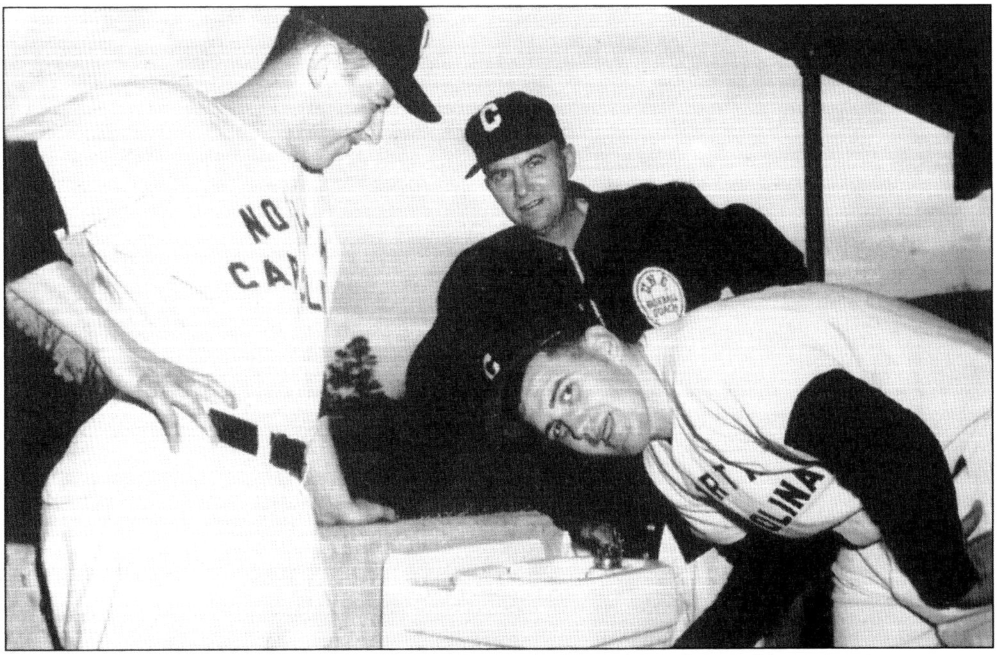

Pictured here is University of North Carolina baseball coach Walter Rabb at the dugout water fountain with 1957 team captains Jim Raugh and Tom Maultsby. Both players were top pitchers for the team and Raugh earned Second Team All-American honors that season. Rabb served as the school's head baseball coach for more than 30 seasons. (From the collection of the author.)

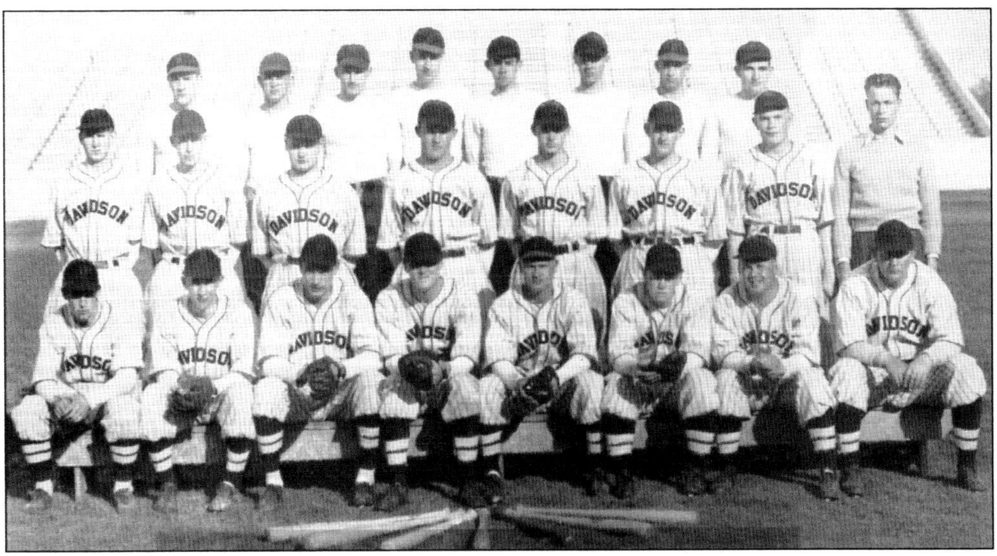

Davidson College has a long history of involvement in collegiate baseball. This is the Wildcats team of 1938. From left to right are the following: (front row) Grey Hunter, Ellwood Moyer, J.D. Hicks, Fielding Clark, Eddie Steere, Tubby Hand, Joe Kellam, and Coach Flake Laird; (middle row) Jim Thomas, Jim Dunford, Walter Fitzgerald, Dave McLean, Hugh Verner, John Rudisill, Sam Hemphill, and Maizie Hall (manager); (back row) Horace McCall, Russell Hellekson, Parker Connor, George Ficklen, James Currie, Charles Mashburn, Dick Lindsey, and Bill Manson. (From the collection of the author.)

Duke University third baseman Jeff Becker was named 1996 Freshman of the Year in the Atlantic Coast Conference and earned First Team All-Honors in both 1997 and 1998. Becker also played in the Coastal Plain League, a collegiate summer league for top players, for the Durham Braves. (From the collection of the author.)

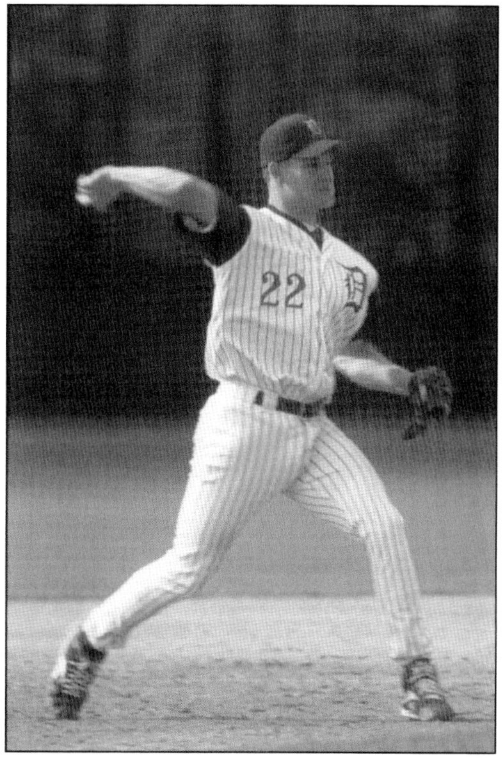

Below is a 1997 schedule for the Campbell University baseball team that features All-Conference infielder Scott Jackson. Campbell, located in the town of Buies Creek, has a long history in the game of baseball and the school has produced many top players including former big leaguers Jim Perry and Cal Koonce. (From the collection of the author.)

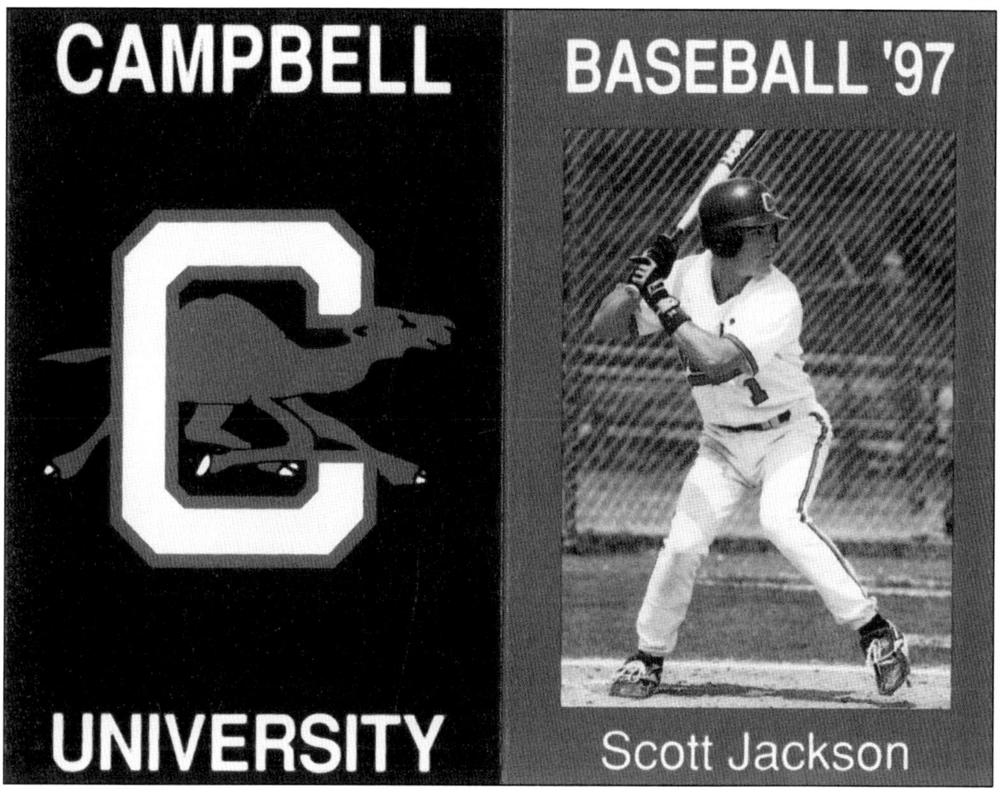

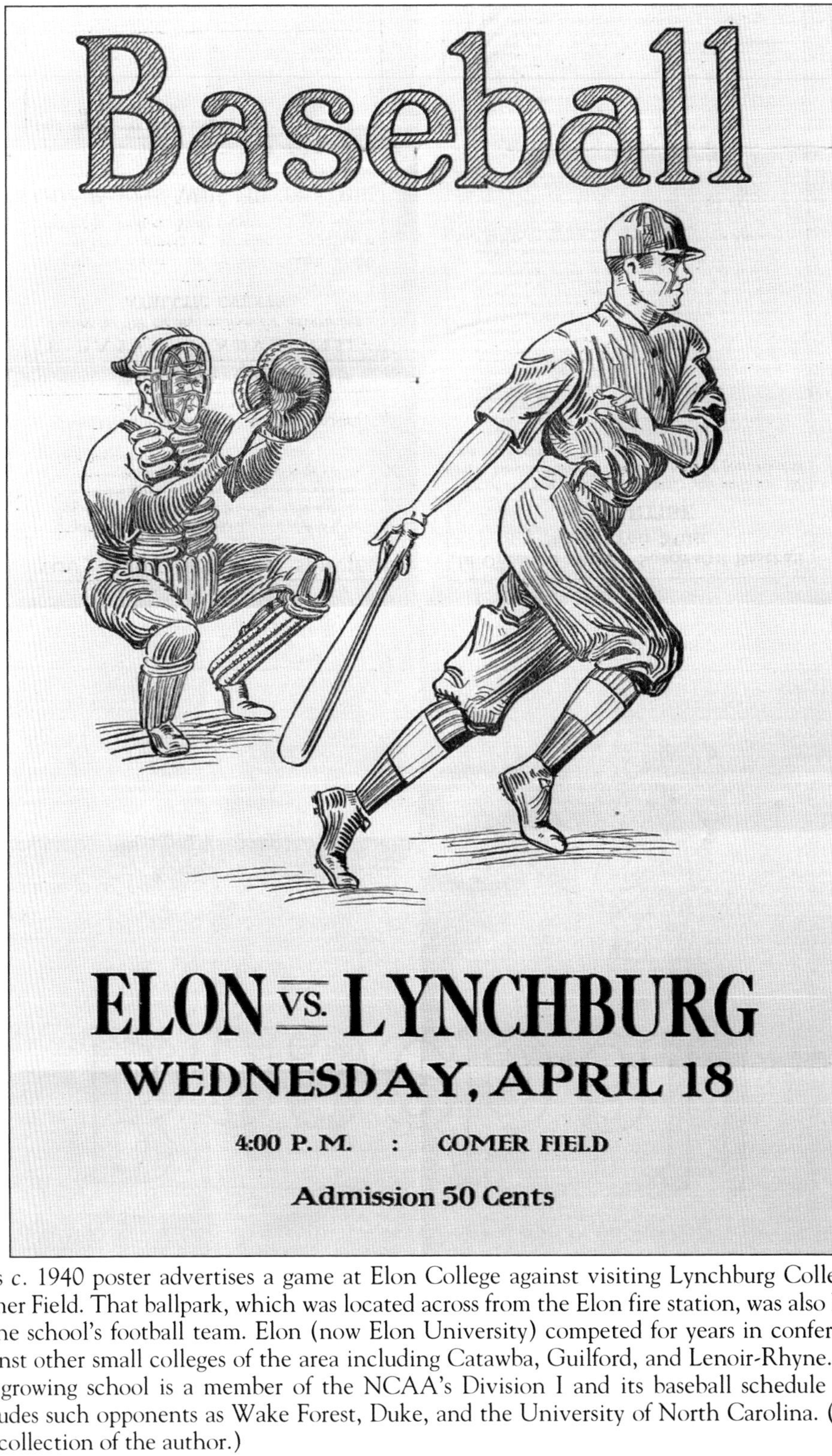

This *c.* 1940 poster advertises a game at Elon College against visiting Lynchburg College at Comer Field. That ballpark, which was located across from the Elon fire station, was also home to the school's football team. Elon (now Elon University) competed for years in conferences against other small colleges of the area including Catawba, Guilford, and Lenoir-Rhyne. Now the growing school is a member of the NCAA's Division I and its baseball schedule often includes such opponents as Wake Forest, Duke, and the University of North Carolina. (From the collection of the author.)

Three

Town Teams, Mill Teams, and More

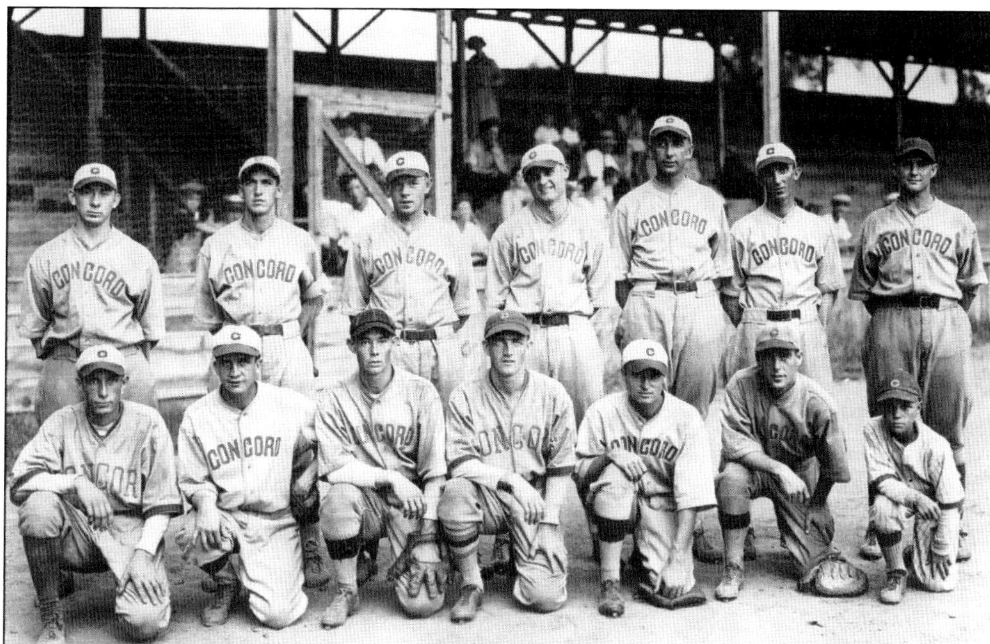

The 1929 Concord Weavers were a team composed primarily of college players looking to make a few dollars over the summer playing semi-pro baseball. The players, from left to right, are (front row) Richard Whittington, Murray Greeson (Wake Forest), Art Hord (Wake Forest), Ernie Jenkins (Duke), Boyd Hatley (UNC), and Charley Eatman (NC State); (back row) Willie Duke (NC State), Howard Briggs (Elon), Harry Lloyd (Auburn), Billy Laval (University of South Carolina), Manley Llewellyn, (manager), Lefty Sherrill, and Mutt Miller. The batboy is Penny Brown. (Courtesy of Hank Utley.)

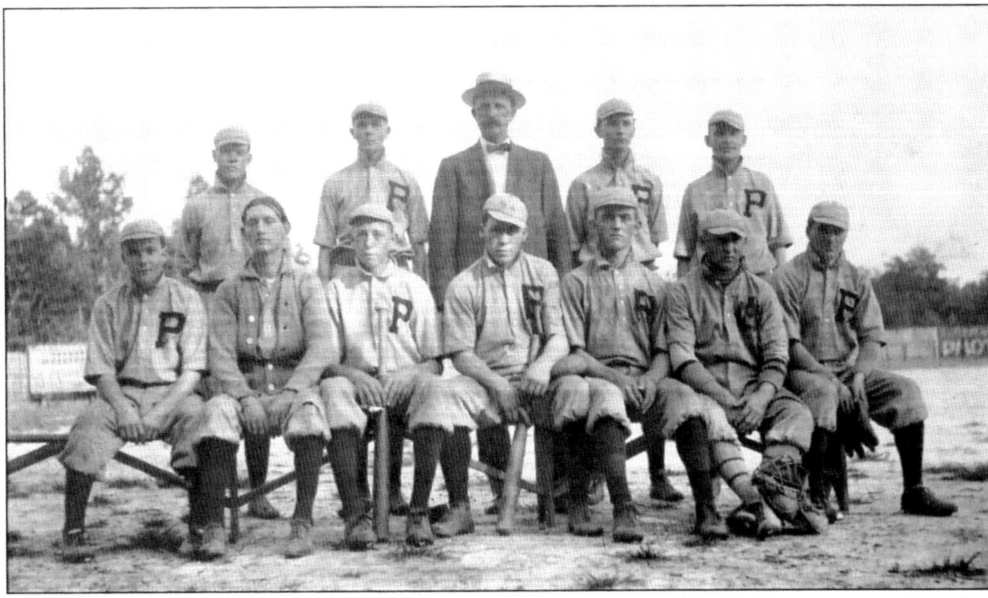

These are two photos of Greensboro textile teams from 1908. The players were not identified but Proximity Mill (upper) were named on the photo as season "Winners" while White Oak Mill (lower) were designated as "Losers." (Courtesy of Barry Smith.)

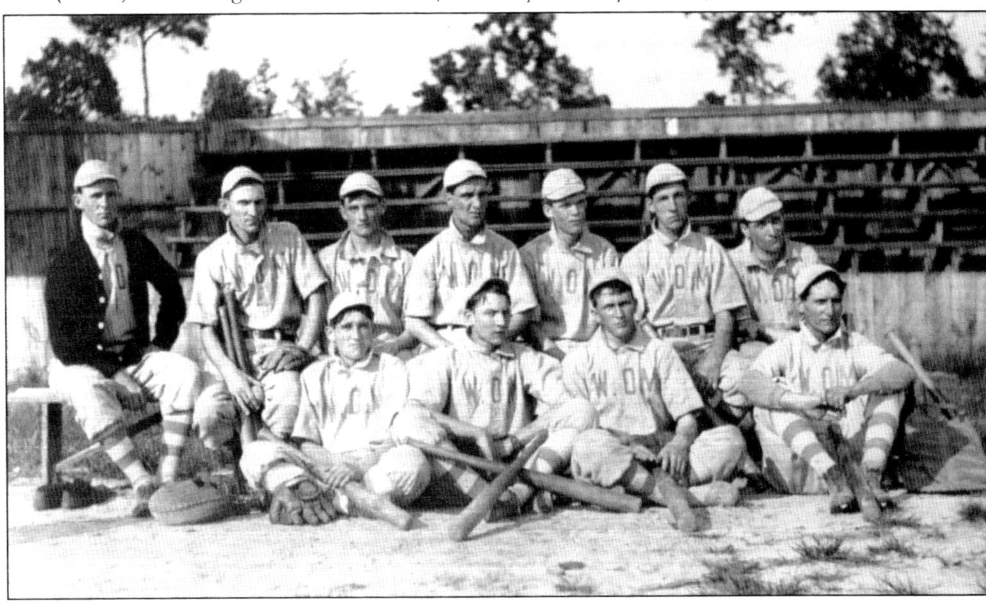

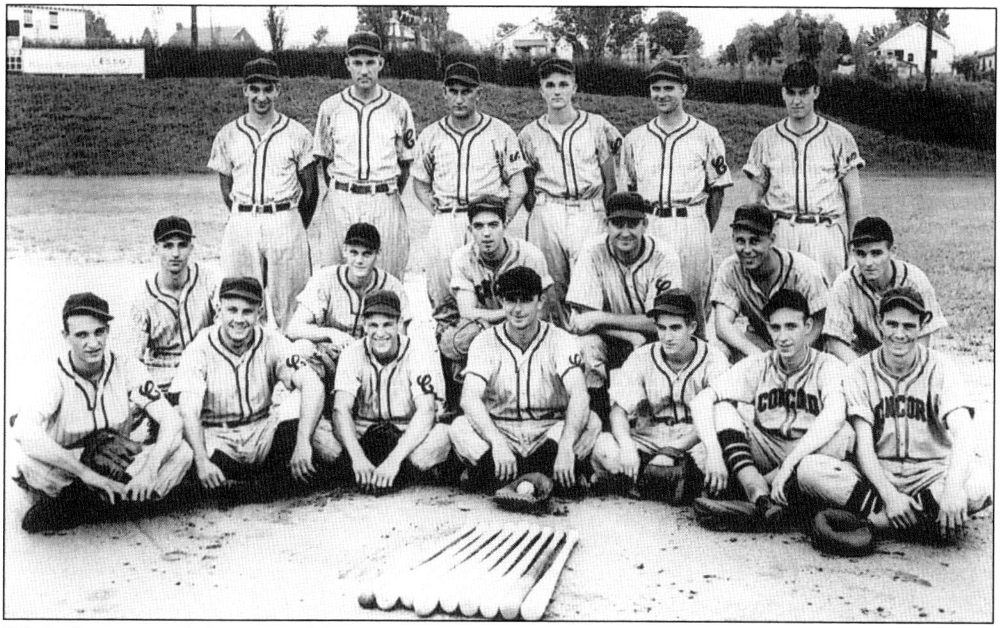

With the entry of the United States into World War II, most minor leagues across the country suspended operations. The North Carolina State League shut down as well but several members wanted to go on playing in an unofficial league with the purpose of keeping area morale up. Thus, the Victory League was formed in 1943, a loop which included this Concord team. Concord native Billy Goodman, only 17 years old in this photo, would go on to win the 1950 American League batting title for the Boston Red Sox. From left to right are the following: (front row) Richard Mauney, Bob Boger, Billy Goodman, Herman "Ginger" Watts (manager), Harold McNaulty, Ralph Ritchie, and Johnny Tallent; (middle row) Chaver Alred, Troy Furr, Boots Fletcher, Archie White, Bill Kluttz, and Leroy Stewart; (back row) Toots Rogers, Harry "Slim" Ingram, Virgil Taylor, Don Harwood, Marvin Watts, and Shade Honeycutt. (Courtesy of Hank Utley.)

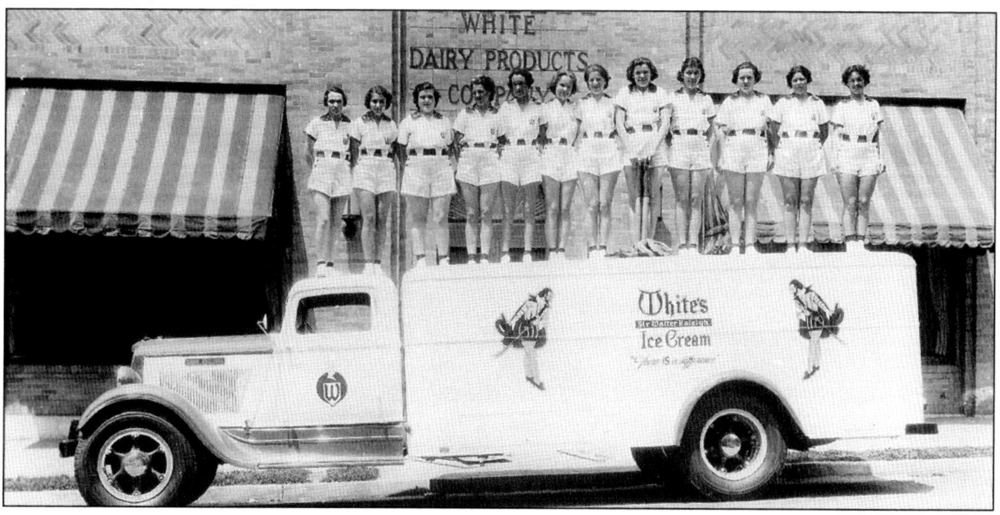

It wasn't only the men who played baseball. This photo from the 1930s shows the girls' baseball team sponsored by the White Diary Products Company of Raleigh. (Courtesy of the North Carolina Department of Archives and History.)

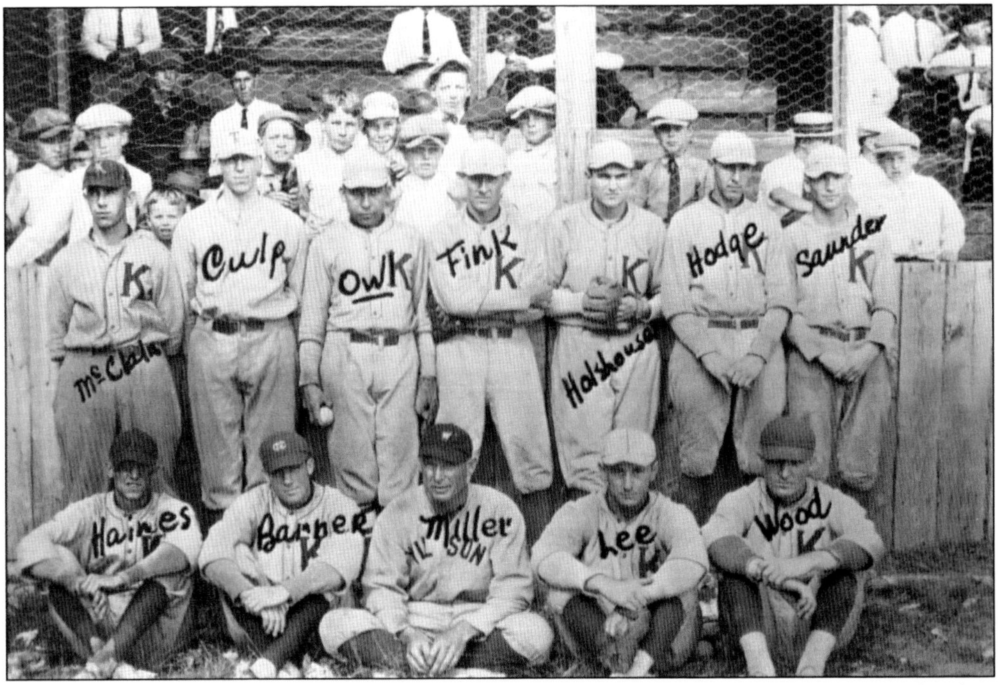

This 1925 Kannapolis team competed in the semi-pro leagues of the area. Most of the first names are unknown; official statistics were not kept and newspapers usually referred to players by last name only. Some were former minor leaguers looking to earn a few dollars per game; McClain had played professionally for Charlotte, and Miller, shown here wearing the uniform of the Piedmont League's Wilson club, was called "a former big leaguer" in the newspapers. Some were college players unofficially working "summer jobs," including Saunders from Duke University, Hodge from Lenoir-Rhyne College, and Owl, who was reportedly an "Indian from the University of Oklahoma." Pitcher Herman Holshouser would go on to spend the 1930 season with the St. Louis Browns of the American League. The players, from left to right, are (front row) Mack Haines, Barber, Miller, Russell "Runt" Lee, and Wood; (back row) McClain, Culp, Owl, Homer Fink, Herman Holshouser, Hodge, and Saunders. (Courtesy of Hank Utley.)

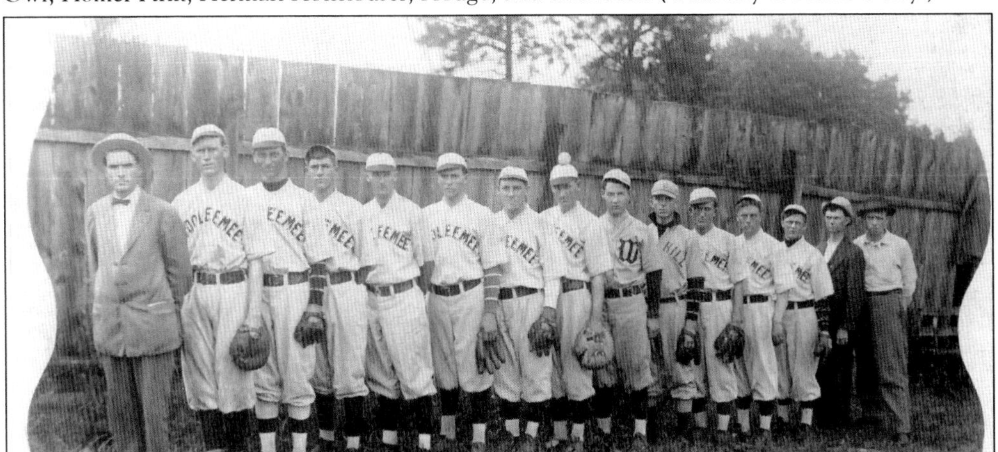

A *c.* 1920 photo shows members of a Cooleemee team that played against other communities; note the non-matching uniforms. (Courtesy of Cooleemee Textile Heritage Center Archives.)

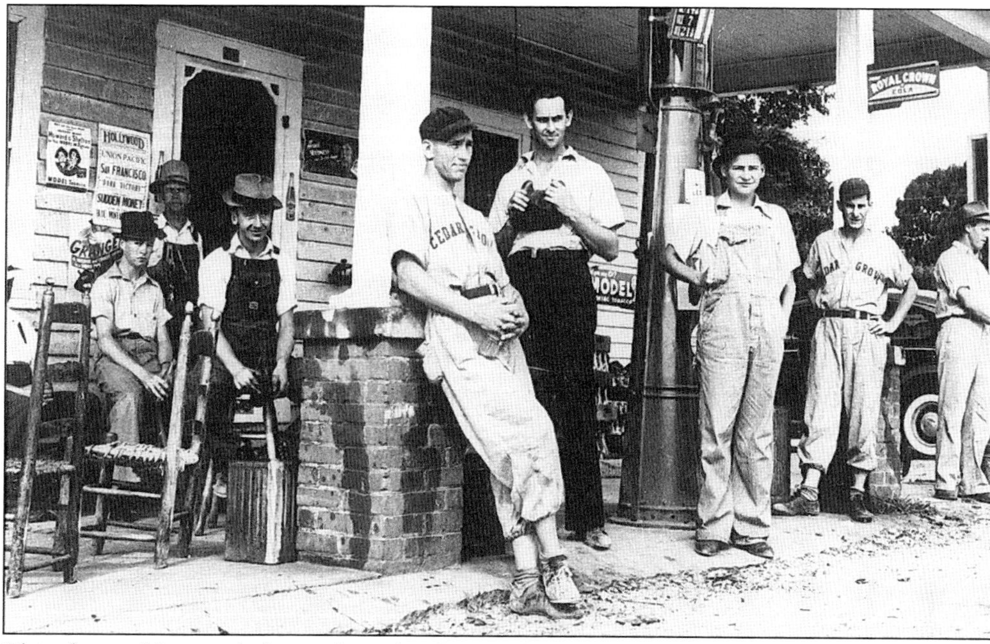

This photo of fans and players from the Orange County town of Cedar Grove was taken after a game at a local filling station and general store on July 4, 1939. Pictured from left to right are W.P. "Billy" Roberts, Jim Crabtree, Brodie Crabtree, David "Bo" Wells, Gordon "Boss" Anderson, Percy Terry, Aubrey Terry, and Tom Roundtree. (Courtesy of the North Carolina Department of Archives and History.)

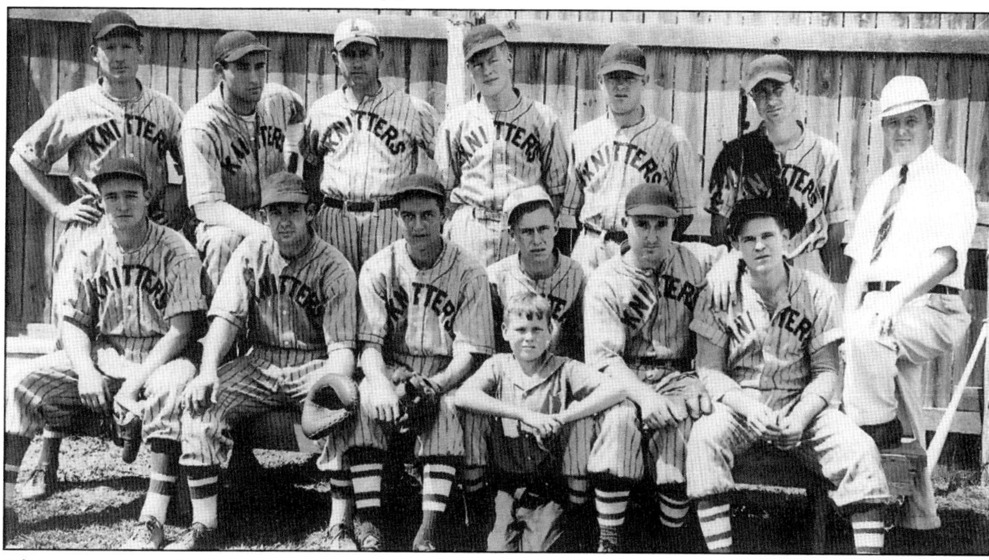

The 1935 Wiscassett Knitters, a prominent textile mill team from Albemarle, included the following players, from left to right: (front row) Ike Williams, Jim Staton, Claude Hathcock, two unidentified bat boys, Snook Cooper, and Bruce Staton; (back row) Rip Tudor, Orge "Pat" Cooper, Shelby Burleson, Monk Watson, Skin Hatchcock, Bob Kendall, and Hoyle Blalock (business manager). Pat Cooper—seen here at age 18—would go on to the major leagues more than a decade later. In 1946–1947 he played in 14 games as a first baseman for the Philadelphia Athletics. (Courtesy of Bob Kendall.)

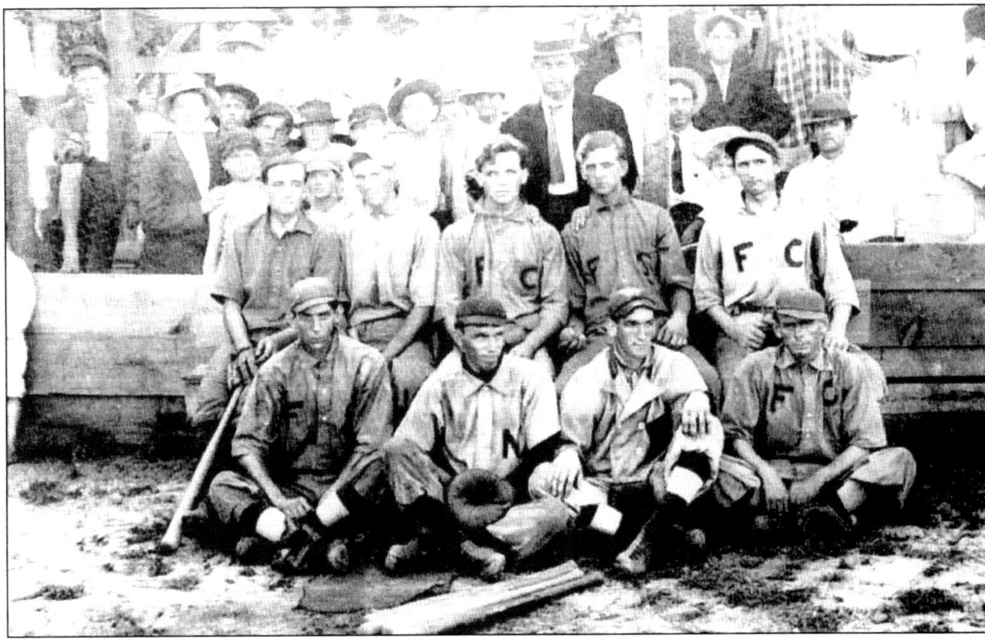

Many small communities once fielded semi-pro "town teams." Players were local men rather than full-time professionals but they might have been paid a few dollars from the gate receipts for each game they took part in. This team represented the Rutherford County town of Forest City in 1907 or 1908. (Courtesy of Hank Utley.)

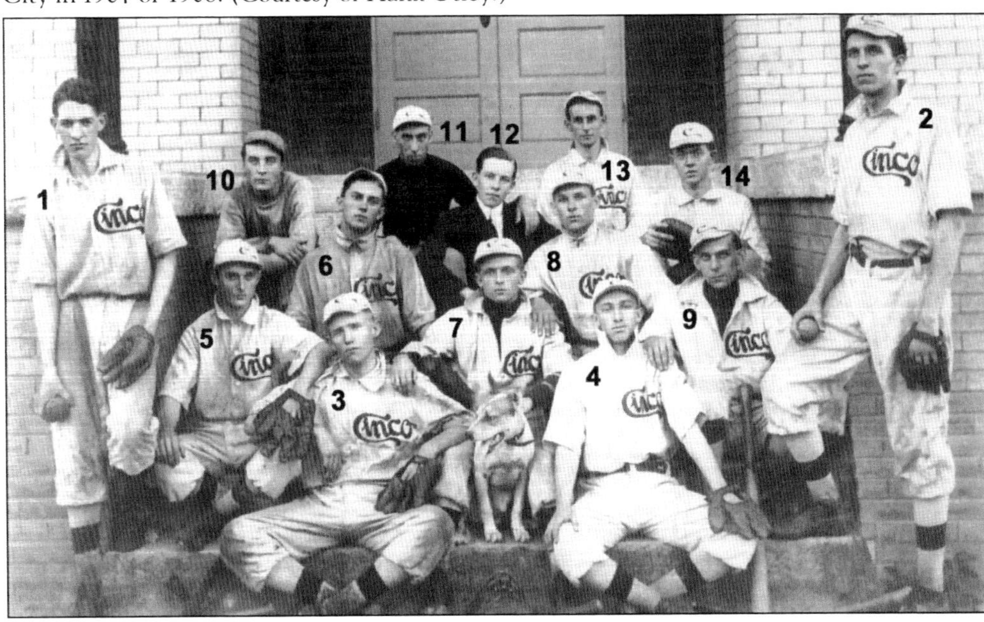

The 1911 Cincos were Concord's first town team. The team's uniforms were provided by Jones Yorke, a distributor of a brand of 5¢ cigars called Cincos—hence the team name. The players, from left to right, are Leslie Bell (1), Campbell Cline (2), ? Wood (3), Pearlie Cook (4), Oscar Sappenfield (5), Fred Patterson (6), Luke Sappenfield (7), Bill Wadsworth (8), Charley Barrier (9), Gowan Dusenberry (10), ? Clark (11), Ray Bell (12), Bill Bingham (13), and ? Grier (14). (Courtesy of Hank Utley.)

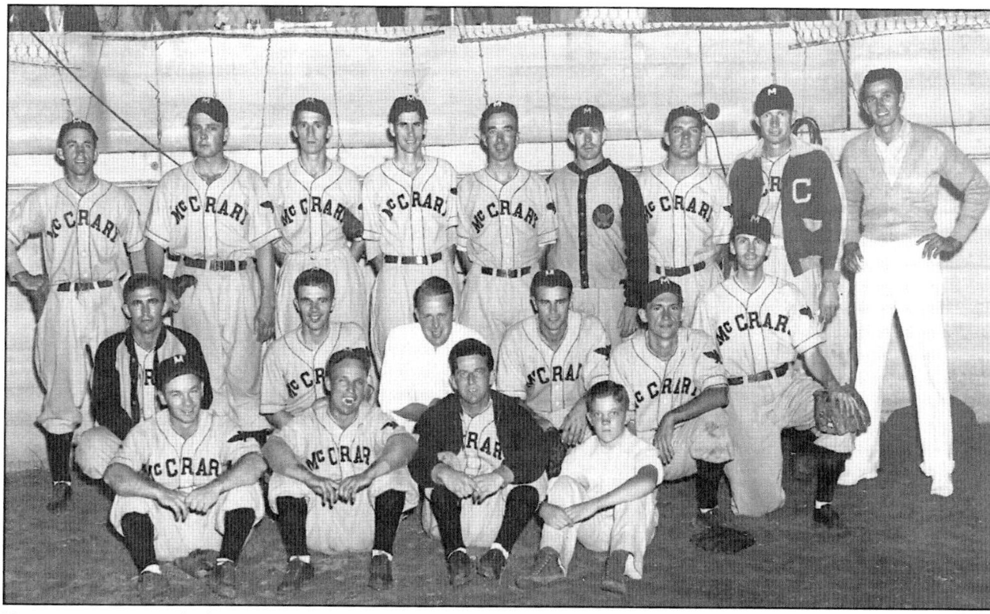

Representing Asheboro's McCrary Hosiery Mills, the 1937 McCrary Eagles won the North Carolina semi-pro state title and competed in the national championships in Wichita, Kansas, where this photo was taken. From left to right are (front row) Forrest "Pat" Short, Hayes Harrington, Sam Lankford, and Jack Underwood (mascot); (middle row) Mal Craver, Guy Clodfelter, Neely Hunter (manager), John Griffin, Jack Cox, and Bob MacFayden; (back row) Paul Cheek, Lester Burge, Hal Johnson, Mike Briggs, Gates Smith, Lawrence "Hooks" Calloway, Tom Burnett, Red Norris, and Charlie Barnes (trainer). (Courtesy of Ada Burge.)

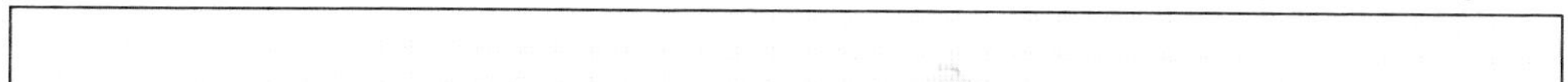

From the Rowan County town of Spencer, this 1922 team represented Spencer Shops, Southern Railway Company's largest steam locomotive servicing facility. The team members, from left to right, are (front row) Williams, Smith, and unidentified; (back row) Wagner, Zachary, Briggs, Killingsworth, two unidentified, and Troutman. (Courtesy of the North Carolina Department of Archives and History.)

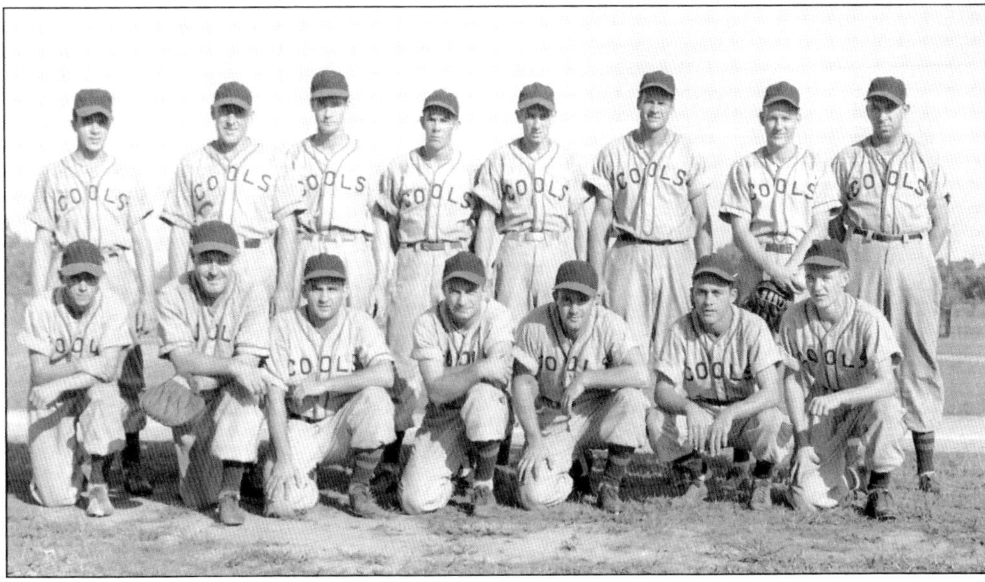

This photo of the Cools, a mill team from the town of Cooleemee, was taken sometime in the 1940s. From left to right are the following: (front row) George Jordan, Luther Whitlock, Hubert "Thang" Shoaf, J.F. "Effie" Grimes, Clarence Myers, Fred Pierce, and Henry Shoaf; (back row) J.W. "Booger" McClannon, Clanard "Firpo" Creason, Fred Dunn, Hayden Benson, Bob Jordan, Grimes "Fat" Parker, Jim Brinegar, and Ed Clawson. (Courtesy of Cooleemee Textile Heritage Center Archives.)

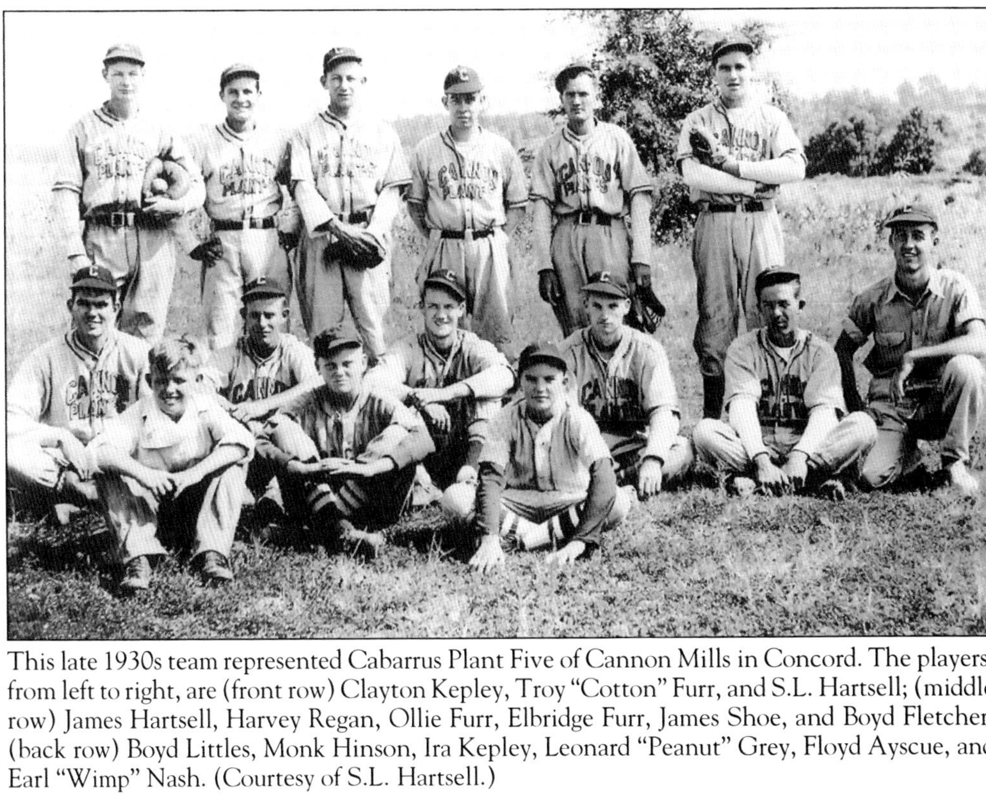

This late 1930s team represented Cabarrus Plant Five of Cannon Mills in Concord. The players, from left to right, are (front row) Clayton Kepley, Troy "Cotton" Furr, and S.L. Hartsell; (middle row) James Hartsell, Harvey Regan, Ollie Furr, Elbridge Furr, James Shoe, and Boyd Fletcher; (back row) Boyd Littles, Monk Hinson, Ira Kepley, Leonard "Peanut" Grey, Floyd Ayscue, and Earl "Wimp" Nash. (Courtesy of S.L. Hartsell.)

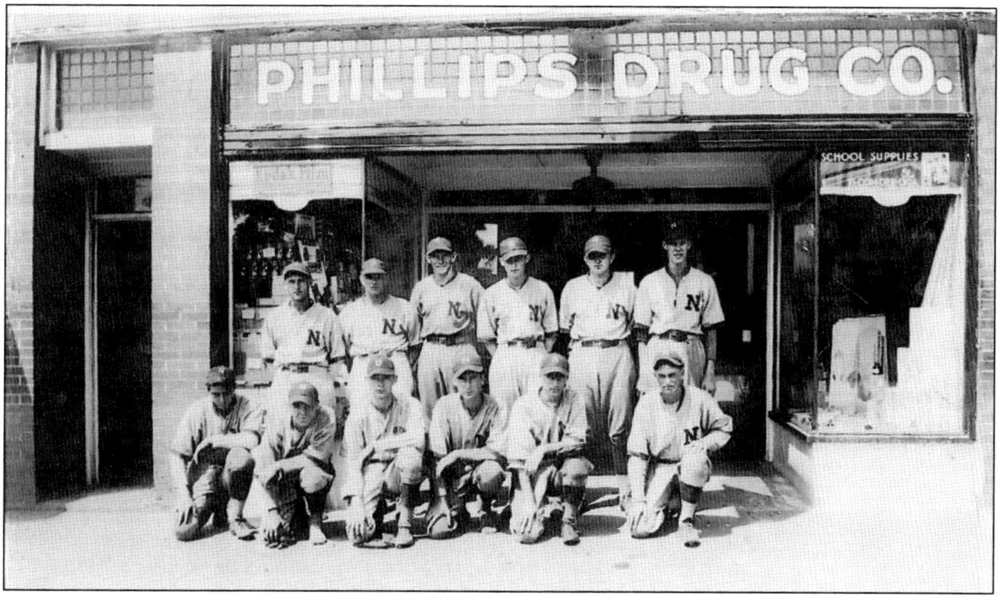

This 1933 semi-pro team from Norwood in Stanley County featured future big leaguer Buck Ross. The Norwood native, a right-handed pitcher, made his big league debut with the Philadelphia Athletics in 1936 and won 56 games over 10 seasons with the Athletics and White Sox. Included in the picture are Uriah Norwood (front row, second from left), Bob Kendall (front row, fourth from left), and Buck Ross (back row, sixth from left). (Courtesy of Bob Kendall.)

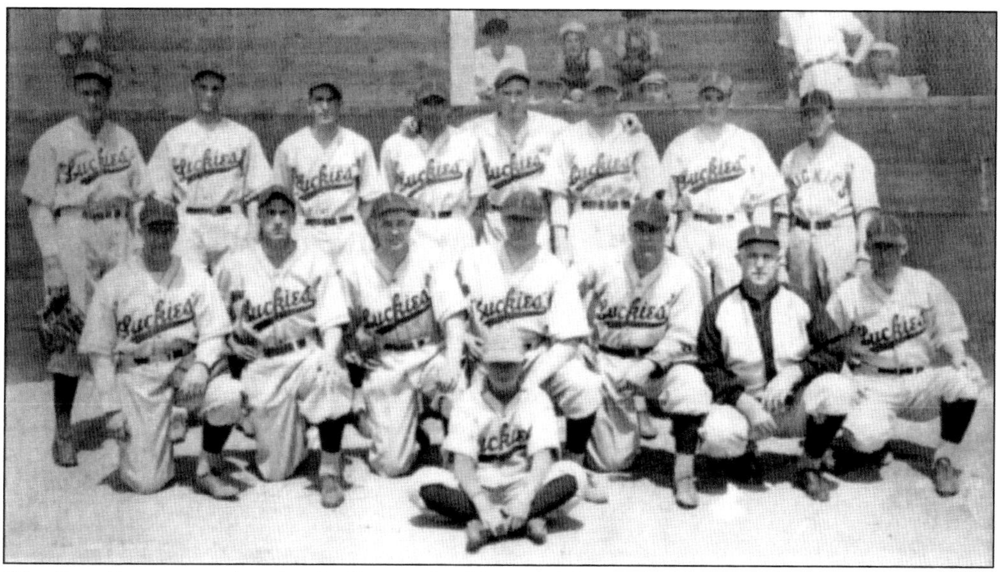

Wes Ferrell, a star pitcher for the Boston Red Sox and Greensboro native, held out on reporting to his team in 1934 in hopes of better contract terms. While waiting, he was hired by American Tobacco in Reidsville to pitch a couple of games for their team, the Luckies. The Luckies team members, from left to right, are (front row) Willie Wagoner, Howard Briggs, Al Shaw, Marvin Coker, Van Howard, and G.C. Deviney (manager); (back row) Wes Ferrell, Nap Lufty, John Briggs, Sherman Hoggard, Flop Beaver, Pat Brady, Pat Griffin, and Howard Lamberth. The batboy is James Deviney. (Courtesy of Sherman Hoggard.)

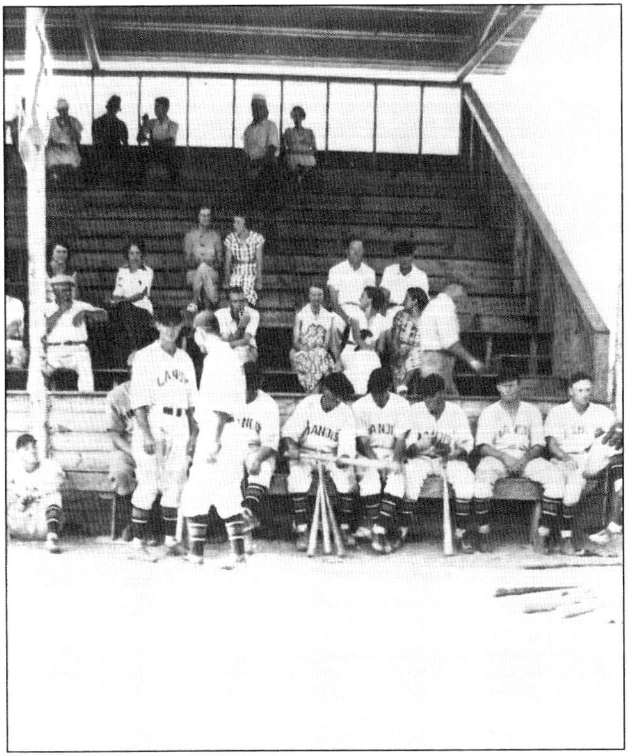

In this 1935 photo, Landis Cardinals' bench manager and catcher, Ginger Watts, is standing at left, facing the camera. The Cardinals were champions of the Carolina Textile League that season with a record of 49-24. (Courtesy of Hank Utley.)

This early 1900s team represented the Iredell County communities of Troutman and East Monbo. From left to right are the following: (front row) Sid Lyton, Henry Hartline, Joe Clark, John Clark, P.W. Brown, and Rome Clark; (back row) Worth Williamson, Claude Troutman, Rome Lyton, Charlie Hartline, Hyde Lyton, and Troy Cavin (manager). (Courtesy of Mac Lackey.)

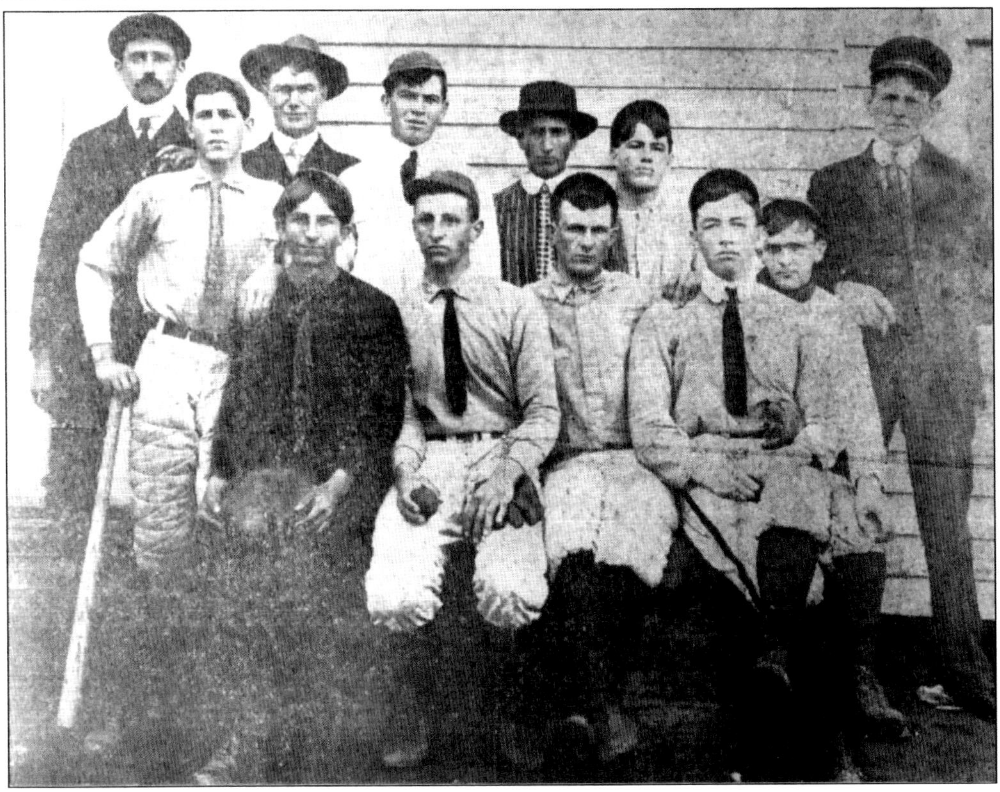

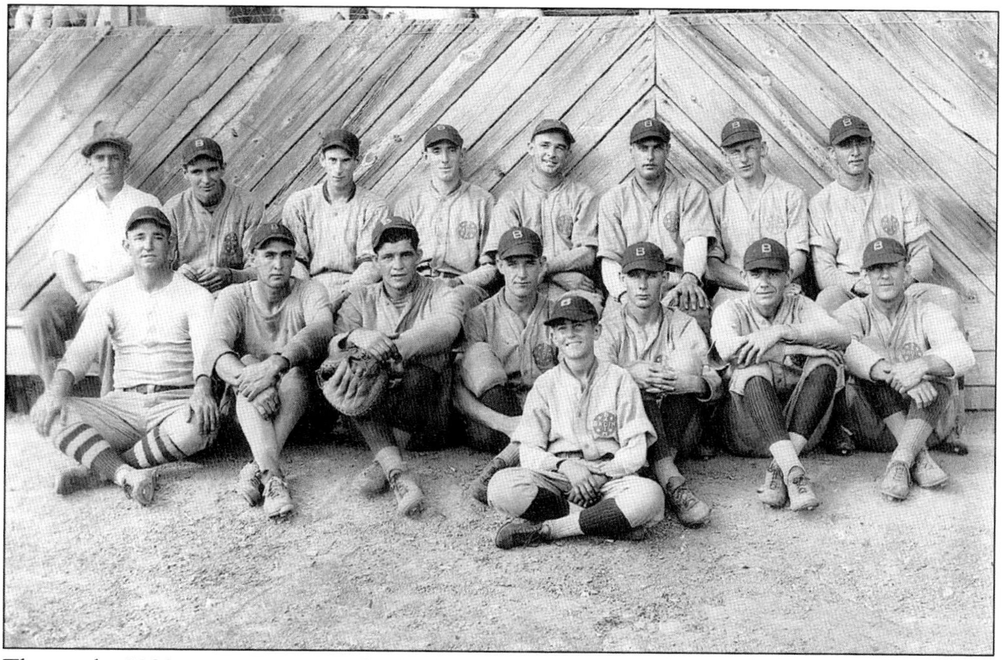

This early 1930s semi-pro team from Badin was sponsored by the Aluminum Company of America, the town's primary employer. Team members, from left to right, are (front row) George Rhinehardt, David Shoe, Carl Owens, Sherman Hill, Luke Ross, Luke Saunders, and Ralph Neely; (back row) Jimmie Black, Bob Frye, Buren Scarboro, Charlie Wentz, Oscar Fary, Carl Motley, Joe Cresswell, and Fred Lisk. (Courtesy of Bob Kendall.)

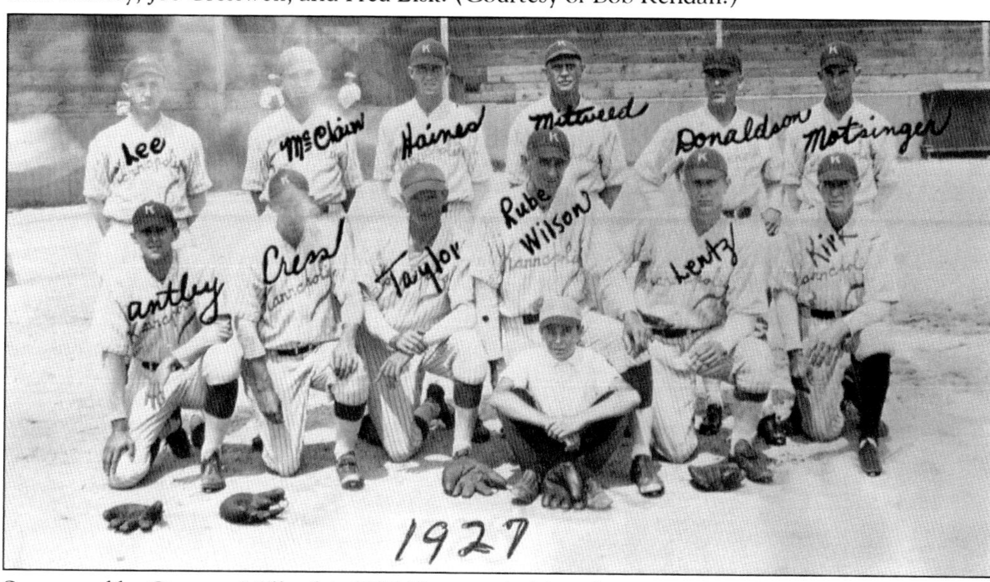

Sponsored by Cannon Mills, this 1927 Kannapolis Towelers team played in the semi-pro textile leagues that were so common in the central part of the state. The team got its name from the items most commonly produced by Cannon Mills—towels. The players, from left to right, are (front row) Shuler Antley, ? Cress, ? Taylor, Rube Wilson, ? Lentz, and ? Kirk; (back row) Russell "Runt" Lee, ? McClain, Mack Haines, ? Mitweed, ? Donaldson, and Robbie Motsinger. (Courtesy of Hank Utley.)

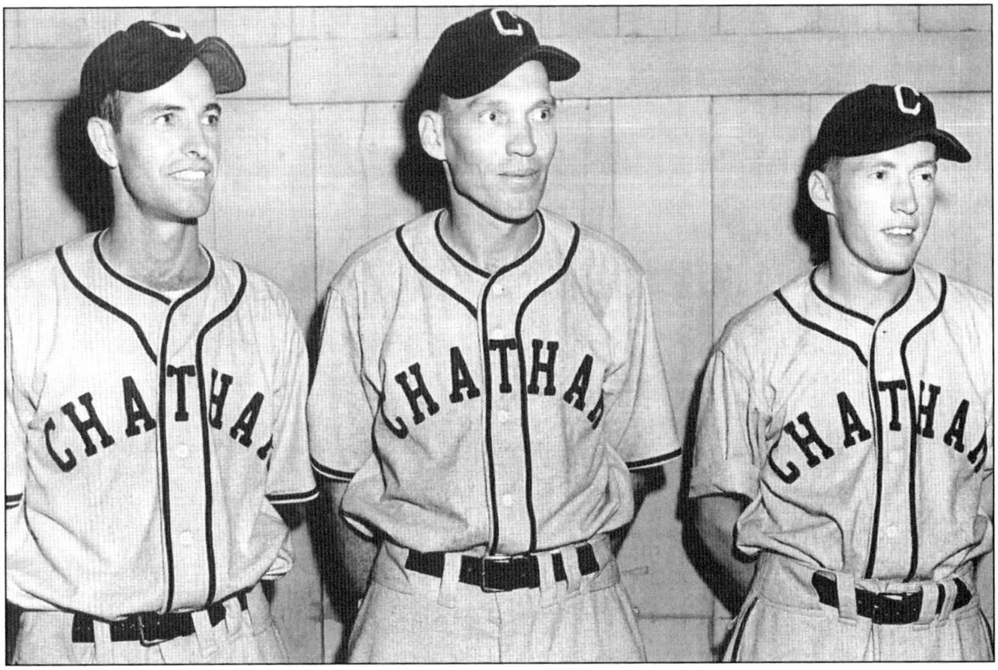

Wayne "Tige" Harris (center) and Henry "Shorty" Brown (right), members of the 1948 Chatham Blanketeers from the town of Elkin, are pictured here with an unidentified teammate. When Elkin decided to enter a franchise in the professional Blue Ridge League the following season both Harris and Brown played important roles; Harris served as playing manager while Brown was an All-Star outfielder. (Courtesy of Henry Brown.)

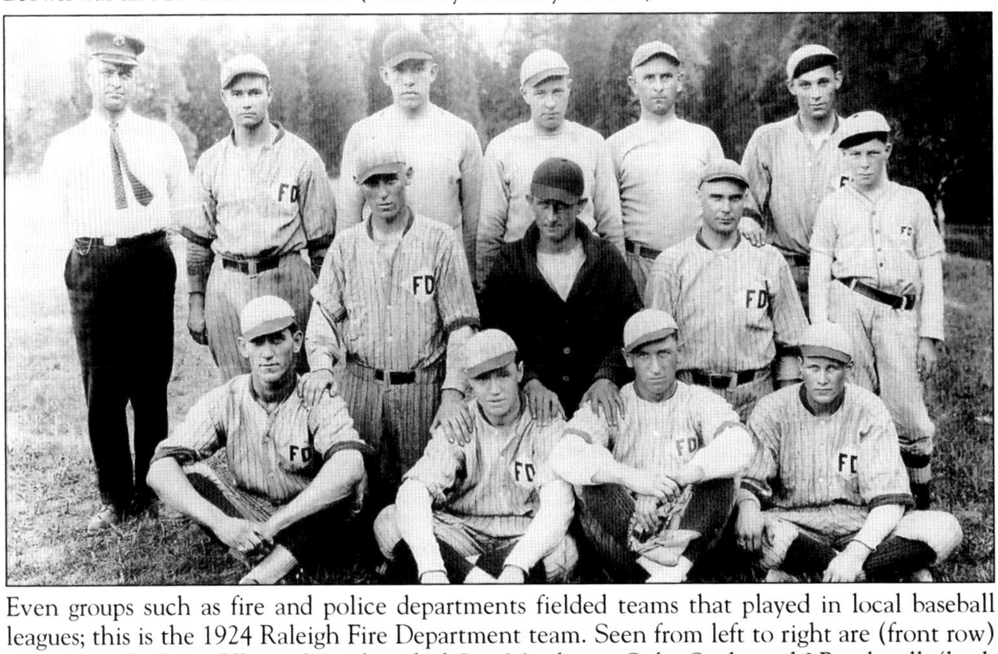

Even groups such as fire and police departments fielded teams that played in local baseball leagues; this is the 1924 Raleigh Fire Department team. Seen from left to right are (front row) all unidentified; (middle row) unidentified, Lee Matthews, Gales Sauls, and ? Brockwell; (back row) Chief Hicks, ? Canole, Bruce Holloway, ? Poole, and two unidentified. (Courtesy of the North Carolina Department of Archives and History.)

Bob Kendall was a star player in the semi-pro leagues of central North Carolina during the 1930s. Though he had the talent, he never pursued a professional career and preferred to play for and manage teams like Wiscassett Mills near his hometown of Albemarle. (Courtesy of Bob Kendall.)

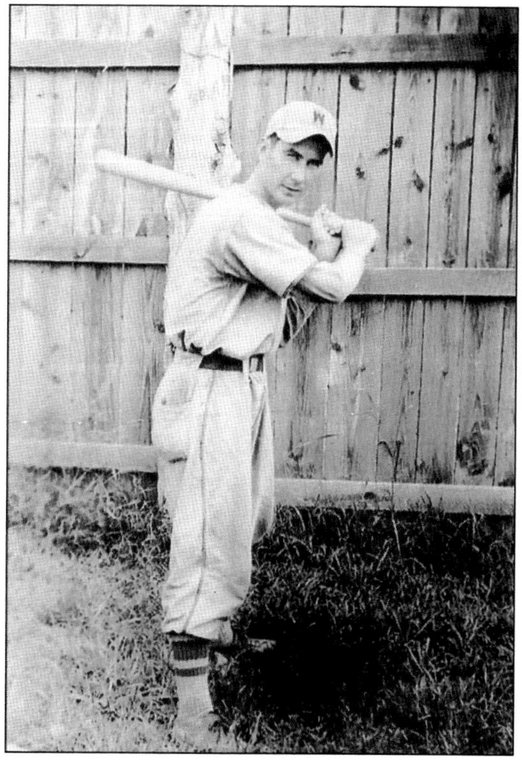

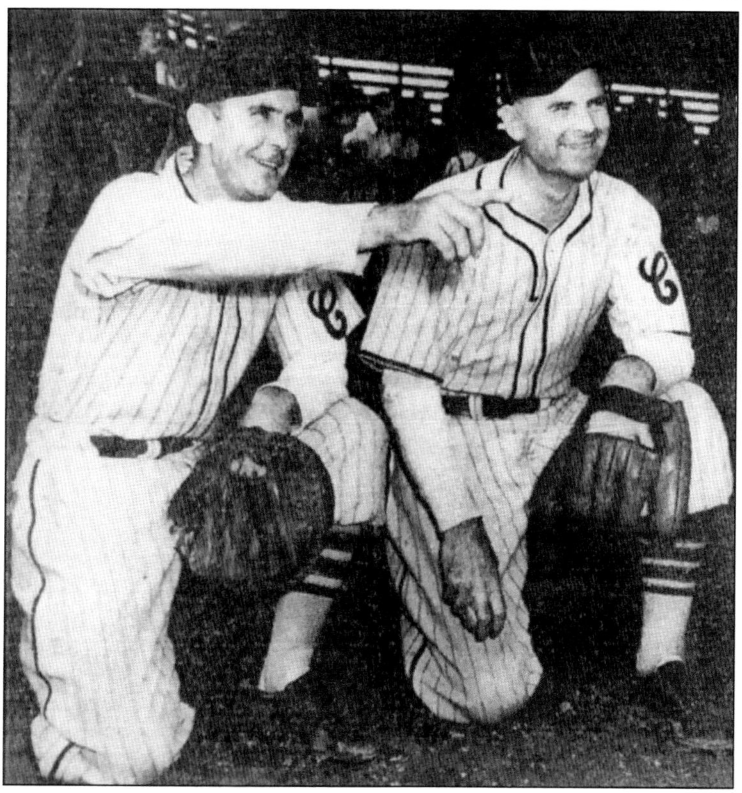

For nearly 20 years the Watts brothers played baseball for both professional and semi-pro teams around their Concord-area homes. Every summer from the 1930s into the 1950s, it was common to see one or both of the brothers playing for area teams. Ginger, left, often managed and played catcher while Marvin held down the hot corner. (Courtesy of Hank Utley.)

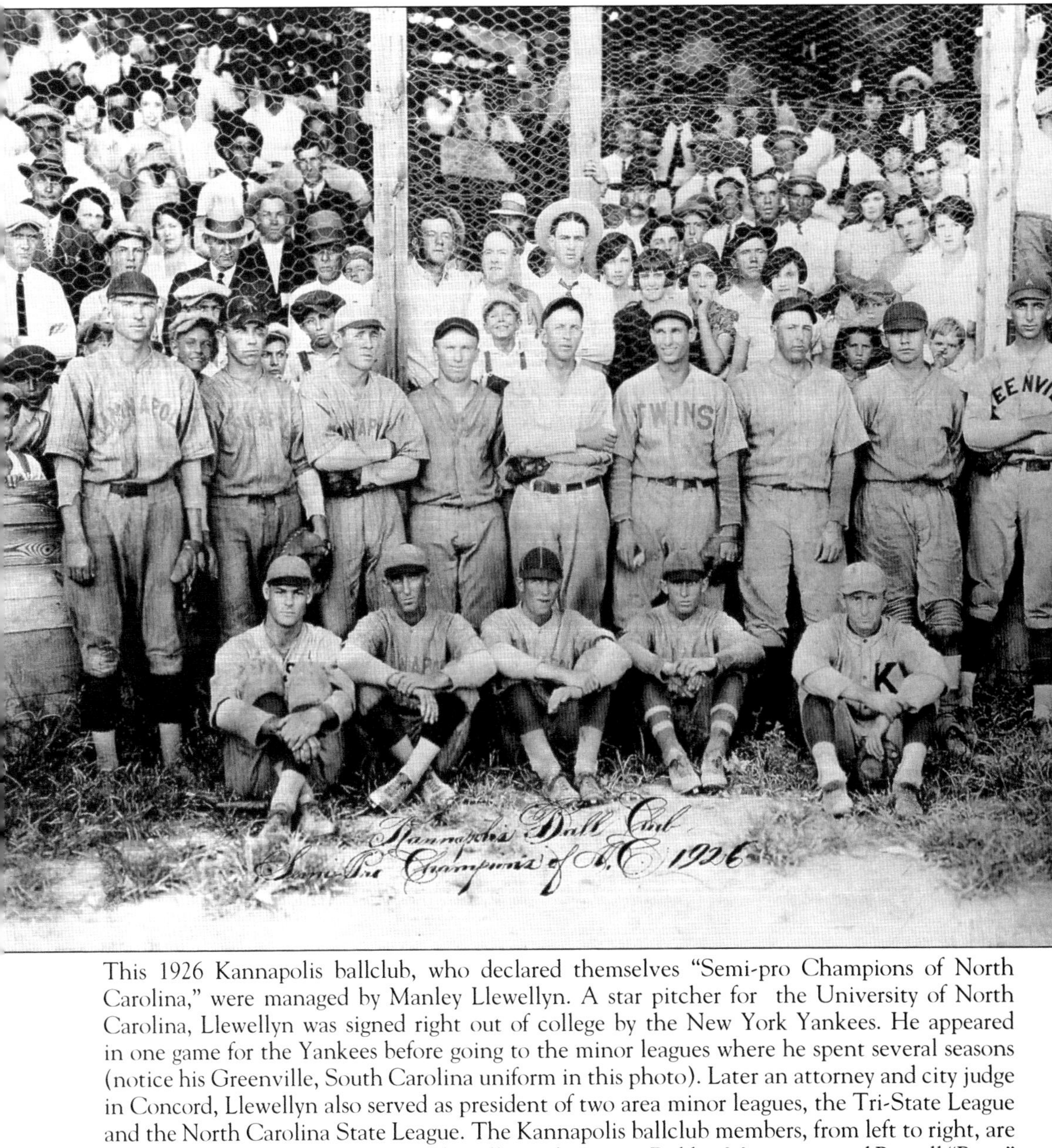

This 1926 Kannapolis ballclub, who declared themselves "Semi-pro Champions of North Carolina," were managed by Manley Llewellyn. A star pitcher for the University of North Carolina, Llewellyn was signed right out of college by the New York Yankees. He appeared in one game for the Yankees before going to the minor leagues where he spent several seasons (notice his Greenville, South Carolina uniform in this photo). Later an attorney and city judge in Concord, Llewellyn also served as president of two area minor leagues, the Tri-State League and the North Carolina State League. The Kannapolis ballclub members, from left to right, are (front row) Shuler Antley, Bryant Sherrill, Mack Haines, Robbie Motsinger, and Russell "Runt" Lee; (back row) Pat Glass, Mack McClain, Homer Fink, Red Irby, Bob Kirk, Carl Smith, Tiny Pheltes, Harvey Johnson, and Manley Llewellyn. (Courtesy of Hank Utley.)

Four

The Professionals

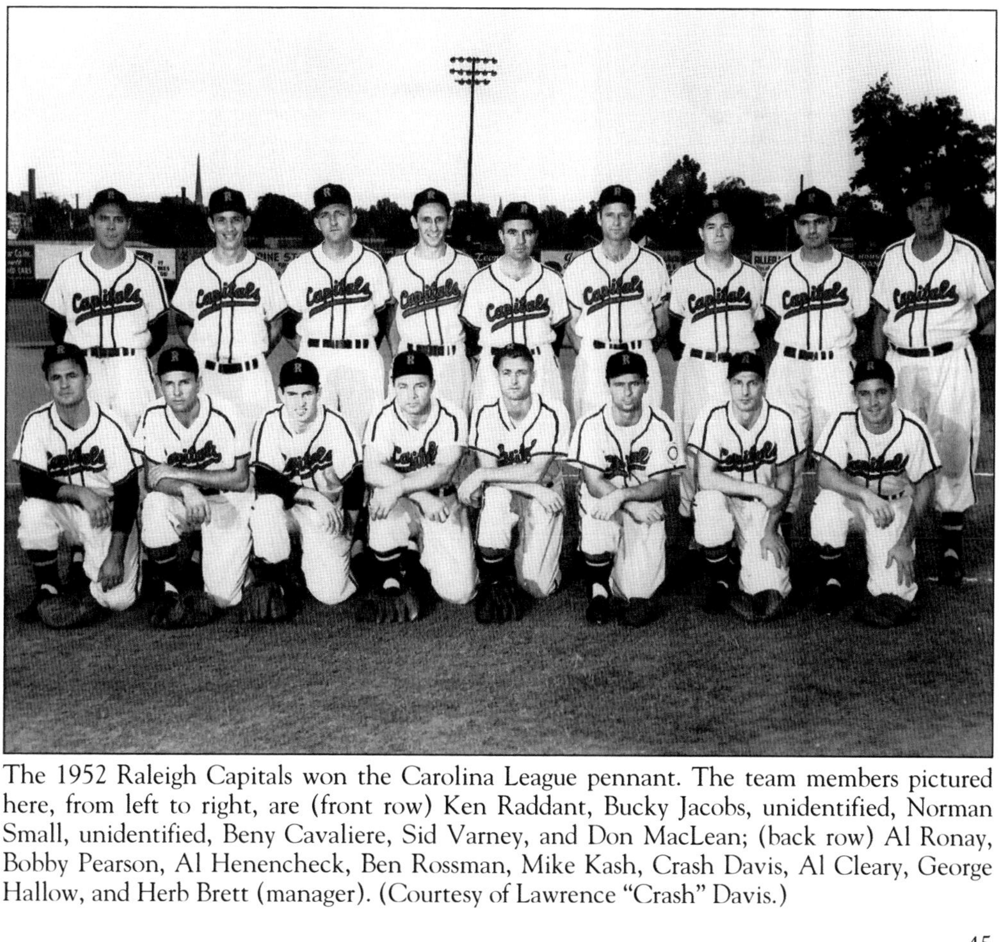

The 1952 Raleigh Capitals won the Carolina League pennant. The team members pictured here, from left to right, are (front row) Ken Raddant, Bucky Jacobs, unidentified, Norman Small, unidentified, Beny Cavaliere, Sid Varney, and Don MacLean; (back row) Al Ronay, Bobby Pearson, Al Henencheck, Ben Rossman, Mike Kash, Crash Davis, Al Cleary, George Hallow, and Herb Brett (manager). (Courtesy of Lawrence "Crash" Davis.)

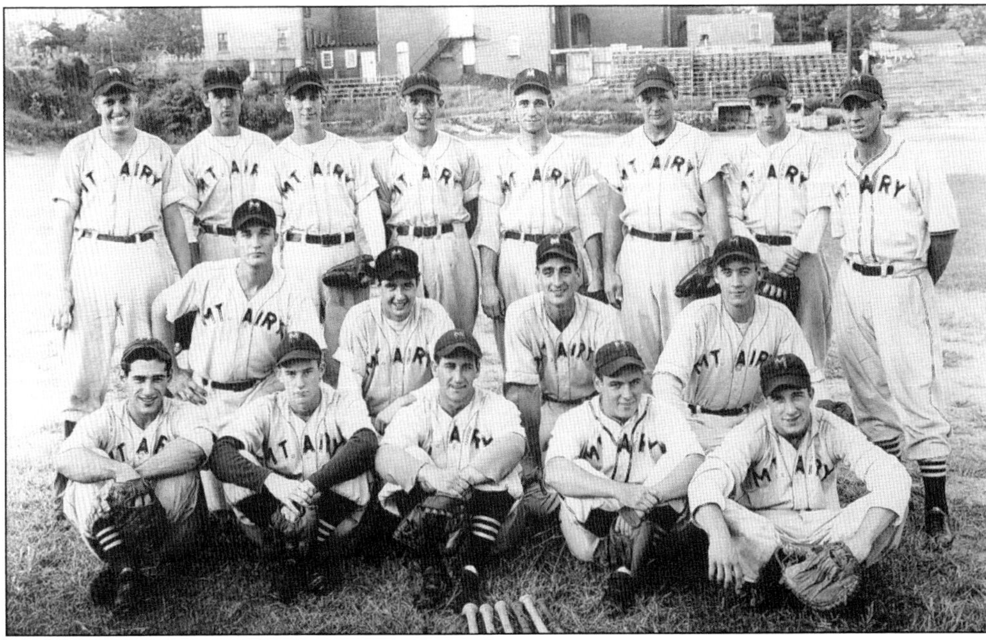

The 1948 Mount Airy Graniteers defeated the Galax Leafs from Virginia, four games to three, in the playoff finals to take the Blue Ridge League title. They are, from left to right, (front row) Marvin Zwelling, Harold Teer, Pete Treece, George Holmes, and Allen Yearick; (middle row) Reavis Marshall, John Williams, Frank Solters, and John Nixon; (back row) Charles Hall, Jack Holt, Stanley King, Robert Davis, Francis Essic, Dub Akins, ? Jackson, and Noel Casbier (manager). (Courtesy of David Beal.)

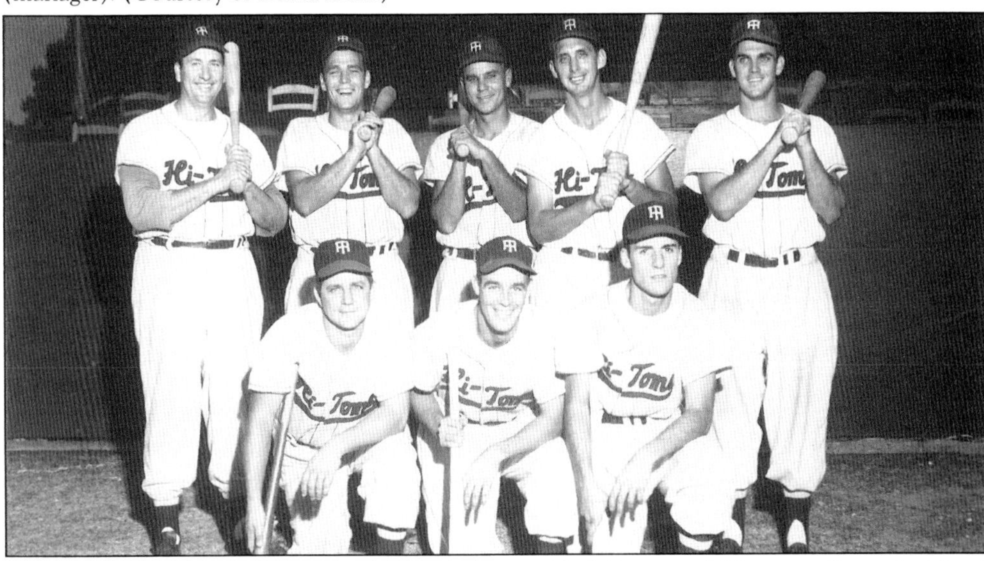

One team represented the two neighboring cities of High Point and Thomasville in the North Carolina State League from 1948 to 1952, the Tar Heel League in 1953, and the Carolina League from 1954 to 1958 and again from 1968 to 1969. Neither city has been home to professional baseball since. This photo shows members of the 1954 High Point-Thomasville Hi-Toms including, from left to right, (front row) all unidentified; (back row) Woody Rich, two unidentified, Don Stafford, and unidentified. (Courtesy of High Point Museum Archives.)

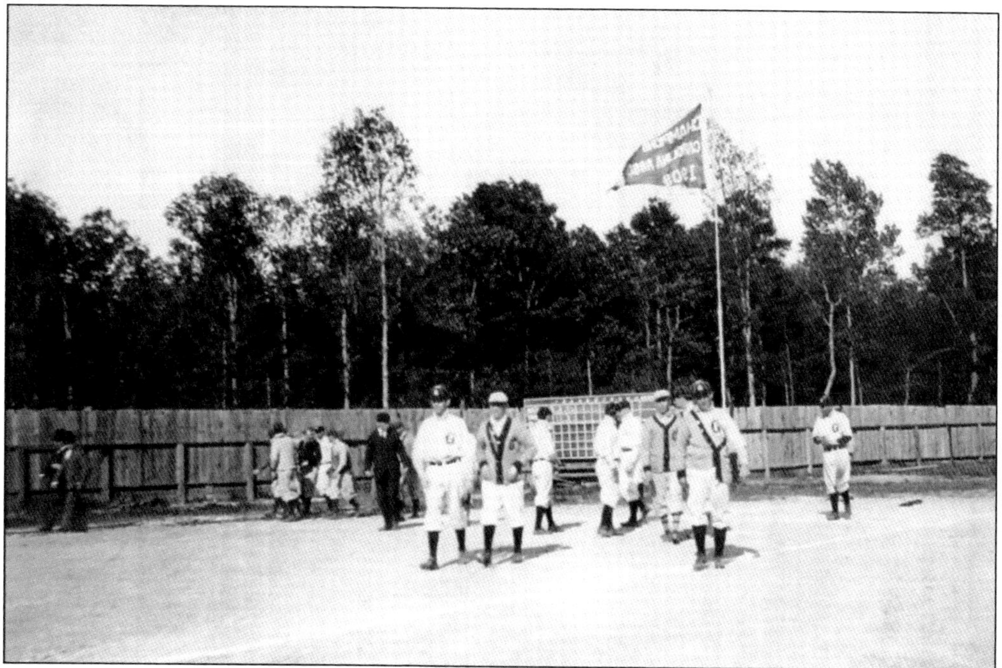

The two photos on this page show views of the 1910 Greensboro Champs, members of the Carolina Association, before a game at Cone Park. In the upper photo the pennant the Champs won for taking the 1909 league title is visible flying above the scoreboard. The team was not so fortunate in 1910, however, and finished last in the six-team league. (Courtesy of Greensboro Historical Museum Archives.)

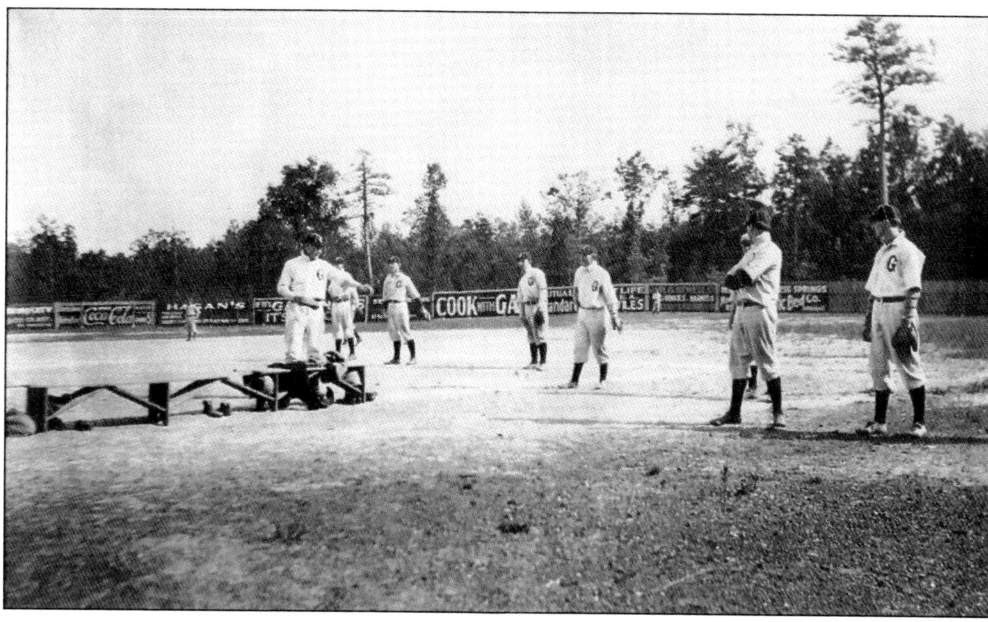

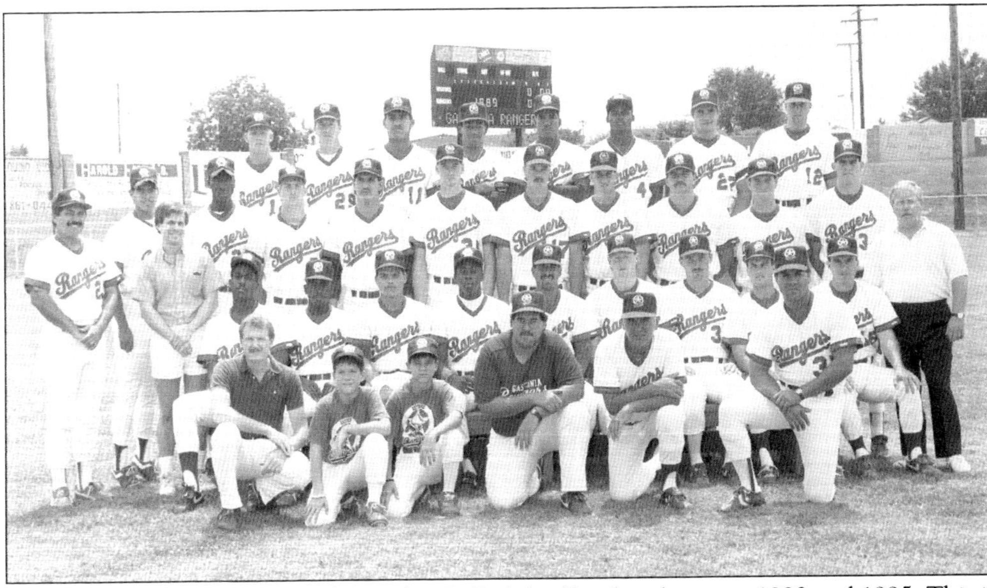

Gastonia was home to a minor league baseball club off and on between 1923 and 1995. This is the 1989 Gastonia Rangers of the South Atlantic League, a farm club of the big league Texas Rangers. Winners of the league's northern division that season, the Gastonia club featured catcher Ivan Rodriguez (second row, third from left), who developed into one of the best backstops in the history of the game. (From the collection of the author.)

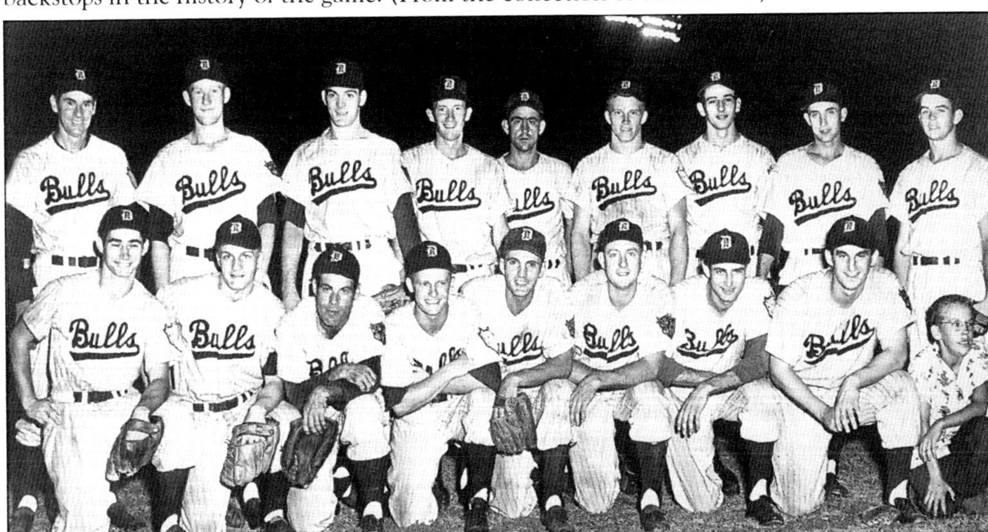

The 1953 Durham Bulls, a farm club of the Detroit Tigers, featured future big league pitcher Duke Maas. Catcher Ralph Caldwell never made it to the major leagues but his son Mike had a long standout career as a pitcher, primarily with the Milwaukee Brewers. The members of the Durham Bulls in 1953, from left to right, are (front row) Harry Durkin, Joe Lewis, Eddie Neville, Maurice Mikesell, two unidentified, Duane "Duke" Maas, and Bill Radulovich; (back row) Marv Owen, Herb Grissom, Larry Donovan, Andy Frazier, Ralph Caldwell, Fred Fleming, George Alusik, Dan Searle, and unidentified. (Courtesy of Miles Wolff.)

Minnie Mendoza spent a total of 10 seasons and most of the 1960s in a Charlotte uniform. After retiring from the playing field he returned to serve as coach for his old team. He also coached the Burlington Indians of the Appalachian League and served as manager of that team in 1992. (From the collection of the author.)

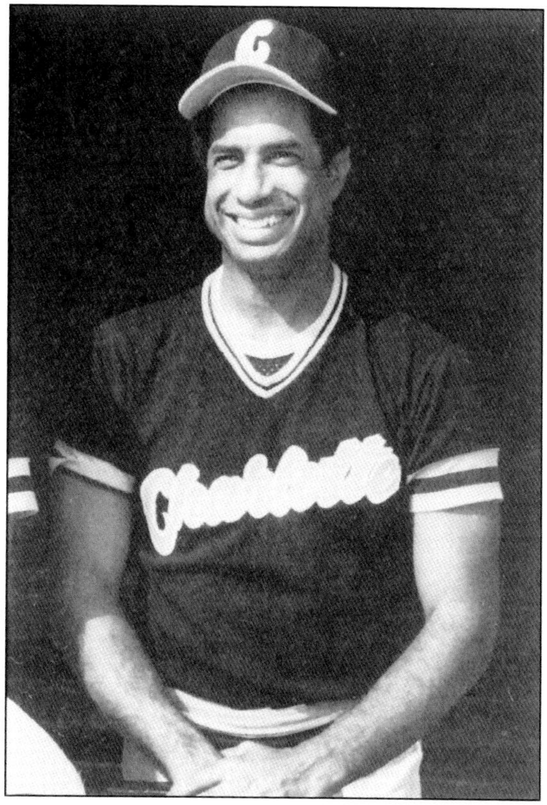

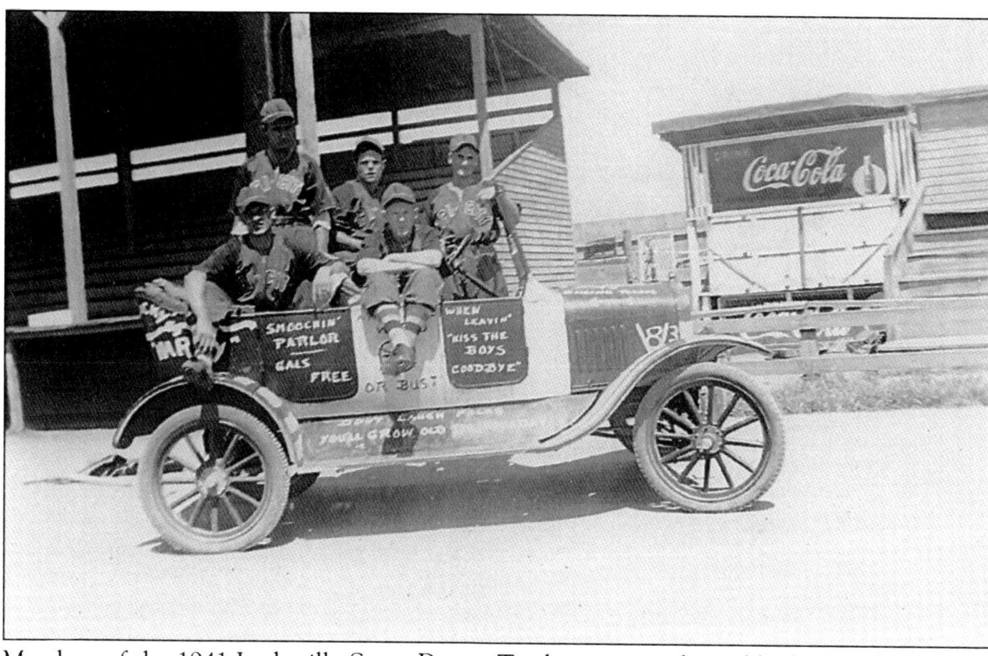

Members of the 1941 Leaksville-Spray-Draper Triplets pose in their old jalopy in front of the grandstand. From left to right are Al Letrick, J.D. Holt, Harry Land, Cotton Powell, and Ken Rhyne. (Courtesy of Cotton Powell.)

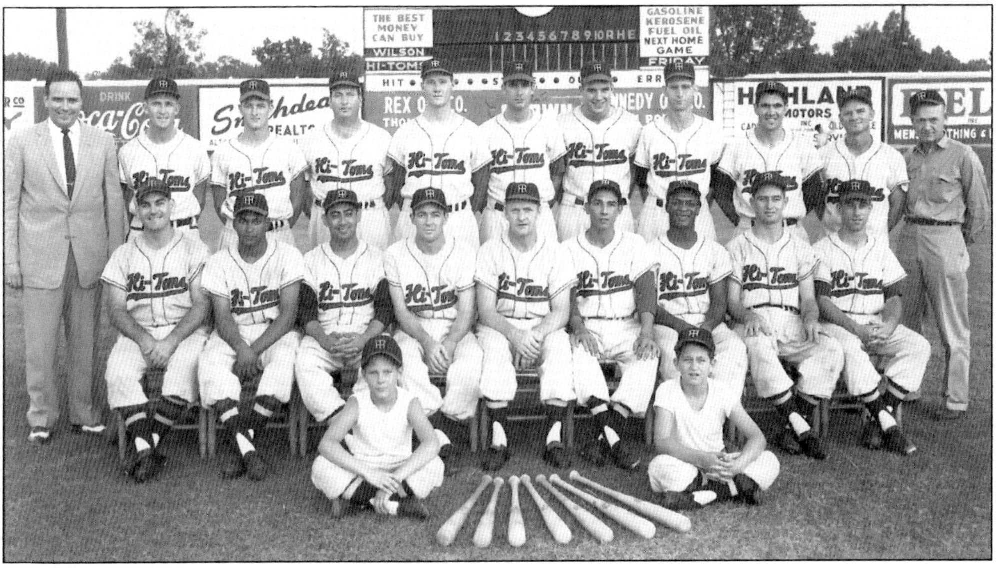

The 1956 High Point-Thomasville Hi-Toms featured 18-year-old outfielder Curt Flood, who would go on to become a three-time All-Star with the St. Louis Cardinals. Forty-year-old pitcher Woody Rich, on the other hand, was near the end of a long professional baseball career that had seen him spend parts of four seasons in the big leagues. From left to right are the following: (front row) Mike Goocy, Bo Bossard, Rene Solis, Bill Ford, Bert Haas (manager), Orlando Pena, Curt Flood, Karl Keuhl, and Charlie Brown; (back row) George Erath (business manager), Nelvin Cooper, Gail Thomas, Woody Rich, Bud Cooke, Amiel "Lefty" Solomon, Haven Schmidt, Jack Taylor, Gus Carmichael, Fred Harrington, and Austin Kearns (groundskeeper). (Courtesy of High Point Museum Archives.)

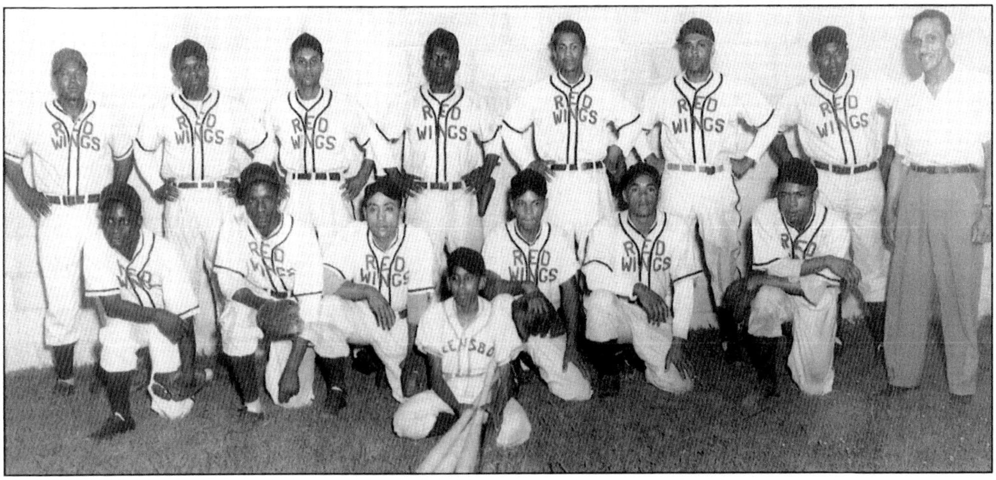

The 1948 Goshen Red Wings were a Greensboro team that played in the Negro Leagues of the state. Pictured here, from left to right, are (front row) Clemente Verona, Joe Siddle, William Davis, Spud Chandler, Ed Ledwell, and John Tonkins; (back row) Charles Parks, Charlie Roach, Hubert Simmons, Benny Harrison, Herman Taylor, ? Johnson, Scooter Watkins, and Brian Morris (business manager). Pitcher William Davis had previously played for Negro big league teams in Washington and Philadelphia and third baseman Charlie Roach would be one of the first players to integrate the white minor leagues in North Carolina when he signed with New Bern of the Coastal Plain League in 1952. (Courtesy of William Davis.)

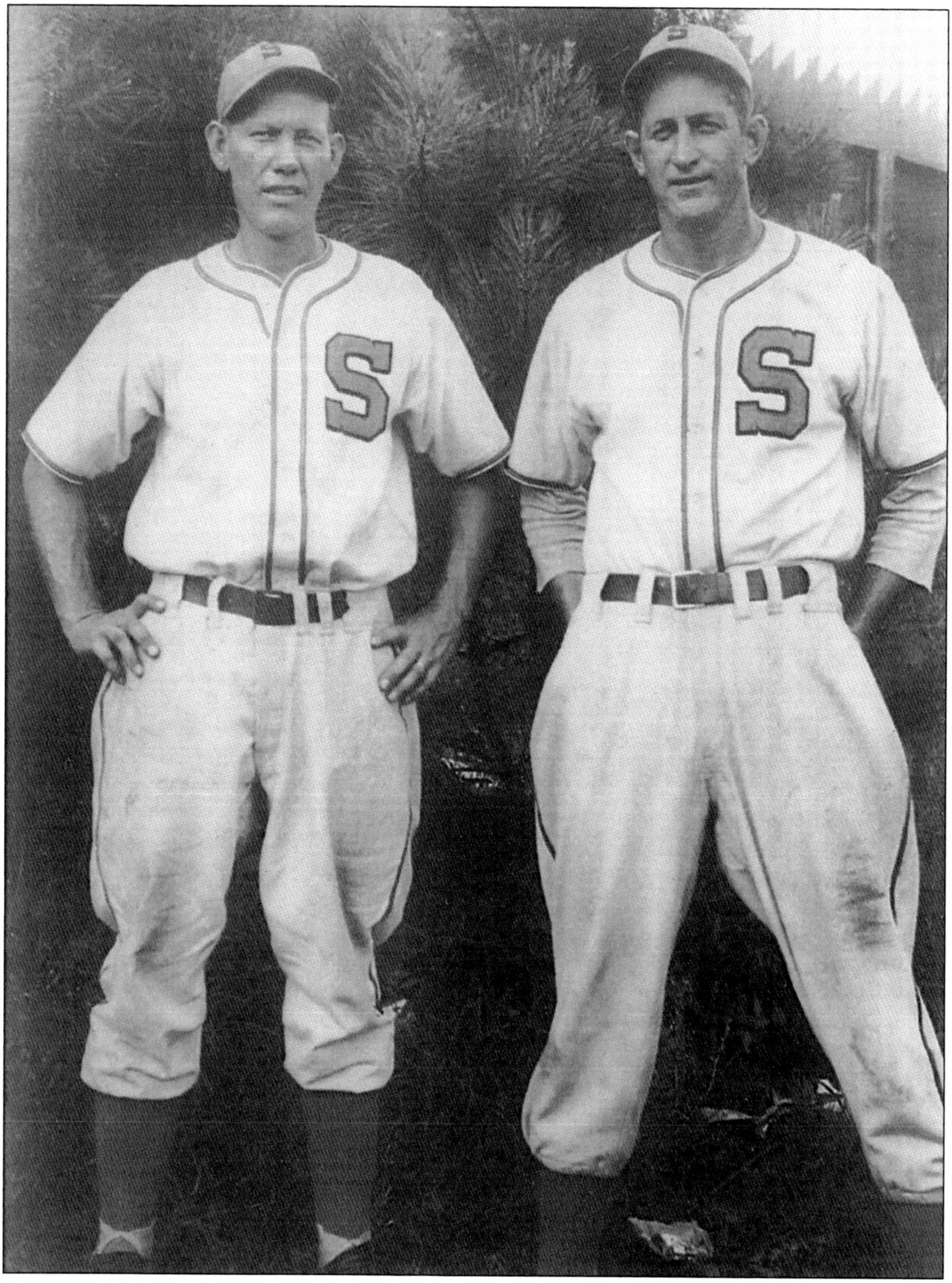

Manager Gaither Riley and outfielder Hank Nesselrode were members of the Sanford Spinners in 1946. Nesselrode had been on his way upward in the minor leagues when World War II came along and he missed four seasons while serving in the United States Army. When discharged he resumed his playing career but the frostbite damage he suffered to his feet during the war robbed him of his speed. No longer a hot prospect, Nesselrode signed with the Tobacco State League's Sanford club, and from 1946 through 1948 he led the league in homeruns and runs batted in and never hit for an average below .350. (Courtesy of Gaither Riley.)

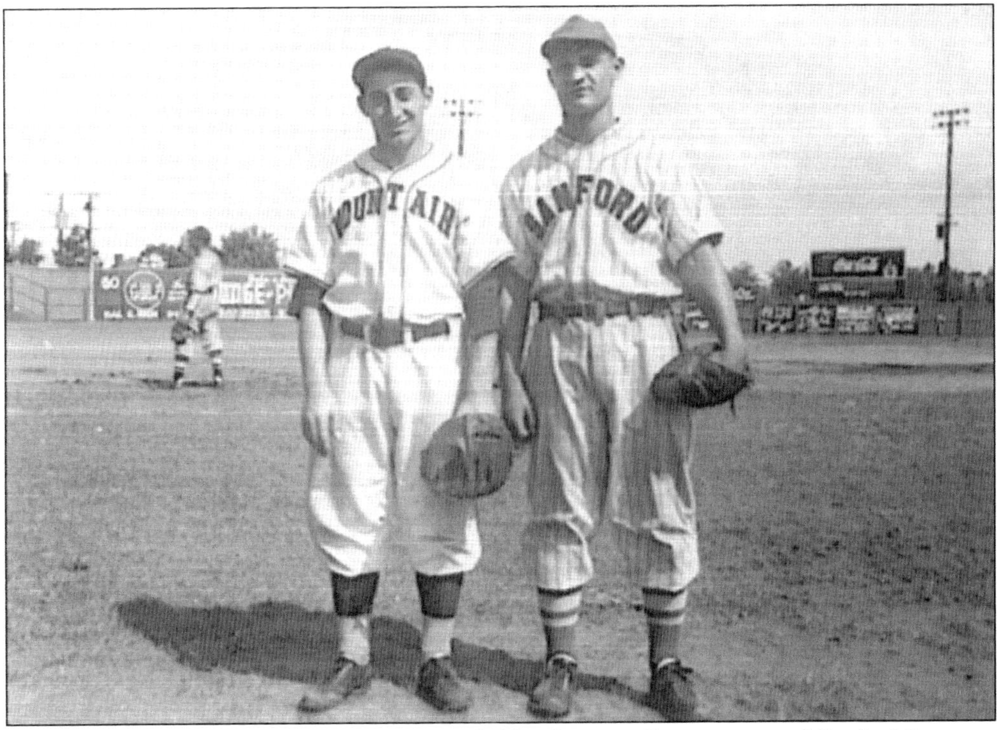

This is a photo of Mount Airy Graniteers outfielder Carmine Dispenziere and Sanford Spinners catcher J.B. Ruark chatting before a Bi-State League game in 1941. (Courtesy of Harry Land.)

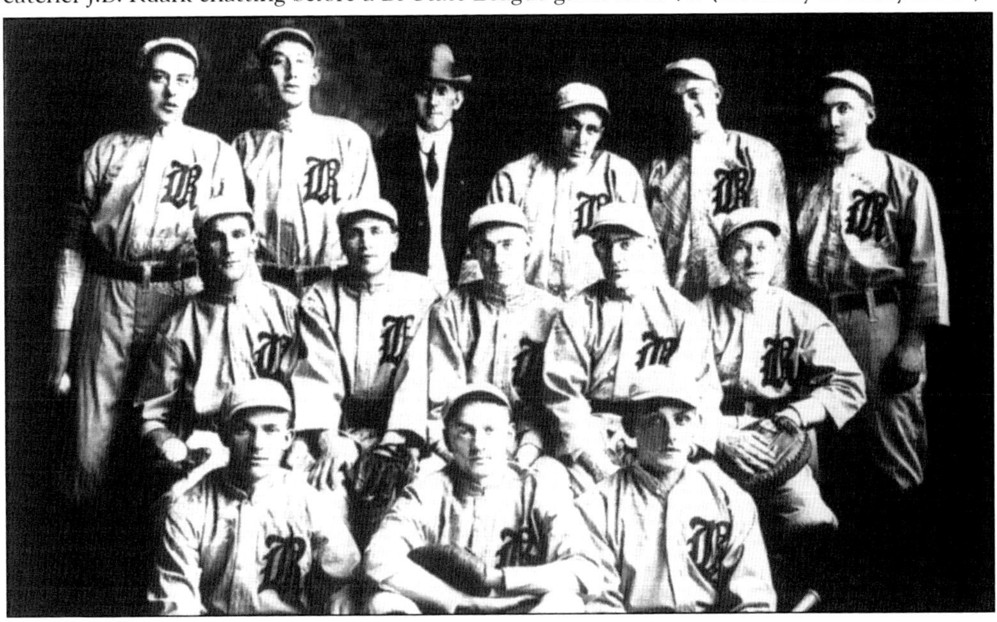

This Raleigh Capitals baseball team competed in the North Carolina State League sometime in the 1910s. It is very possible that the man in the suit on the back row is Earle Mack, who managed the Capitals from 1913 to 1915. The son of legendary Philadelphia Athletics manager Connie Mack, Earle Mack went on to work with his father in the big leagues. (Courtesy of the North Carolina Department of Archives and History.)

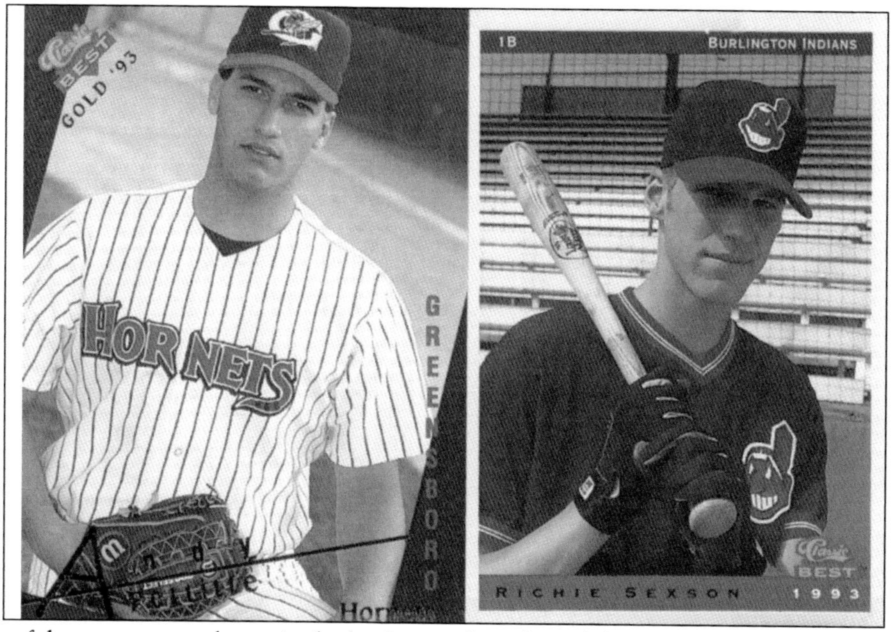

Many of the current top players in the big leagues have honed their skills with the minor league teams of the area including Andy Pettite with the Greensboro Hornets and Richie Sexson with the Burlington Indians, shown here on their 1993 baseball cards. Pettite would go on to become a star pitcher for the New York Yankees while first baseman Sexson developed into a powerful slugger for the Milwaukee Brewers. (From the collection of the author.)

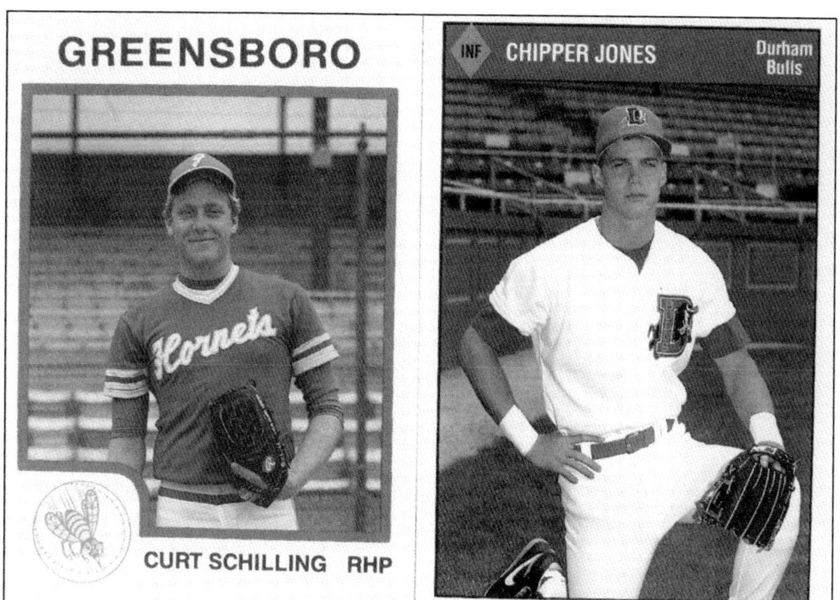

This pair of baseball cards also features two current big league stars in their days with area minor league teams. Curt Schilling, World Series hero for the 2001 Arizona Diamondbacks, pitched for the Greensboro Hornets in 1987 while Atlanta Braves third baseman Chipper Jones played on the left side of the infield for the 1992 Durham Bulls. (From the collection of the author.)

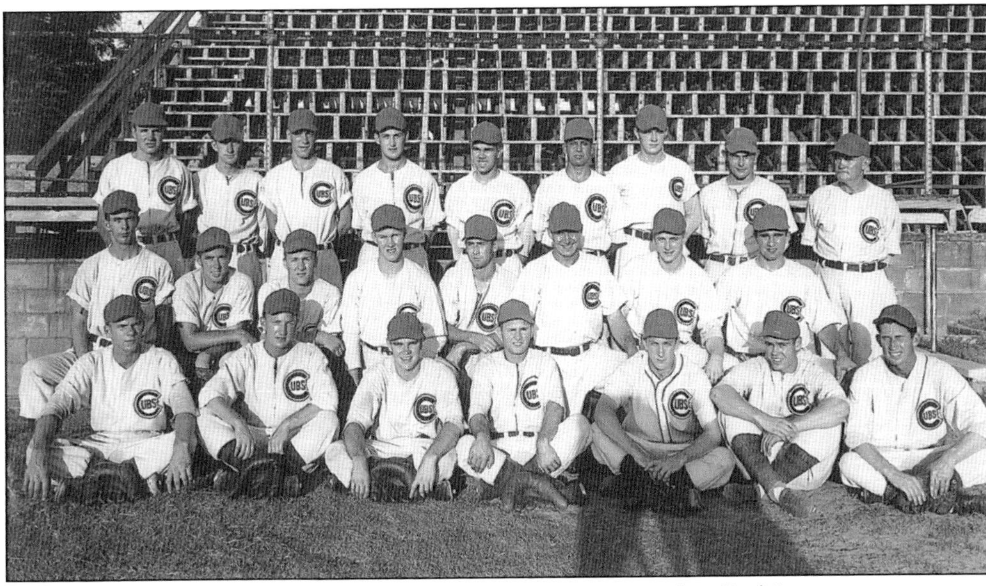

The 1947 Lumberton Cubs, managed by former big league pitcher Red Lucas, were a part of the Tobacco State League. From left to right are (front row) Bill Wood, Doug Lorman, Willard Erhardt, Bob Spicer, unidentified, Shelton Stanley, and unidentified; (middle row) Jerry Cabaniss, Bill Kivett, two unidentified, Willie Crummie, Charlie Jamin, Bill Dalton, and Andy Payonk; (back row) Ralph Dixon, unidentified, Wallace Pearsall, Elzer Marx, John Zmidewski, Manuel Garcia, two unidentified, and Charles "Red" Lucas. (Courtesy of Buddy Frazier.)

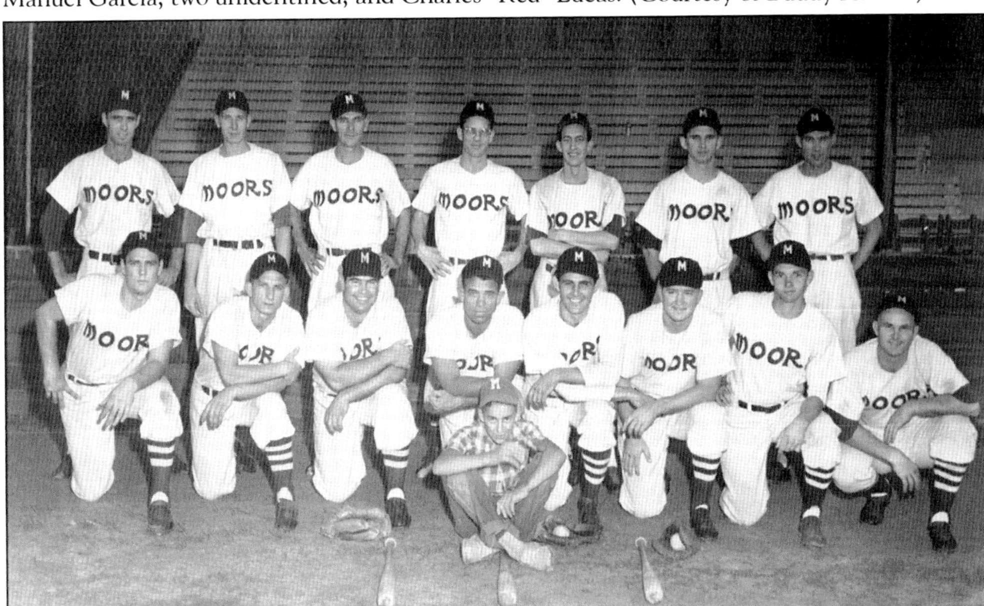

With a 70-39 record, the 1952 Mooresville Moors finished second to High Point-Thomasville in the North Carolina State League standings; next they took the postseason title by defeating Elkin and Salisbury in the playoffs. Pictured from left to right are (front row) Ed Cannon, Charley Richkus, Fred Daniels, Tom Jones, unidentified, Billy Megginson, Joe Brookshire, and Jim Mills (manager); (back row) Tom Griffith, Robert Smith, unidentified, Charlie Suggs, Ozzie Gladden, Henry Lineberger, and Fred Chapman. (From the collection of the author.)

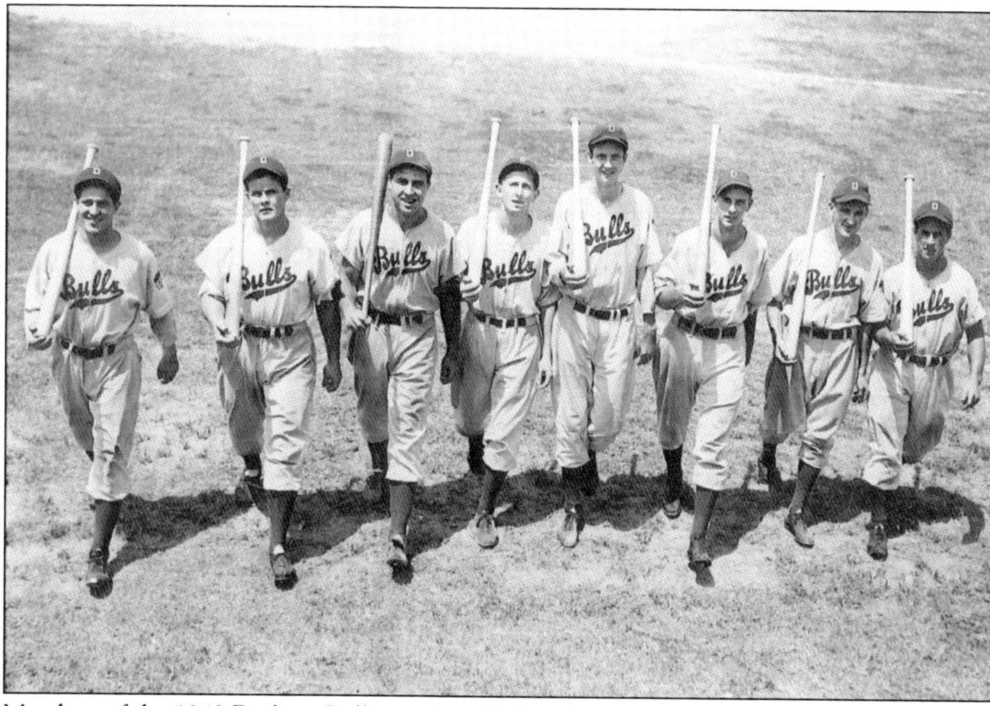

Members of the 1942 Durham Bulls march with their bats as they prepare to go off to war. The players from left to right, are Steve Nagy, Ferrell Anderson, Emo Showfety, Richard Whitman, Charles Welchel, Harold Haub, Lou Welaj, and Bud Kimball. (Courtesy of Emo Showfety.)

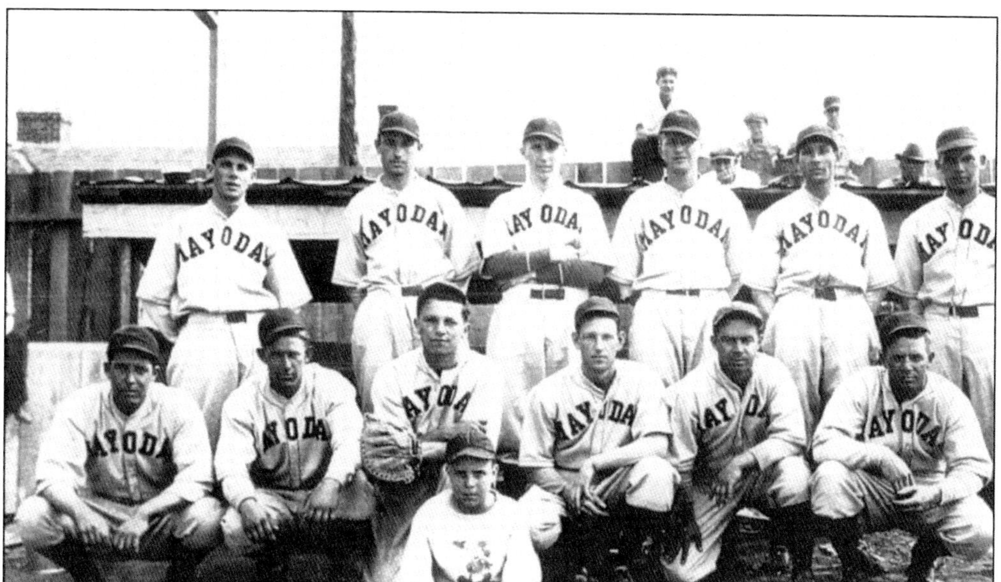

The Rockingham County town of Mayodan was home to professional baseball for eight seasons. The first team, the 1934 Senators, are shown here. From left to right are (front row) ? Eyer, Eddie Weston, C. Stye, Del Breece, J. Dunn, and ? Lindley; (back row) Cecil "Zip" Payne, ? Tate, Lefty Shearin, L. Andrews, A. Brown, and E. Timmers. (Courtesy of Buddy Payne.)

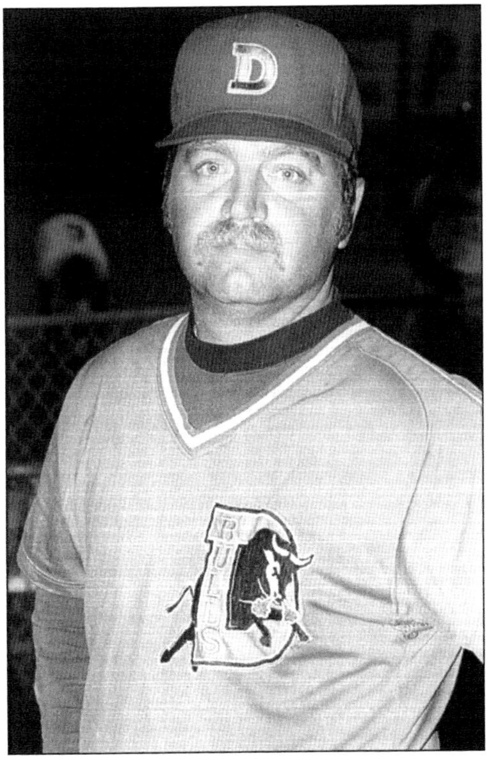

With the Atlanta organization since 1979, Leo Mazzone was assigned as pitching coach for the Durham Bulls, the Braves' Carolina League affiliate, in 1983 and 1984. Since 1990 he has served in that same capacity for the big league club and is credited for much of the success of the Braves' great pitching staff. (From the collection of the author.)

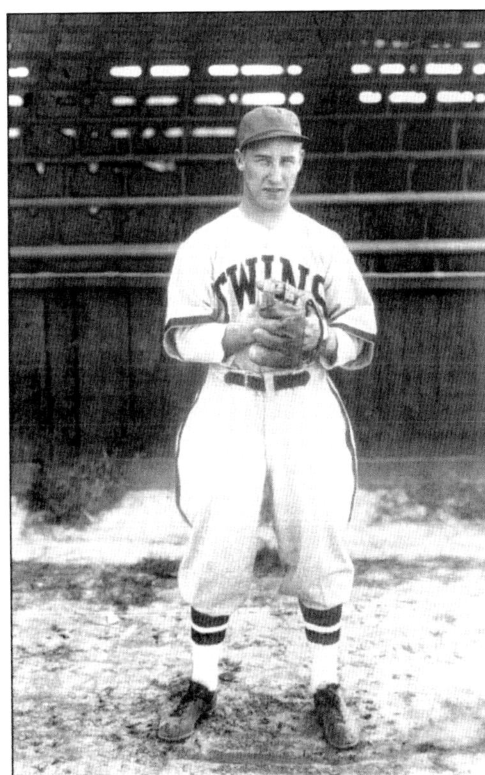

Amil Brinsky was a starting outfielder for the 1940 Winston-Salem Twins of the Piedmont League. (Courtesy of David Beal.)

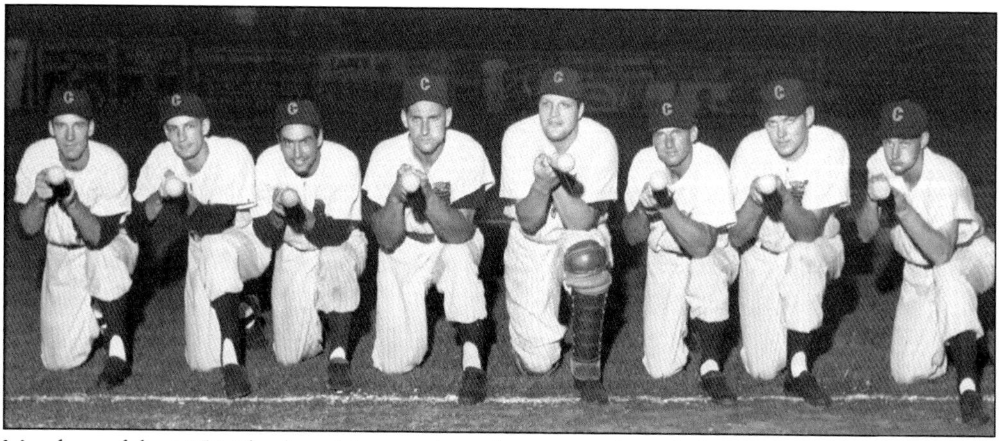

Members of the 1956 Charlotte Hornets show they are ready to do battle on the diamond. From left to right are Phil Mateja, Dickie Harris, Gene Verble, Harry Warner, Joe Montalvo, Johnny Kropf, Ken Wood, and Glenn Zimmerman. (Courtesy of Gene Verble.)

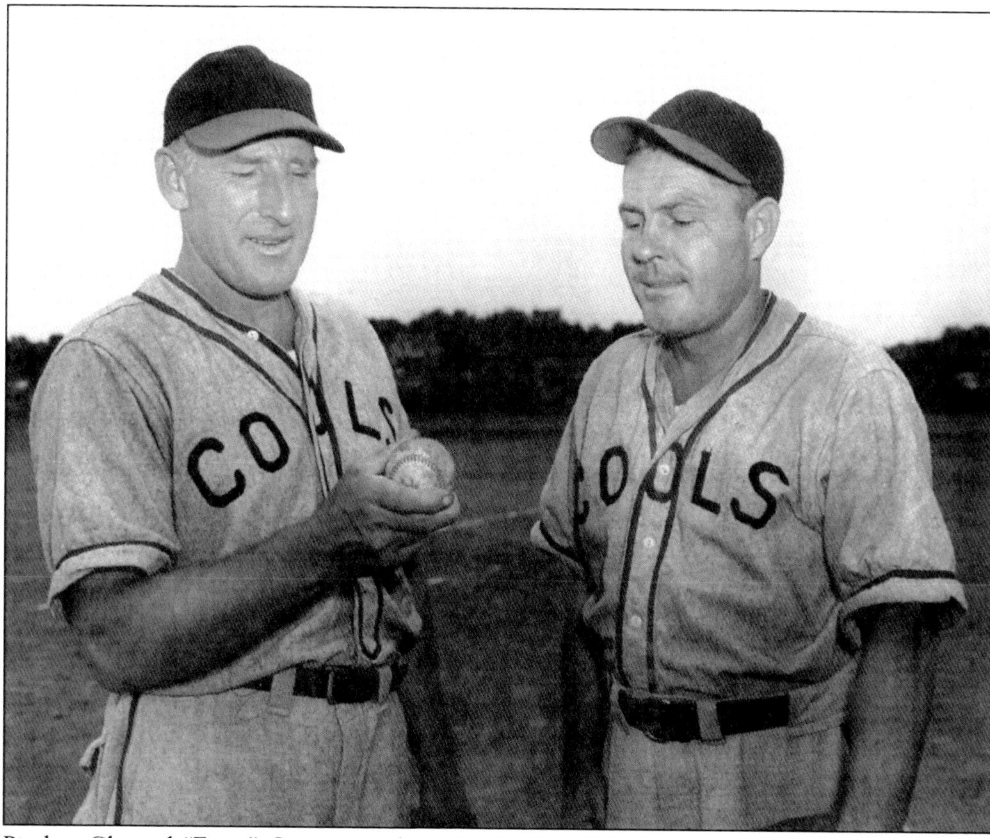

Pitcher Clanard "Firpo" Creason and catcher Luther Whitlock, members of the Cooleemee Cools, discuss strategy before a game in 1939. The Cools played in the North Carolina State League, which included towns like Salisbury, Thomasville, and Landis. (Courtesy of Cooleemee Textile Heritage Center Archives.)

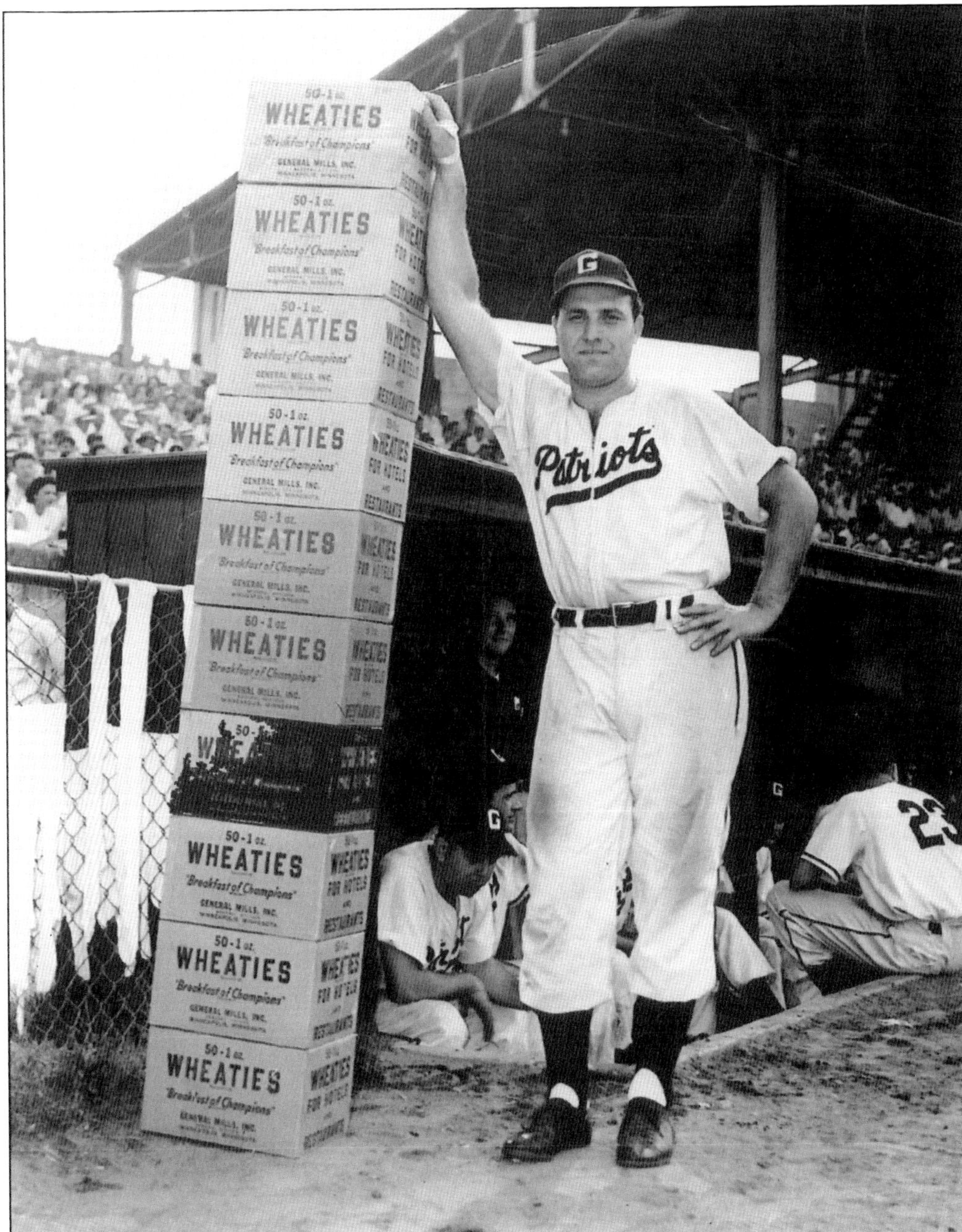

Greensboro native Emil "Emo" Showfety, a graduate of Elon College, was successfully working his way up the minor league ladder when World War II interrupted his career plans. Considered too old to be a major league prospect after three years in the military, he returned to North Carolina where he became a star in the Carolina League. Here he is shown in 1949 as a member of the Greensboro Patriots with cases of Wheaties that he won for hitting homeruns. He would hit 35 round-trippers that season, bat .347, and drive in 120 runs. (Courtesy of Emo Showfety.)

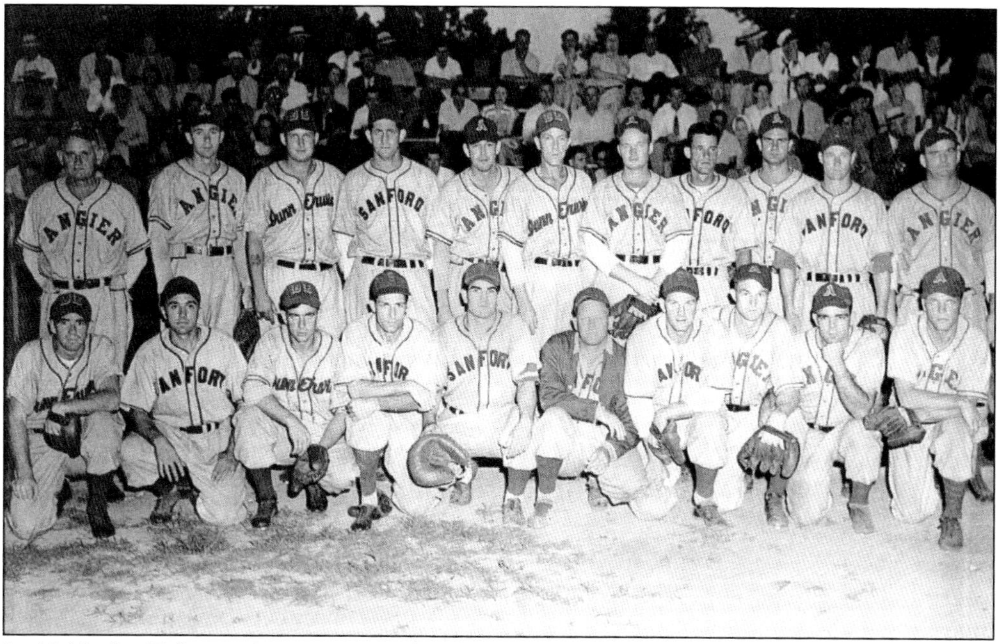

In 1946, the Tobacco State League played an All-Star game at mid-season. Each team was comprised of the top players from three of the league's six-member clubs. This was the All-Star team with members from the towns of Angier-Fuquay Springs, Dunn-Erwin, and Sanford. From left to right are the following: (front row) Andrew Holliday, Phalti Shoffner, Granville "Shamrock" Denning, Jimmy Guinn, Paul Crawford, Zeb Harrington (manager), Joe Nessing, Joe Mills, Ken Jackson, and Paul Hunt; (back row) ? Smith, Marvin Lorenz, Ed Bass, Hank Nesselrode, Jim Taylor, Jim Stephenson, Jim House, Howard Auman, Ray Hardee, Bob Pugh, and Bruce Hedrick. (Courtesy of Howard Auman.)

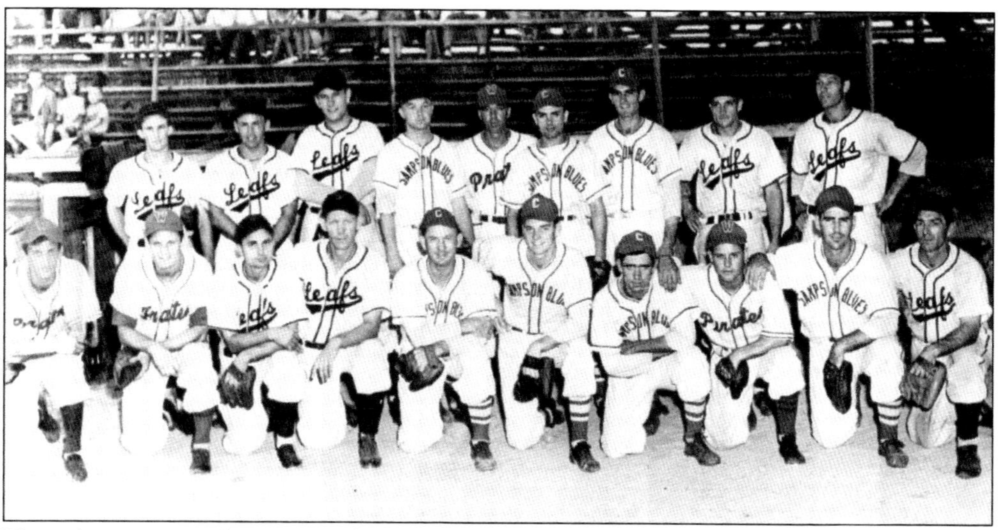

The other team in the 1946 Tobacco State League All-Star game featured the best players from the Smithfield-Selma, Clinton, and Wilmington clubs. Pictured here from left to right are (front row) two unidentified, Mickey Balla, Gaither Riley (manager), Willie Duke, and five unidentified; (back row) Pete Howard, Dick Woodard, Hearn Robinson, three unidentified, Leo Niezgoda, and unidentified. (Courtesy of Gaither Riley.)

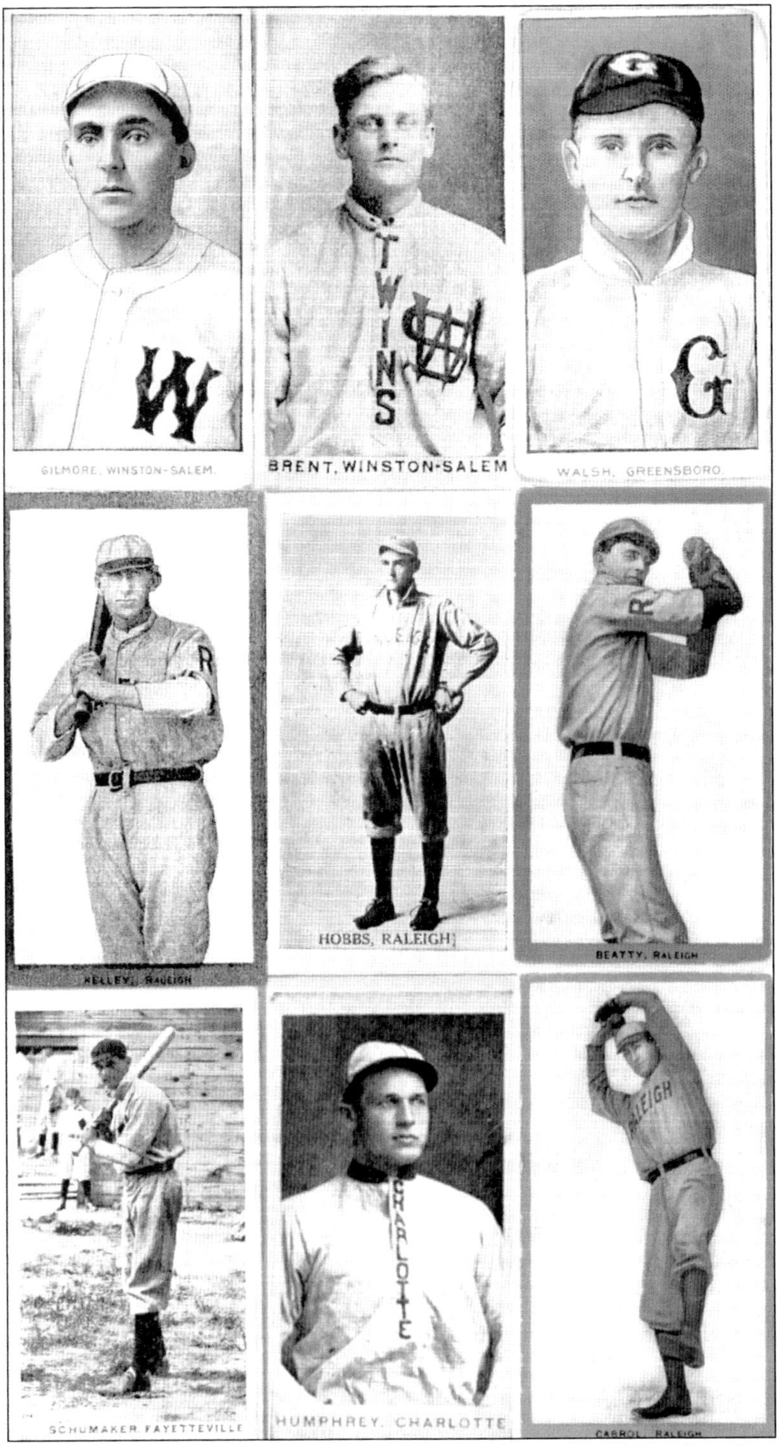

From around 1909 to 1911, several tobacco companies, including Old Mill and Contentnea, produced baseball cards. Inserted into packs of cigarettes, many of these cards featured players from the area's minor league teams. (Courtesy of Doug Klein.)

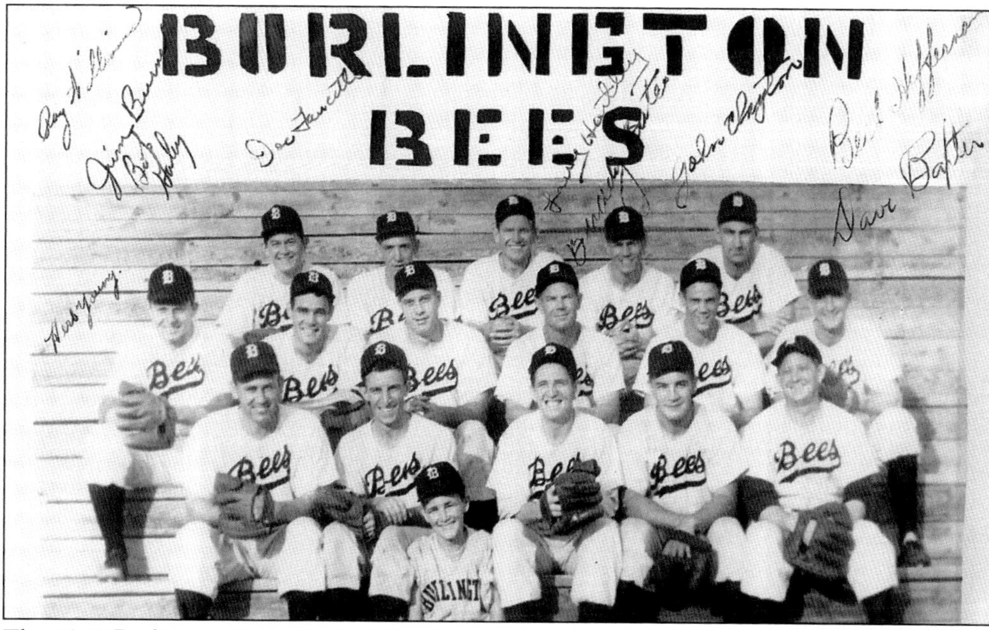

The 1948 Burlington Bees finished third in the Carolina League with an 80-62 record. From left to right are the following: (front row) Dick Woodard, Pete Howard, Mike Hefner, Norm Wilson, and Maxie Wilson; (middle row) Herb Young, Ray Williams, Jim Burns, Buddy Bates, Claude Swiggett, and Bob Falk; (back row) Bob Gailey, Doc Faucette, Larry Hartley, John Clayton, Dave Baxter, and Larry Brammer (batboy). (Courtesy of Pete Howard.)

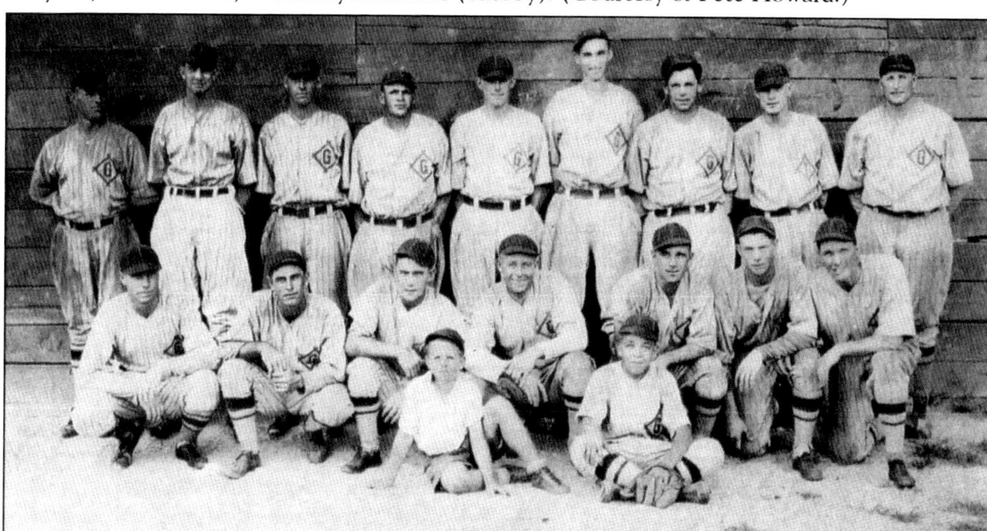

The Greensboro Patriots finished second in the 1929 regular season with an 85-51 record, but in the playoffs they defeated the first-place Durham Bulls to take the Piedmont League championship. Pitcher Jim Tuner would go on to make the big leagues and as a 34-year-old rookie in 1937 he won 20 games for the Boston Braves. The batboys are ? Forbis, and ? Carroll. The players, from left to right, are (front row) Jim Turner, ? Cross, Toots Brandon, Charlie Carroll (manager), ? Kilpatrick, Floyd "Pep" Young, and ? Mayo; (back row) Hobe Brummitt, ? Leight, K. Smith, ? Teague, ? Jeffries, Molly Cox, Henry Parrish, Ulmont Baker, and Rube Crews. (Courtesy of Hank Utley.)

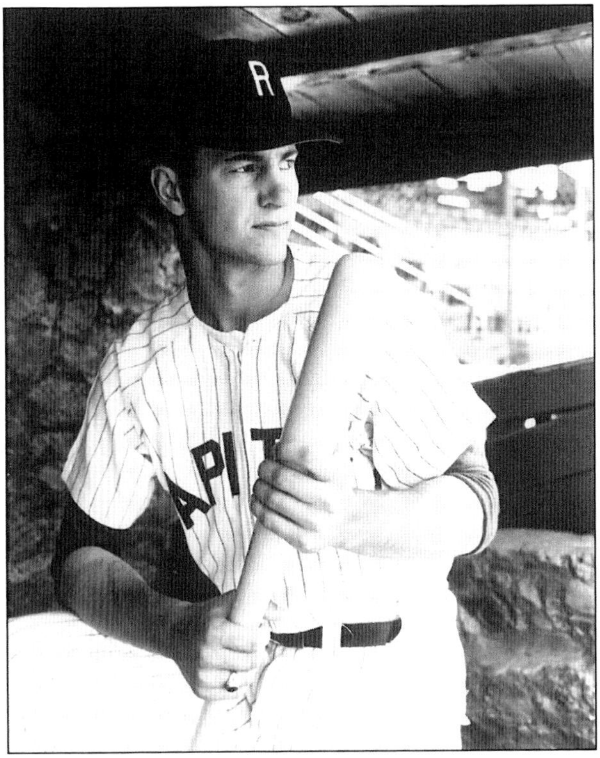

In his first year of professional baseball and just 19 years old when the season began, Carl Yastrzemski won the Carolina League batting title with the 1959 Raleigh Caps. Two years later he made his big league debut for the Red Sox and for 23 seasons was an outfield fixture in Boston. He was elected to the Hall of Fame in 1989. (Courtesy of the North Carolina Department of Archives and History.)

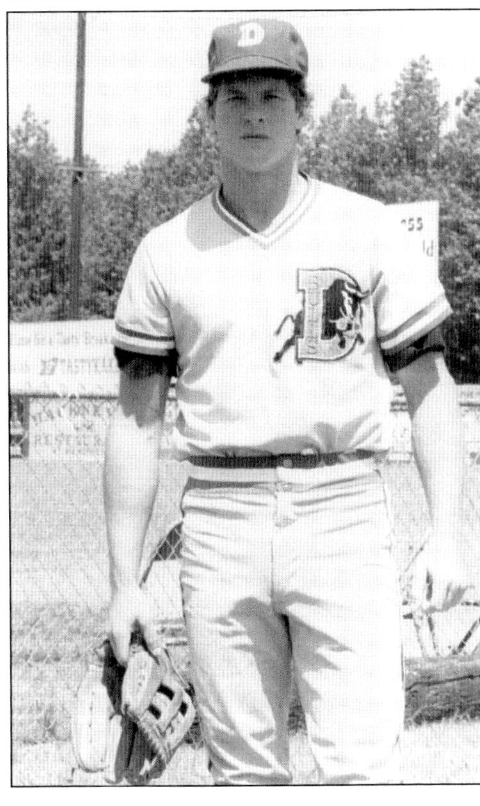

Carl Yastrzemski's son Mike never reached the big leagues but he did spend the 1984 and 1985 seasons as one of the Durham Bulls' top outfielders. (From the collection of the author.)

Santiago Perez was the starting shortstop for the 1995 Fayetteville Generals of the South Atlantic League. A native of the Dominican Republic, Perez worked his way up to the big leagues and spent much of the 2001 season with the San Diego Padres. (From the collection of the author.)

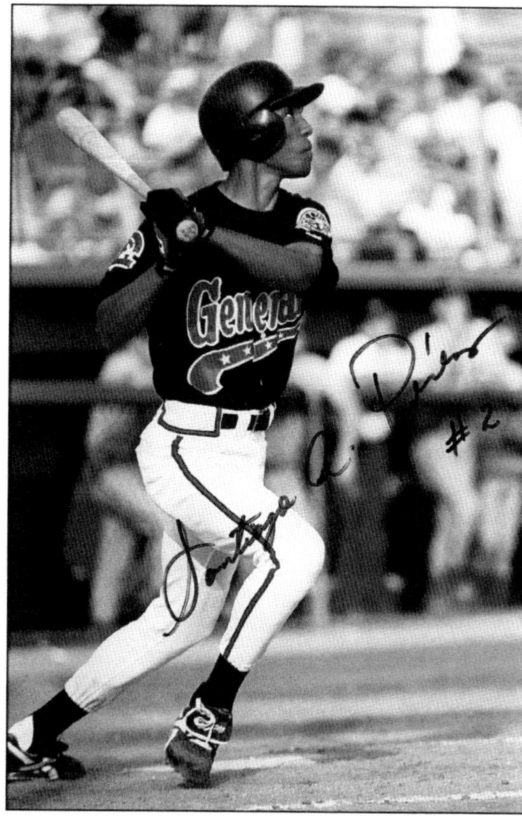

The 1942 Leaksville-Spray-Draper Triplets were led by player and manager Cecil "Zip" Payne (front row, third from left). The team would disband after that season, as would most others in the state, due to World War II. In 1967, the three Rockingham County towns that the Triplets once represented merged to form the town of Eden. (Courtesy of Buddy Payne.)

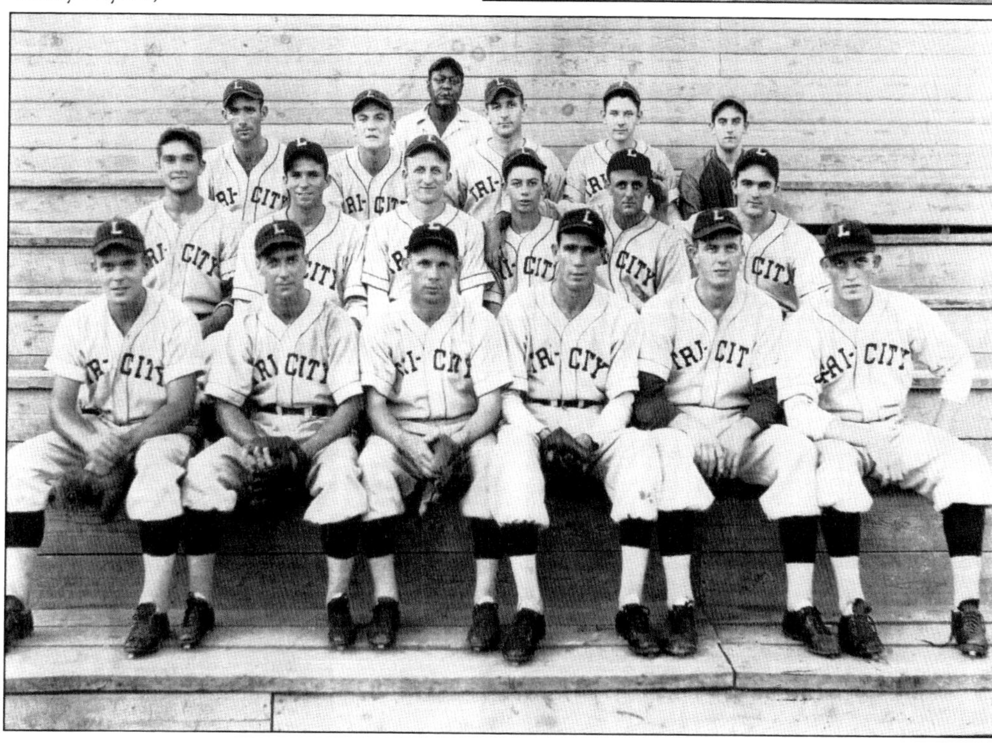

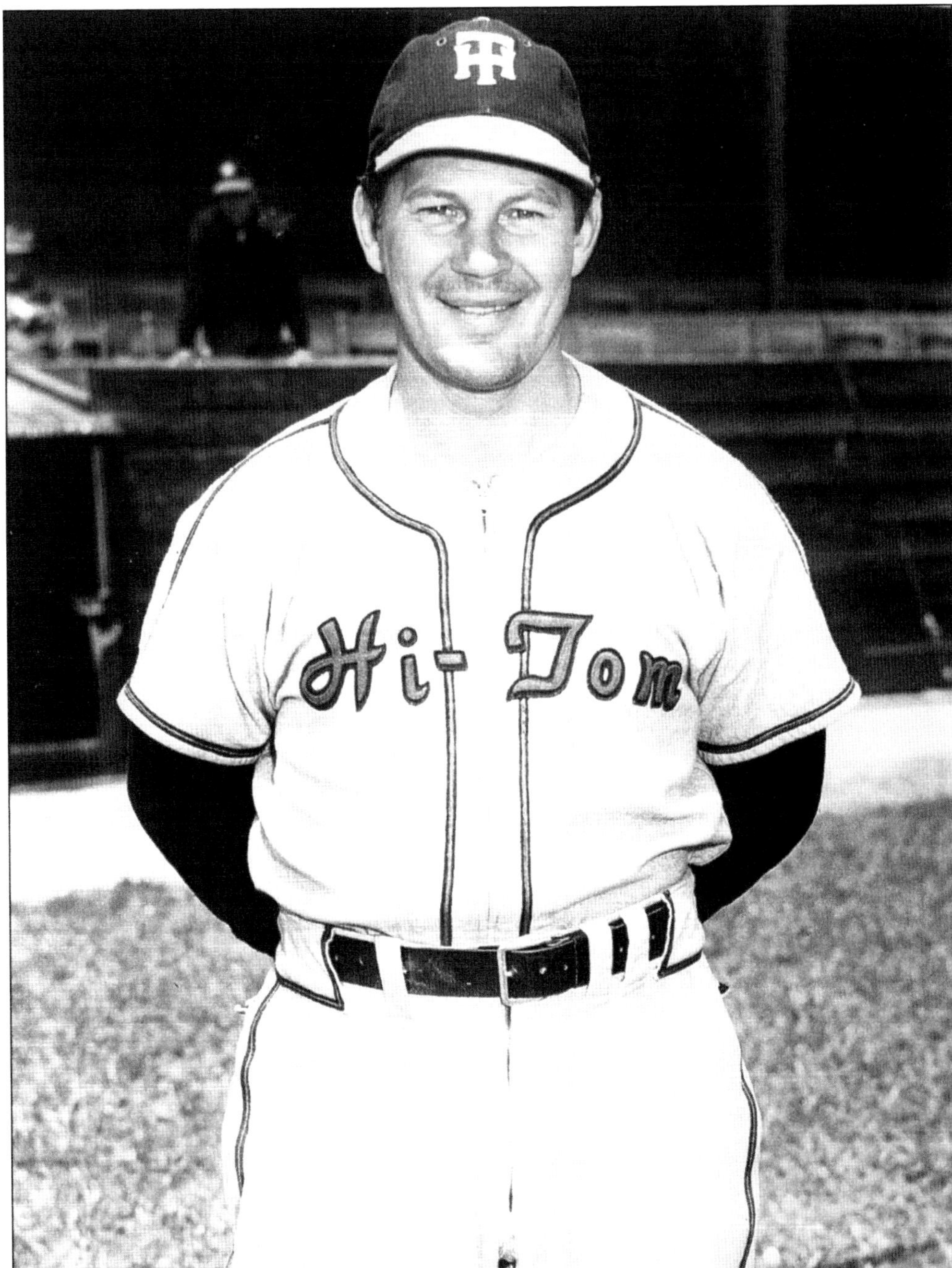

In the 1940s and early 1950s, Jimmy Gruzdis was one of the most familiar faces in North Carolina baseball. A well-traveled veteran, he first became a playing manager with Reidsville in 1940. In 1942, while with the Thomasville Tommies, Gruzdis accomplished a rare feat—his .418 batting average was the highest in all of professional baseball. For his accomplishment he was awarded a full-sized sterling silver bat. He later went on to spend six seasons (from 1948 to 1953) as the playing manager of the High Point-Thomasville Hi-Toms. (Courtesy of High Point Museum Archives.)

Mooresville Moors pitcher Elwood Bringle stares down an opponent from the mound at Moors Park. With a 21-4 record, Bringle was the North Carolina State League's top pitcher in 1949. (From the collection of the author.)

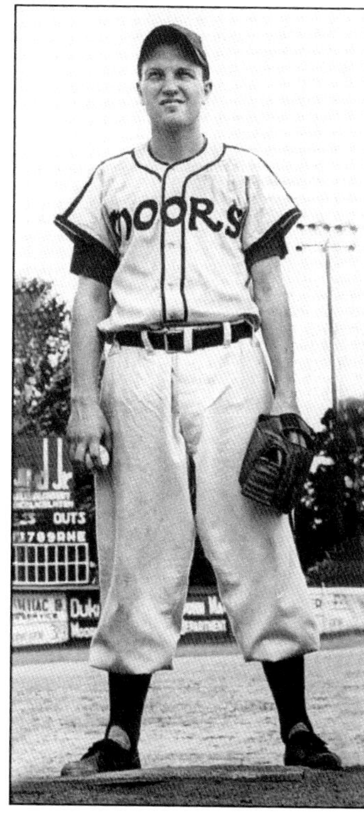

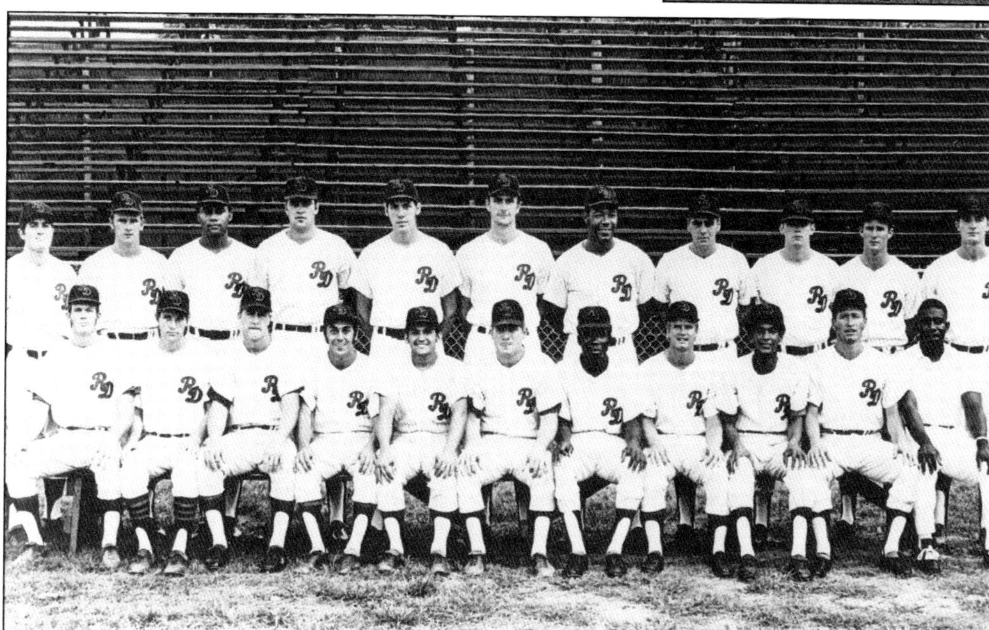

From 1968 to 1971, Raleigh and Durham fielded a joint team in the Carolina League. This is the 1970 Raleigh-Durham Triangles, who played half of their home games at Raleigh's Devereaux Meadow and half at Durham Athletic Park. Catcher Cliff Johnson (back row, fifth from right) was the league's Most Valuable Player that season and would go on to a long big league career. (Courtesy of Miles Wolff.)

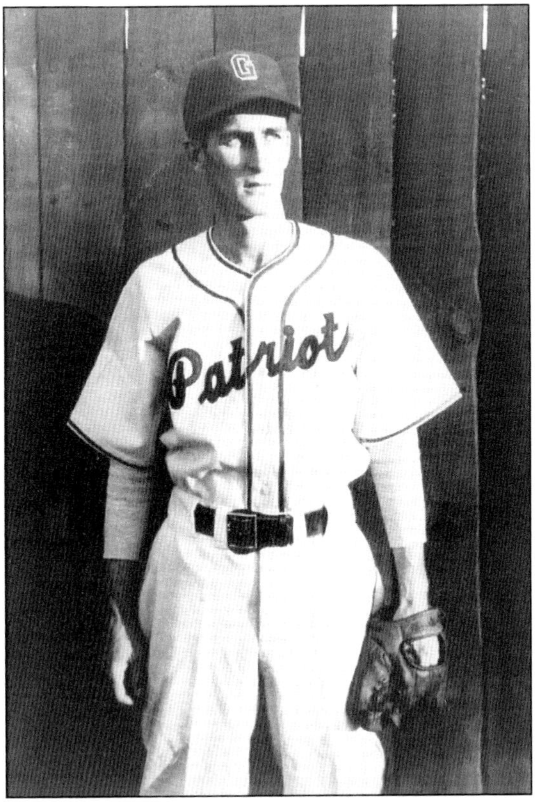

Bernie Keating was a star pitcher for Greensboro in 1946. With a record of 18-7 he helped lead the Patriots to the Carolina League pennant that season. (Courtesy of Bernie Keating.)

Ken Rhyne, Al Letrick, J.D. Holt, Cotton Powell, and Harry Land, all members of the 1941 Leaksville Triplets, line up for a photo at their ballpark. The five players were key participants in the Triplets' capture of the Bi-State League pennant that season. (Courtesy of Cotton Powell.)

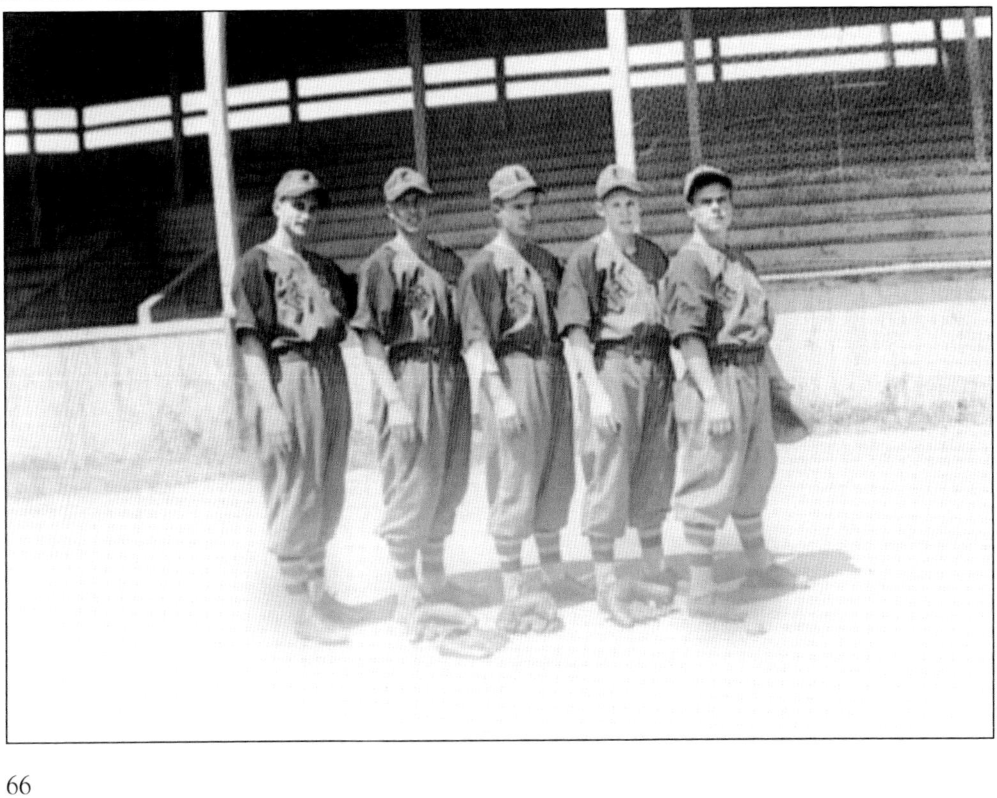

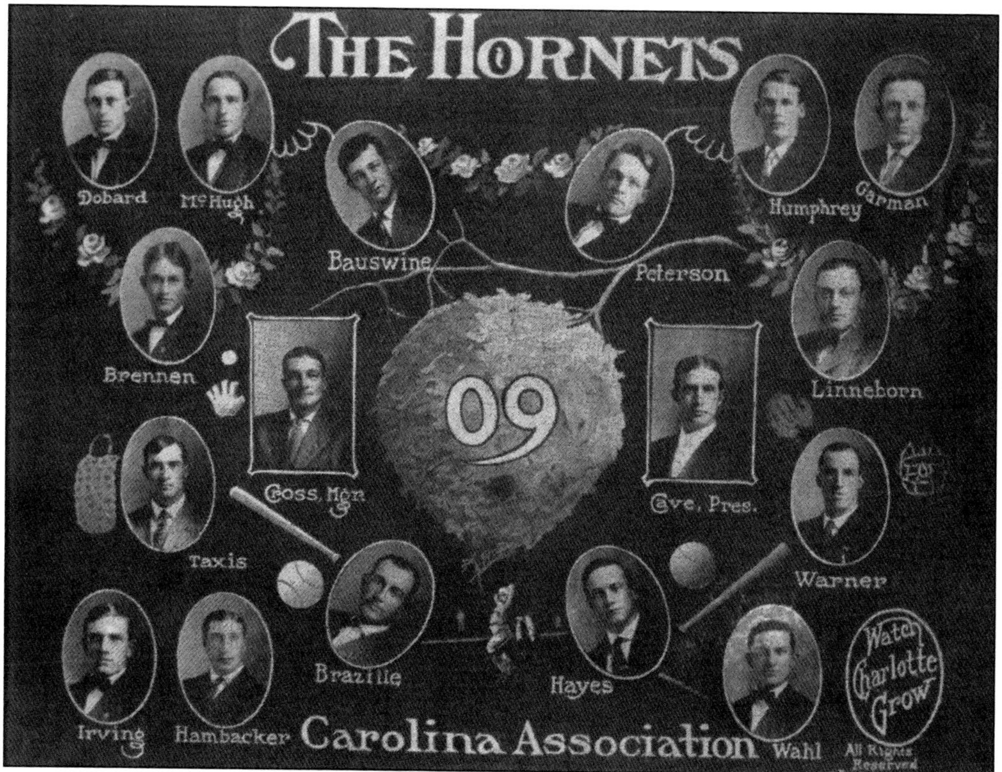

Led by outfielder Al Humphrey, the league's batting champ, the 1909 Charlotte Hornets had good offense, but because of a weak pitching staff they finished only fifth in the six-team Carolina Association. The manager that season was long-time major league star Lave Cross. (From the collection of the author.)

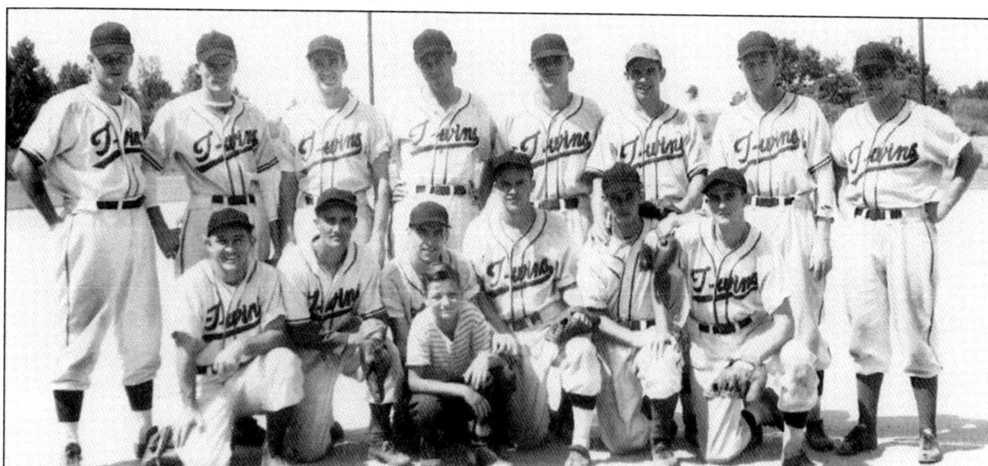

In 1946 the Dunn-Erwin Twins were the first entry of the two neighboring towns of Dunn and Erwin into the world of professional baseball. For four seasons the Twins competed in the Tobacco State League and even won the pennant in 1949. This 1946 team was not so fortunate and finished last, though Eddie Bass (back row, far left) and Granville "Shamrock" Denning (front row, second from right) were two of the best hitters in the six-team league. (Courtesy of Gaither Riley.)

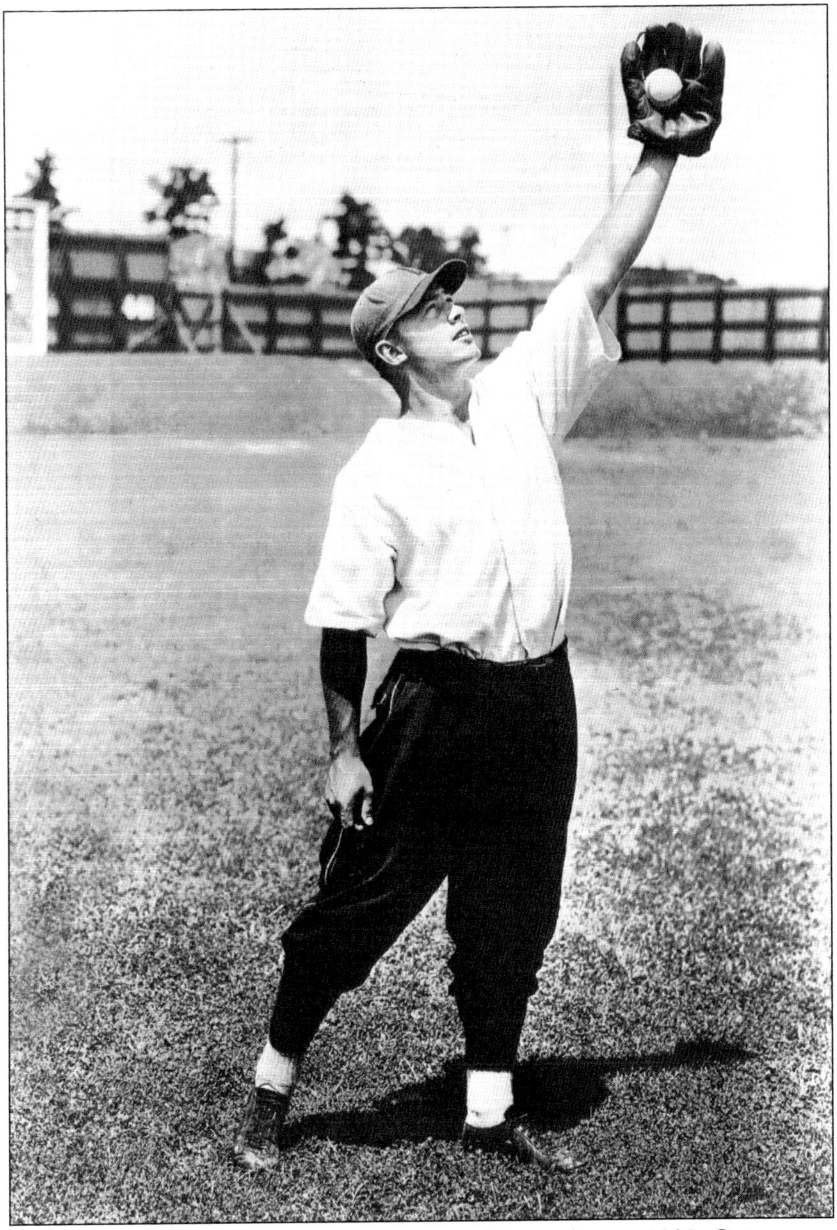

This photo of Durham Bulls outfielder Norman Small was taken in 1938. Quite a controversy arose that season when Bulls team president Paul Florence ordered new uniforms and decided upon the unusual combination of bright red pants and a plain white jersey for home games. The Piedmont League president decided that the uniforms did not comply with the rules of baseball and announced he would fine the Bulls $5 for every game they wore them. According to him, home uniforms were supposed to be completely white, the only color permitted being the hat, the team name or initial on the jersey, and a pinstripe down the side of the pants. Florence protested, saying the rules of organized baseball said only that a team's home and road uniforms had to use the same basic colors, which Durham's did. In the end neither side gave in; Durham ignored the fines and continued to play in their colorful uniforms for the entire season. (Courtesy of Norman Small.)

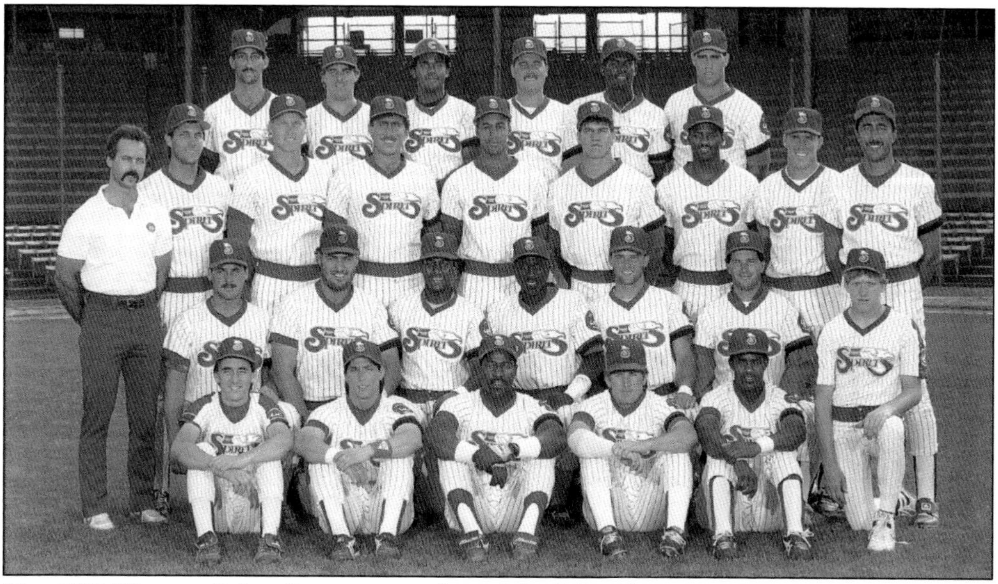

The 1988 Winston-Salem Spirits were a farm club of the Chicago Cubs. From left to right are (first row) Ed Hrynkow (batboy), Steve Hill, Tim Wallace, Eric Woods, and Juan Adames; (second row) Tom Michno, Butch Garcia, Luis Cruz, John Lewis, Greg Smith, Jay Loviglio (manager), and Geoff Burdick (batboy); (third row) Mike Folga (trainer), Bill Kazmierczak, Jeff Schwartz, Brian Otten, Derrick May, Shawn Boskie, Heath Slocumb, Kelly Mann, and Coach Joe Housey; (fourth row) David Rosario, Jim Matas, Henry Gatewood, Phil Harrison, Francisco Tenacen, and Glenn Sullivan. (From the collection of the author.)

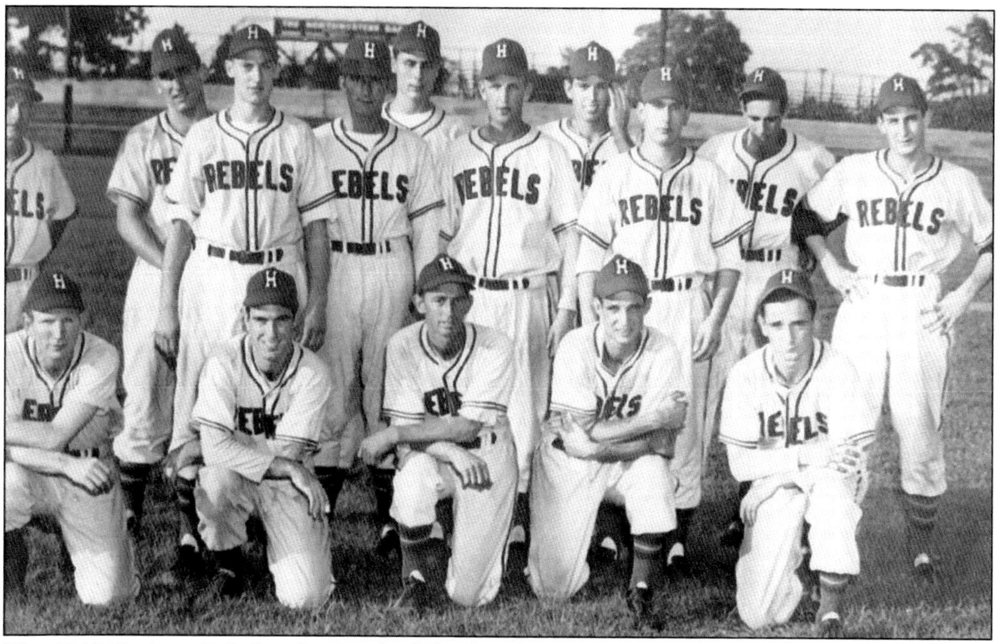

The 1948 Hickory Rebels, who finished third in the North Carolina State League with a 61-49 record, were a farm club of the New York Giants. The only identified player in this photo is outfielder Otis Stephens (back row, fourth from right), who was named to the league's end-of-season All-Star team. (Courtesy of Otis Stephens.)

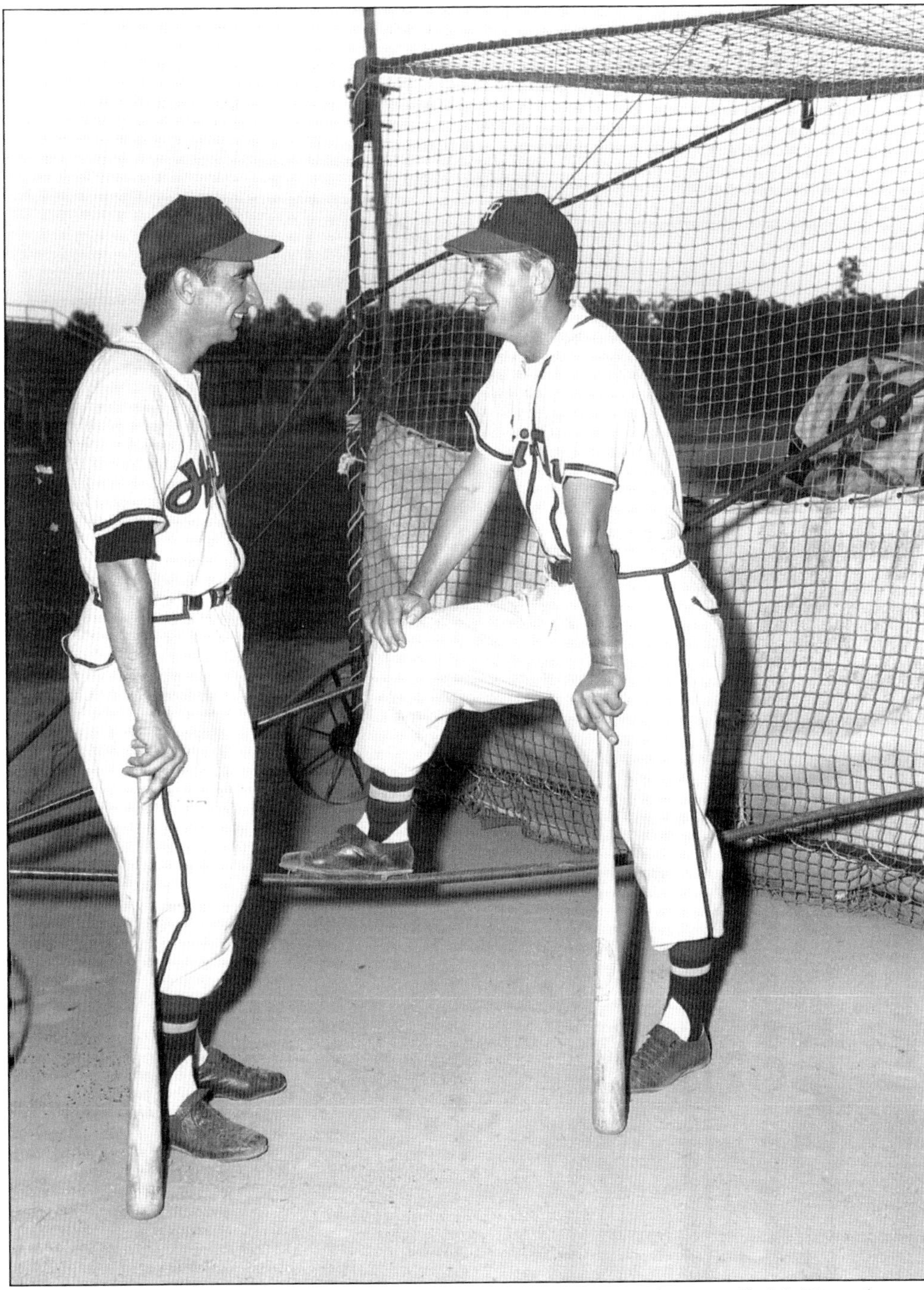

Don Stafford, right, chats with a teammate during a High Point-Thomasville Hi-Toms batting practice in 1953. Stafford, a first baseman, is one of the best hitters to ever play in North Carolina's minor leagues. He began his pro career in 1948 with Newton-Conover, where he hit .388. In 1952, while playing for Salisbury, Stafford won the North Carolina State League batting title with an amazing average of .408. He followed that with a .374 average the following season to win the Tar Heel League title. (Courtesy of High Point Museum Archives.)

An unidentified Mooresville Moors catcher warms up a pitcher in this late 1940s photo. (From the collection of the author.)

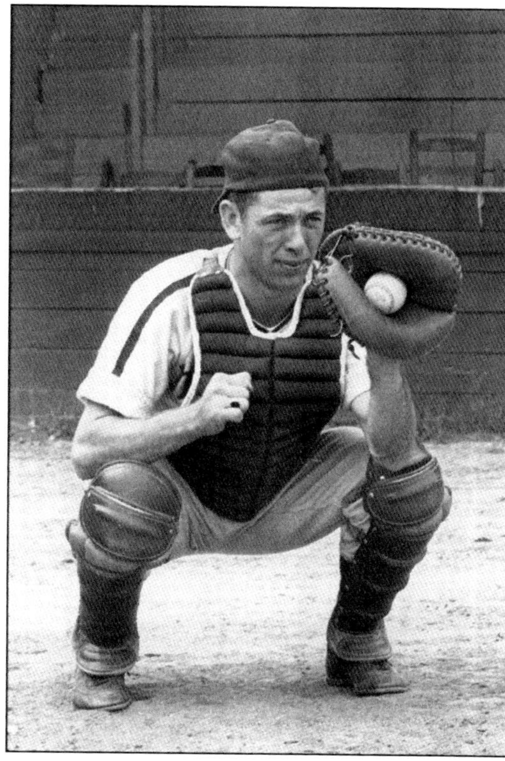

The 1941 Leaksville-Spray-Draper Triplets won the Bi-State League pennant. Team members, from left to right, are (front row) Cecil "Zip" Payne, Cotton Powell, Harry Land, Charlie Cuellar, and unidentified; (back row) Vinnie Fernandez, Lynwood "Hank" Tillotson, unidentified, Harold Scalpini, Al Letrick, Ken Rhyne, unidentified, Joe Frazier, and unidentified. (Courtesy of Harry Land.)

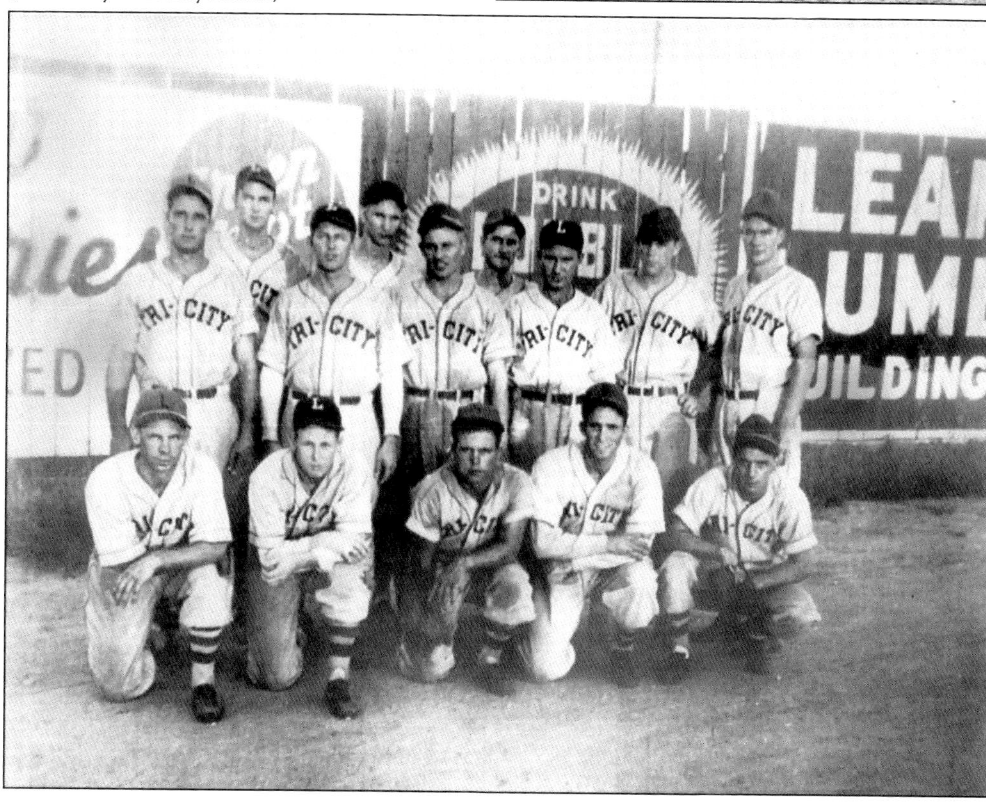

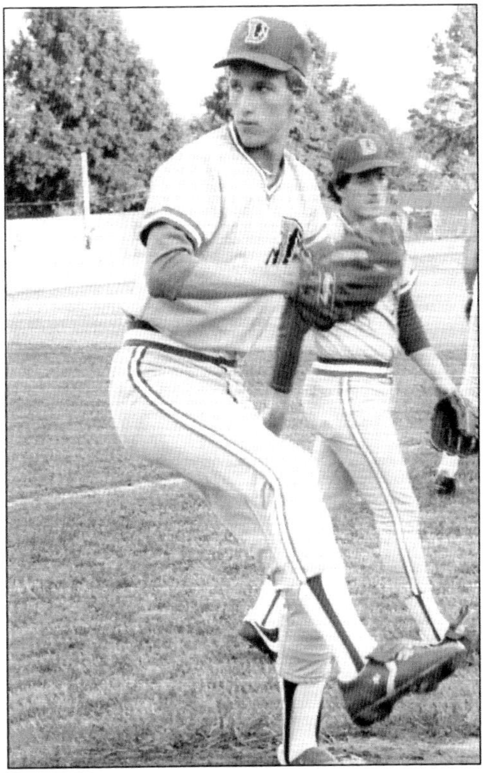

Left-handed pitcher Johnny Cash was a member of the 1985 Durham Bulls. After an outstanding two-thirds of a season with Sumter, Cash was promoted to Durham by the Atlanta Braves. He pitched well for the Bulls and won three games. (From the collection of the author.)

Members of the 1952 Moorsville Moors included, from left to right, Fred Daniels, Joe Brookshire, Henry Lineberger, and Fred Chapman. Both Daniels and Chapman had returned to their native North Carolina to play in the minor leagues after appearing in the big leagues—Daniels played for the Phillies while Chapman was with the Athletics. (From the collection of the author.)

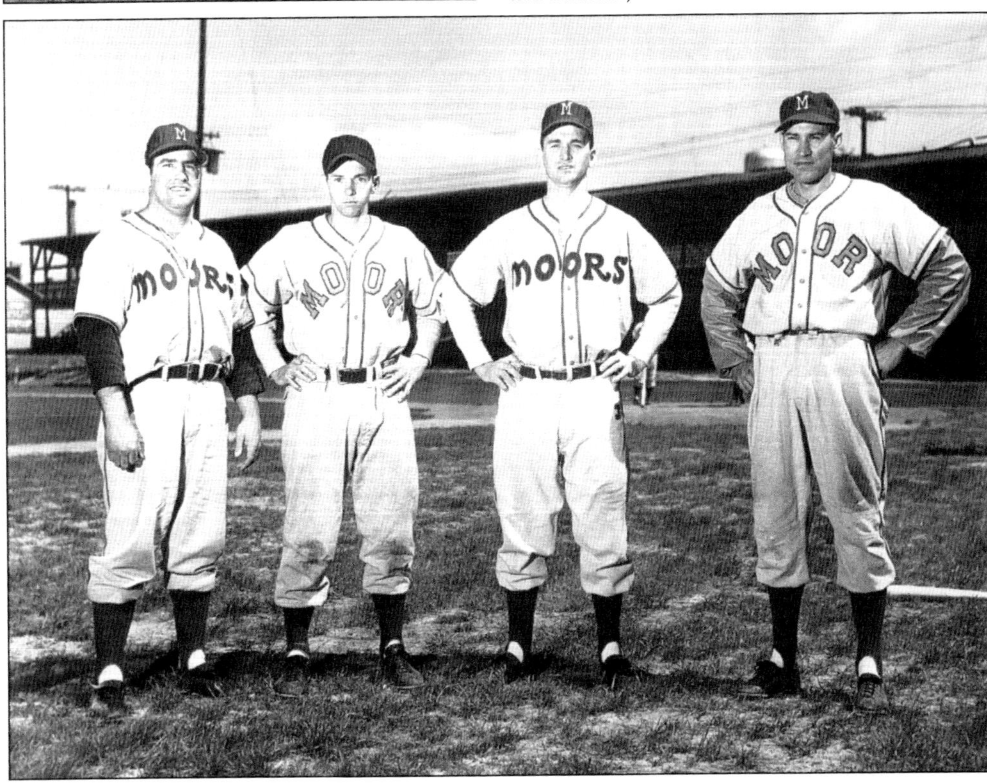

Catcher Harry Land strikes a classic catcher's pose in front of the Leaksville grandstand in 1941. Land, who began his baseball career with Reidsville in 1940, made it as high as Los Angeles in the Pacific Coast League before entering military service during World War II. After the war he served as a playing manager for nearly a decade with clubs including Rock Hill, South Carolina and New Bern, North Carolina. (Courtesy of Cotton Powell.)

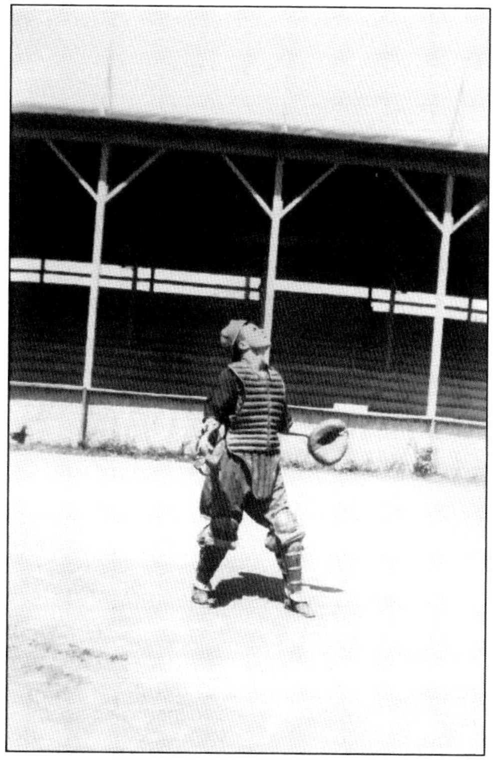

Manager and infielder Gene Verble, pitcher Garland Shiflett, and outfielder Johnny Grice, all members of the 1956 Charlotte Hornets, clown around in the locker room. (Courtesy of Gene Verble.)

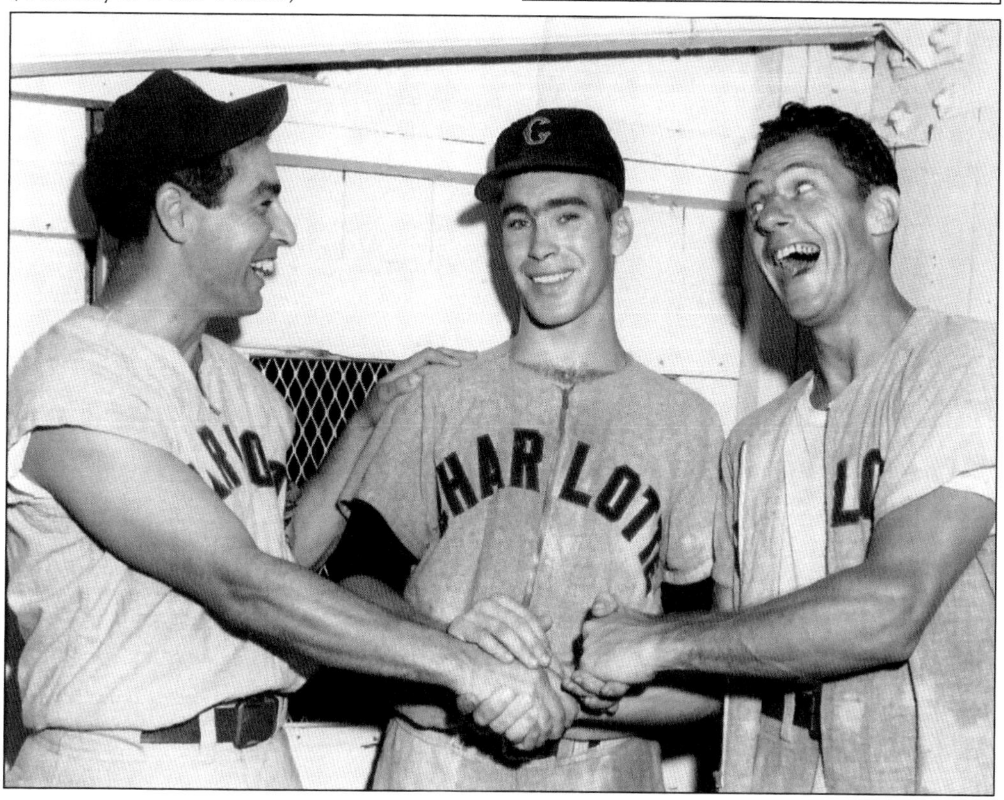

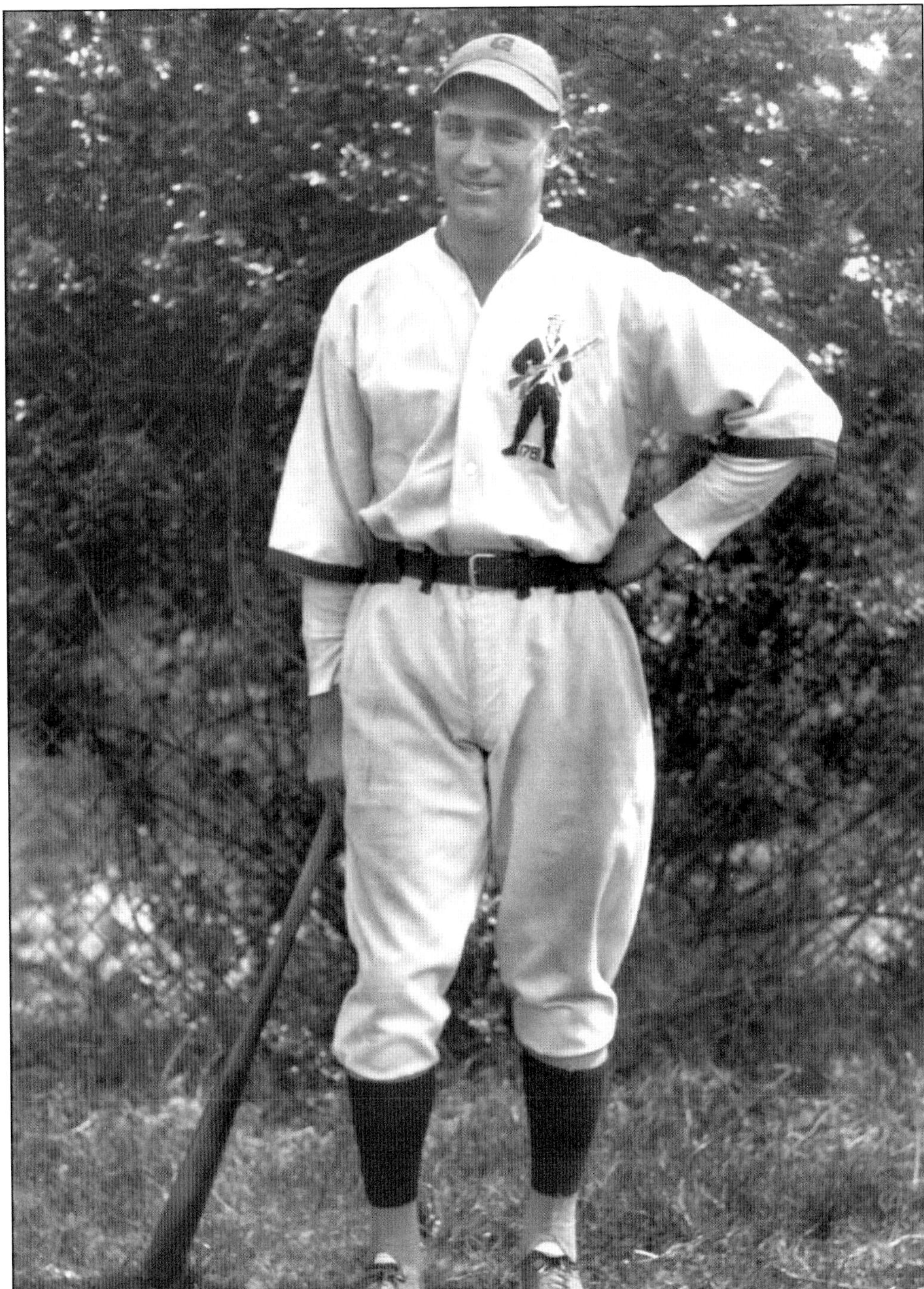

Greensboro Patriots outfielder Johnny Mize was only 18 years old in 1931. A native of Georgia, Mize was working his way up through the St. Louis Cardinals farm system. He made the big league club in 1936 and for 15 seasons was one of the most feared power hitters in the game. With 359 homeruns and a career batting average of .312, Mize was elected to the Hall of Fame in 1981. (Courtesy of Greensboro Historical Museum Archives.)

Mount Airy Graniteers catcher Mike Brelich was the Blue Ridge League's batting champion in 1949 with a .333 average. (Courtesy of Worth Cuthbertson.)

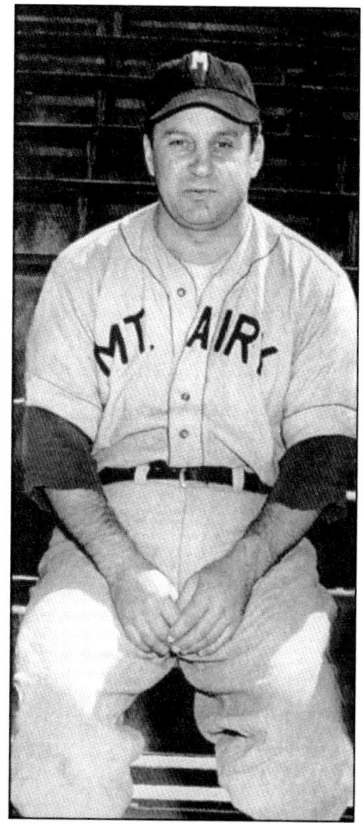

Dean "Spec" Padgett was a well-traveled minor league player in the 1940s and 1950s. Among other teams, the Gastonia native played for Lumberton, Rutherford County, and Charlotte. He is pictured here receiving an award from Charlotte Hornets president Phil Howser *c.* 1957. (Courtesy of Gene Verble.)

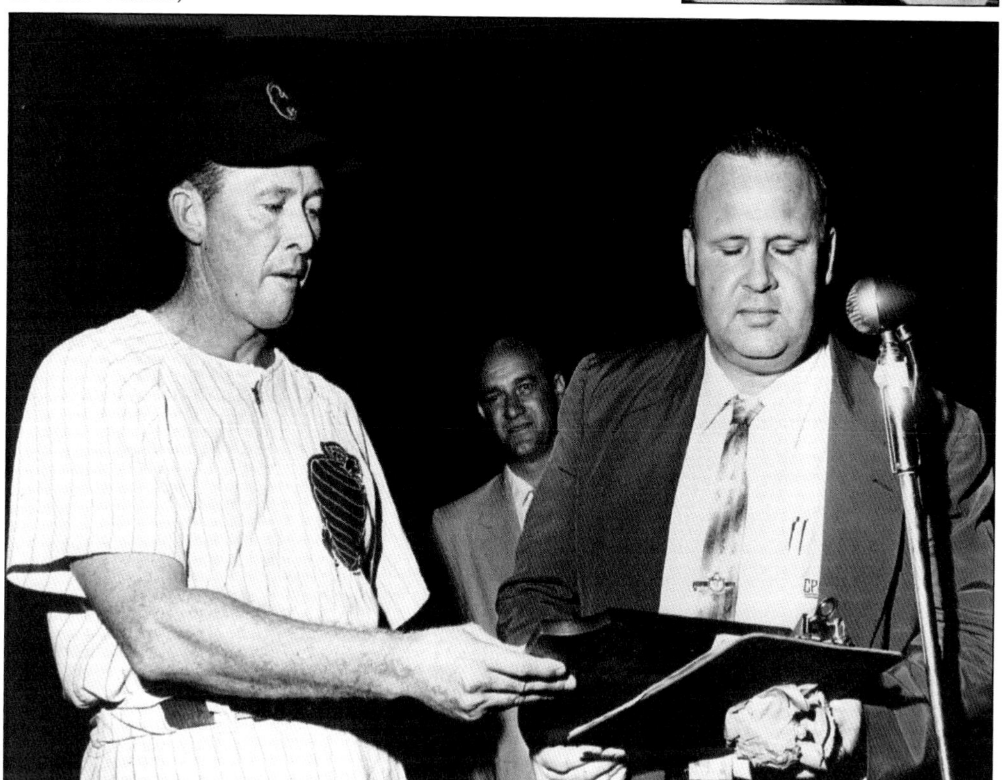

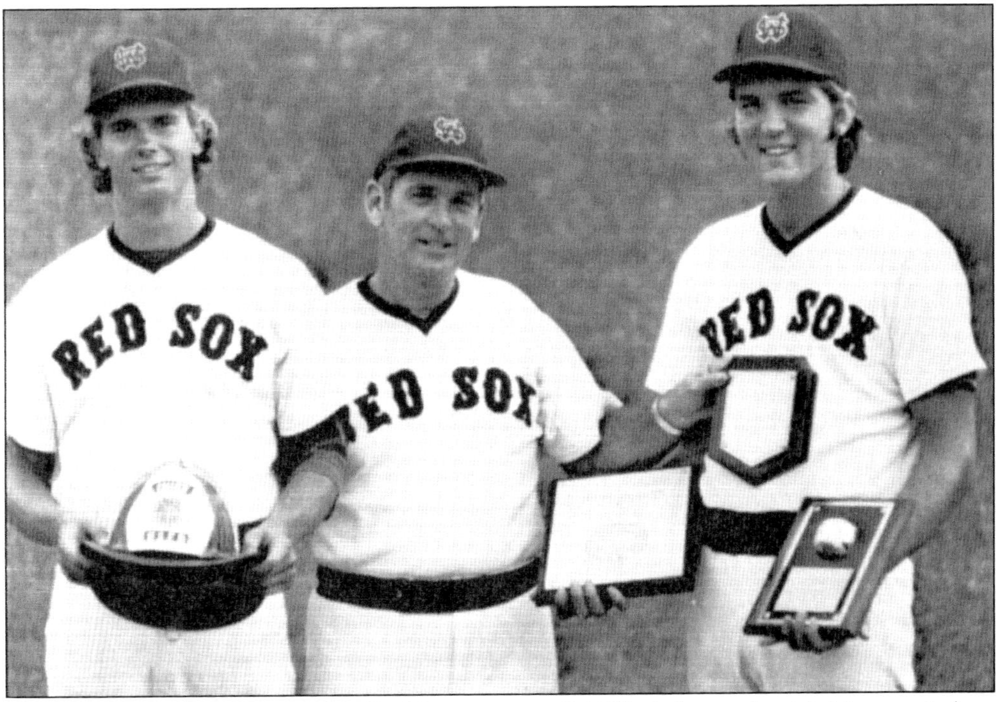

This is a photo of Winston-Salem Red Sox manager Bill Slack (center), with his star pitchers Roz Brayton (left) and Don Aase (right) in 1974. Brayton was named Fireman of the Year as the Carolina League's top relief pitcher while Aase was named Pitcher of the Year. Aase would go on to have a long big league career, primarily as a relief pitcher. (From the collection of the author.)

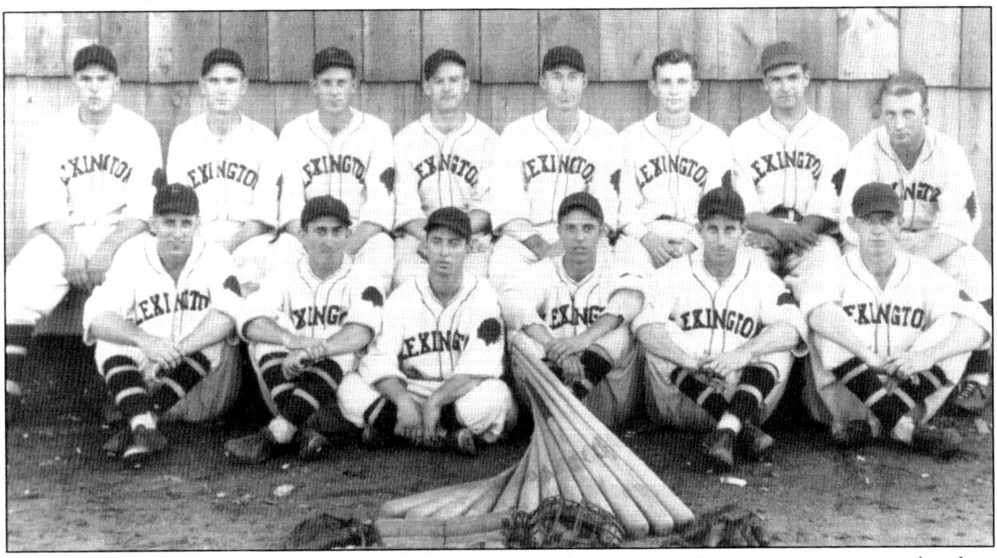

The 1937 Lexington Indians, members of the North Carolina State League, were the first professional team to represent the Davidson County town. From left to right are the following: (front row) Tom Horner, Gus Surdey, Melvin Dry, C.B. Cook, Glenn Payne, and Weldon West; (back row) Chester Novak, John Dellinger, Bill Carrier, Lester McCrabb, Phil Lundeen (manager), Wilbur Reeser, Roy Rohrer, and Frank "Red" Matheson. (Courtesy of Betty Fite.)

The 1986 Durham Bulls's infield featured shortstop Jeff Blauser and first baseman Wayne Harrison, shown here before a game on the road. Blauser would go on to spend a decade as a key member of the Atlanta Braves lineup. (From the collection of the author.)

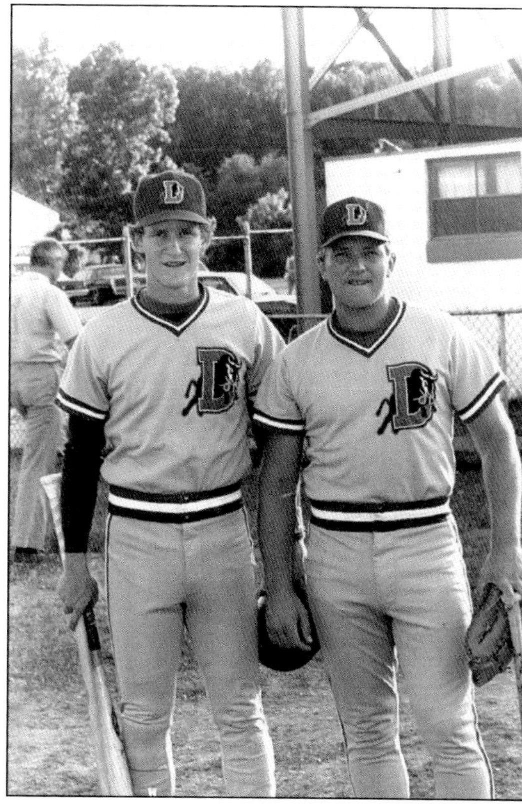

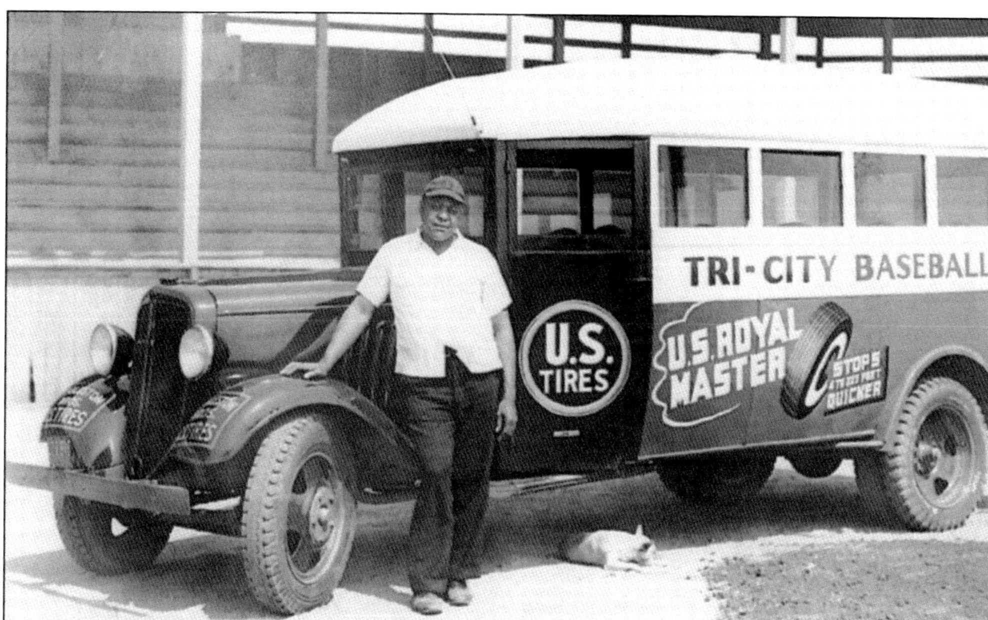

Phillip "Rabbit" Martin, who served as driver and groundskeeper for the Leaksville-Spray-Draper Triplets, poses with the team bus in 1941. (Courtesy of Harry Land.)

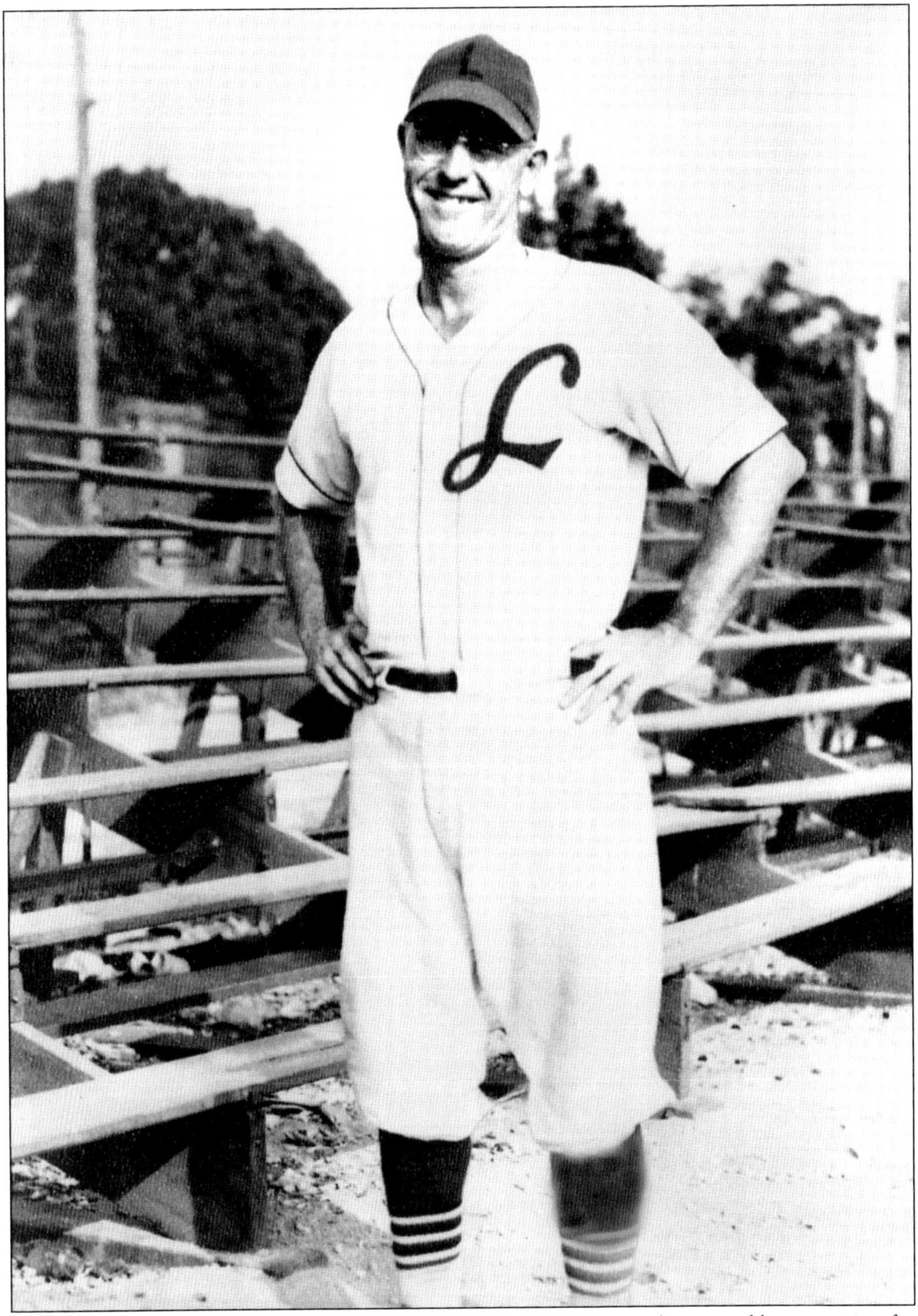

From the early 1930s through the mid-1940s it was common to see the second base position for a Landis ball club being held down by Ed Cross. From the semi-pro textile league teams to the professional minor league teams that represented the town, Cross had a long involvement with the game. (Courtesy of Hank Utley.)

Fair Swaim, shown posing in front of his home dugout, was a pitcher for the 1937 Reidsville Luckies. The Luckies and their ballpark were named after Reidsville's most famous product, the Lucky Strike cigarettes of American Tobacco Company. (Courtesy of Fair Swaim.)

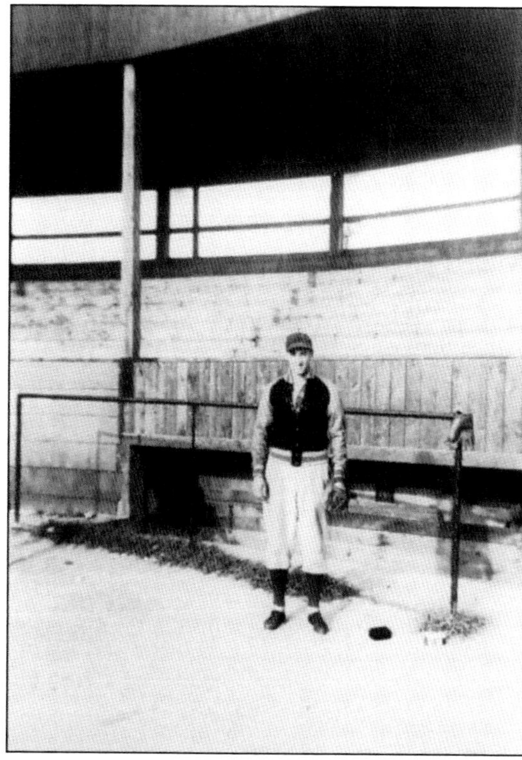

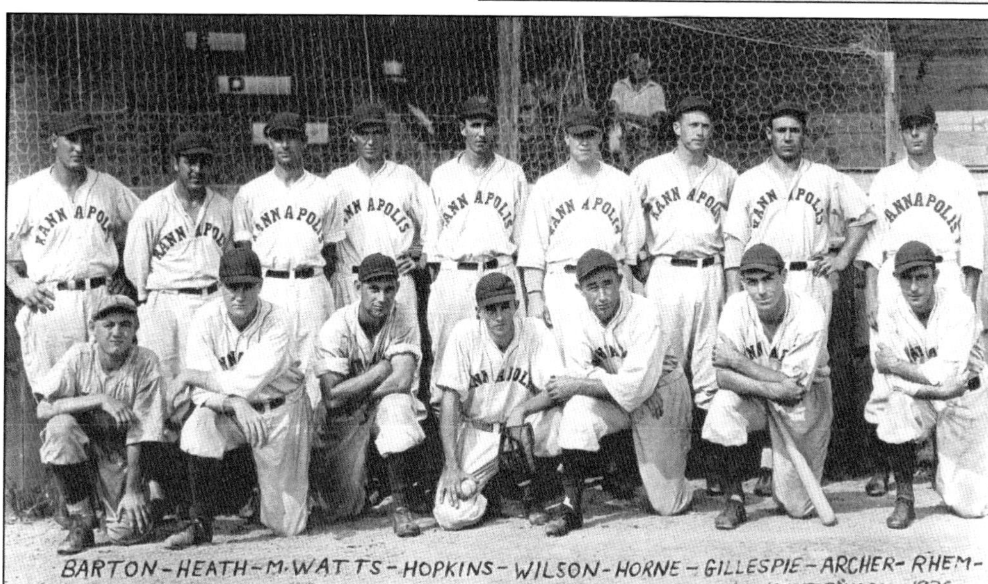

The Carolina League was an independent professional league that existed from 1936 to 1938. The Kannapolis Towelers, shown here, were the league's third place team in 1936. From left to right are (front row) George Barley (manager), Grey Clarke, Glenn "Razz" Miller, ? Reynolds, ? Beams, and Herman "Ginger" Watts (batboy); (back row) Vince Barton, Fletcher Heath, Marvin Watts, Frank Hopkins, ? Wilson, ? Horne, ? Gillespie, Fred "Lefty" Archer, and Bethel Rhem. (Courtesy of Hank Utley.)

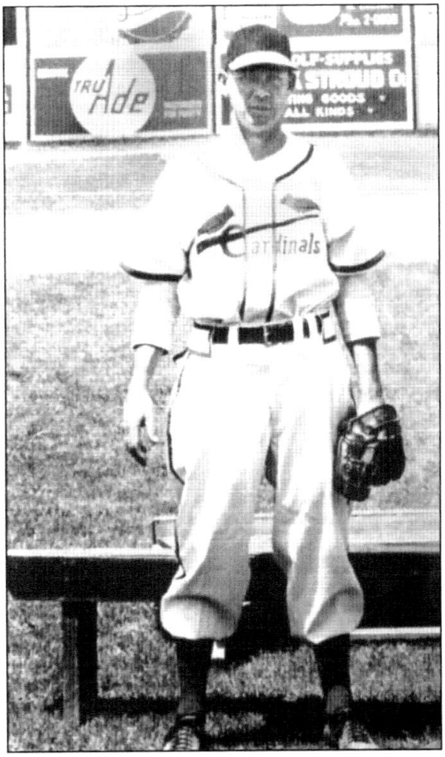

Cecil "Zip" Payne, manager of the 1947 Winston-Salem Cardinals, poses at old Southside Park. Payne had a long career in the North Carolina minor leagues as a player and manager and spent time at Henderson, Mayodan, Leaksville, Winston-Salem, Fayetteville, and Mount Airy. (Courtesy of Buddy Payne.)

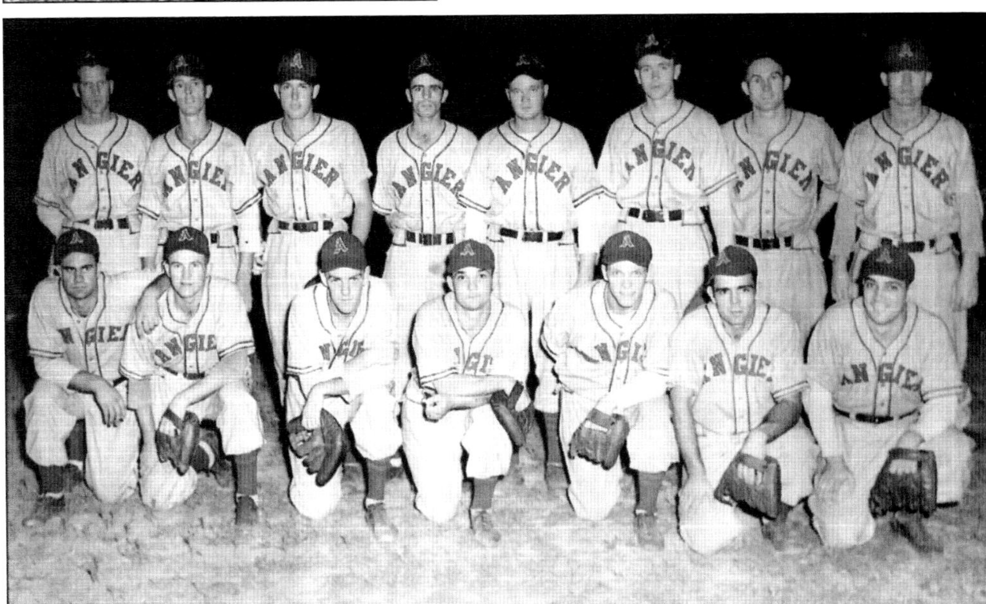

Angier and Fuquay Springs fielded a shared team for one season, the only time either town would be involved in professional baseball. This is the 1946 Angier-Fuquay Springs Colts. The team members, from left to right, are (front row) Ray Hardee, unidentified, Harry Fortune, Sam Sellers, Paul Hunt, Ken Jackson, and Gus Rogers; (back row) Andrew Scrobola, Ray Bomar, Otis Stephens, Roscoe Gentry, James House, Marvin Lorenz, Joe Mills, and Bill Ratteree. (Courtesy of Otis Stephens.)

Leaksville outfielder Joe Frazier was only 19 years old when this photo was taken in 1941. A native of Liberty, North Carolina, he eventually went on to spend parts of four seasons in the big leagues, primarily with the St. Louis Cardinals. (Courtesy of Harry Land.)

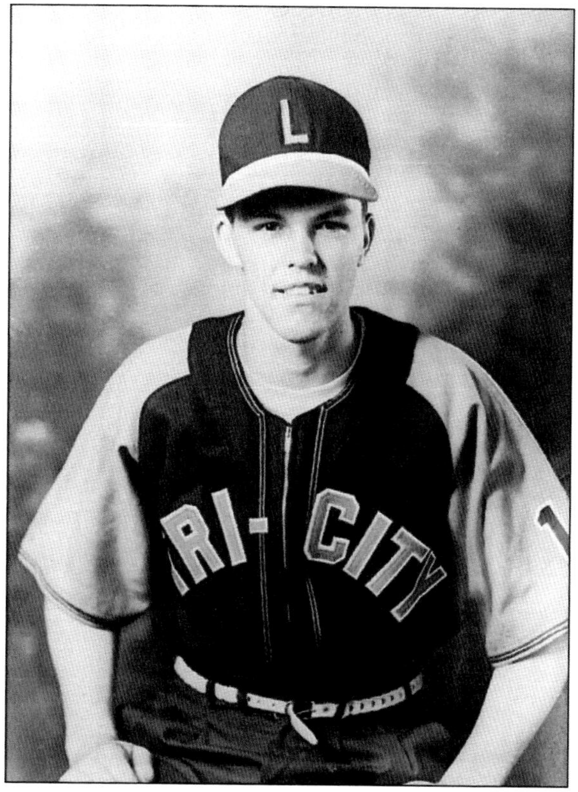

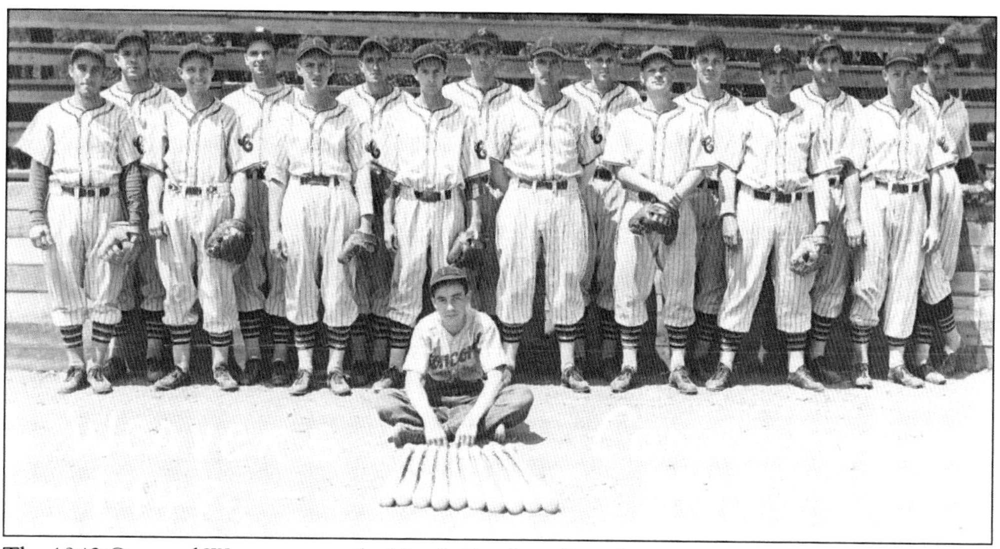

The 1942 Concord Weavers won the North Carolina State League pennant with a 64–34 record but were upset by the Thomasville Tommies in the playoffs. Pictured here from left to right are (front row) Willard Mauney, unidentified, John Shoe, unidentified, Herman "Ginger" Watts (manager), unidentified, George Brown, and unidentified; (back row) Buck Glover, Marvin Watts, Herman Drefs, Glenn "Razz" Miller, Zeke Graham, unidentified, George Motto, and unidentified. (Courtesy of Hank Utley.)

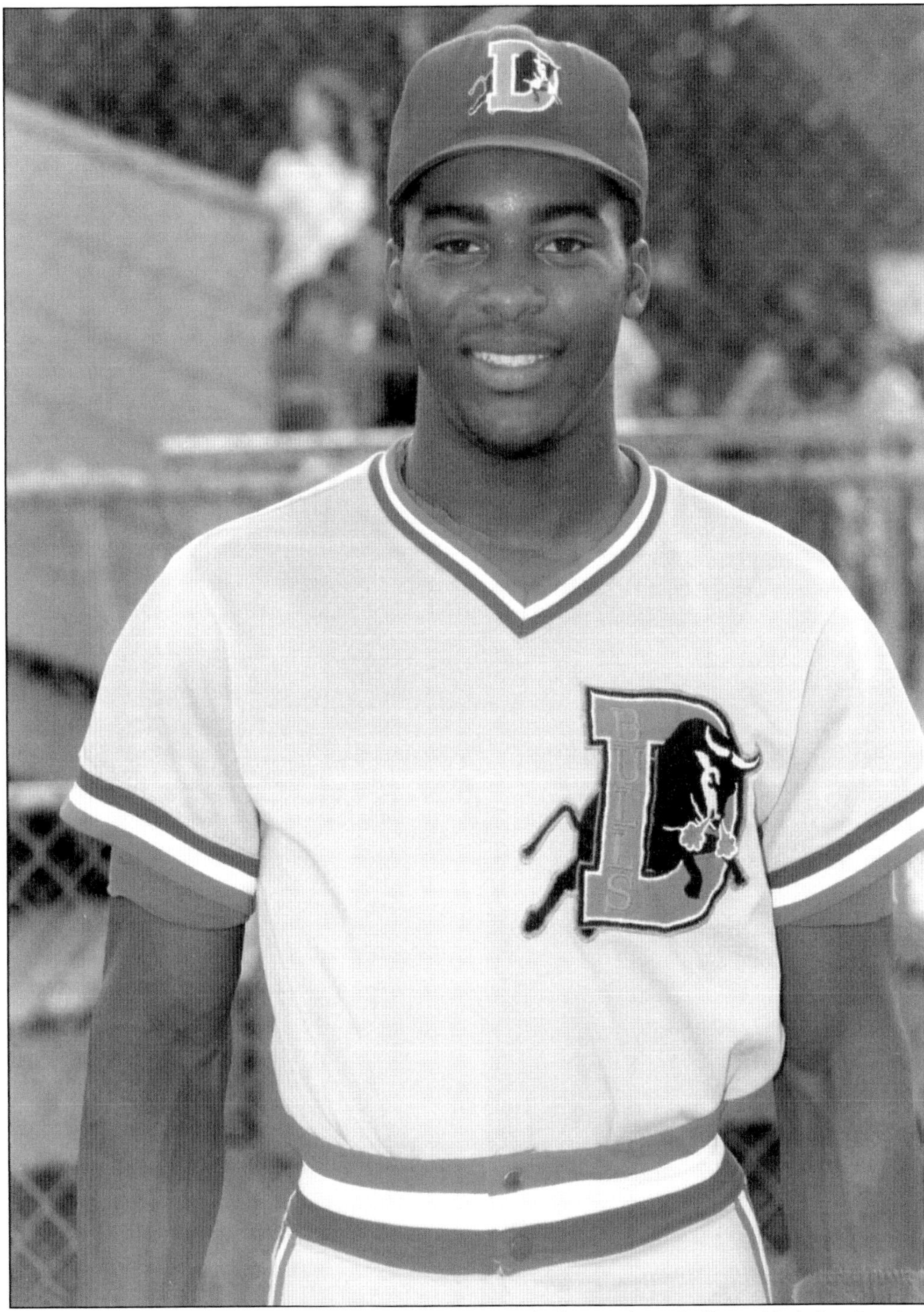

Second baseman Ron Gant spent the 1986 season with the Durham Bulls and led the Carolina League with 26 homeruns. Thanks to his power and his exceptional speed, he was promoted to Atlanta the following season. Eventually converted to an outfielder, Gant became a feared power hitter and slugged over 300 homeruns in his career with the Braves and other teams. (From the collection of the author.)

This 1952 scorecard from the Salisbury Rocots of the North Carolina State League bears the likeness of manager Don Padgett. A native of High Point, the former big league catcher and outfielder guided his team to third place that season with a 64-43 record. (From the collection of the author.)

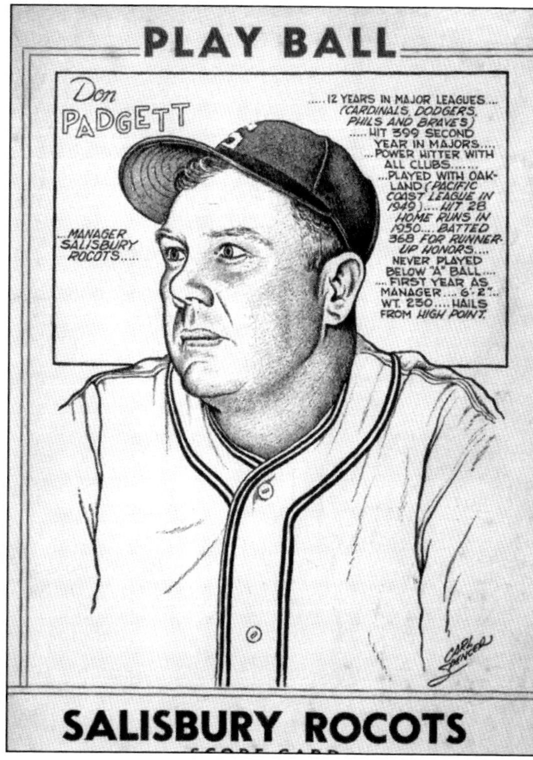

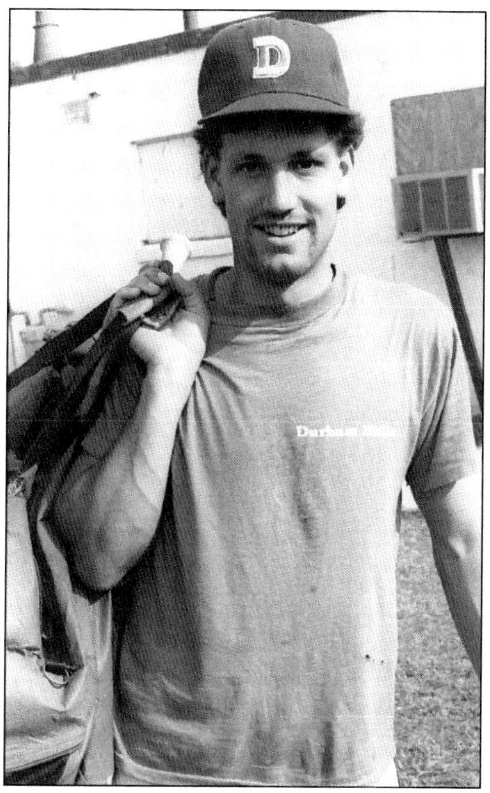

Scott Hood, shown here on his way to batting practice, played catcher for the Durham Bulls for parts of the 1982 through 1984 seasons. Solid behind the plate, Hood tied a Carolina League record with 20 putouts in a 1982 game. (From the collection of the author.)

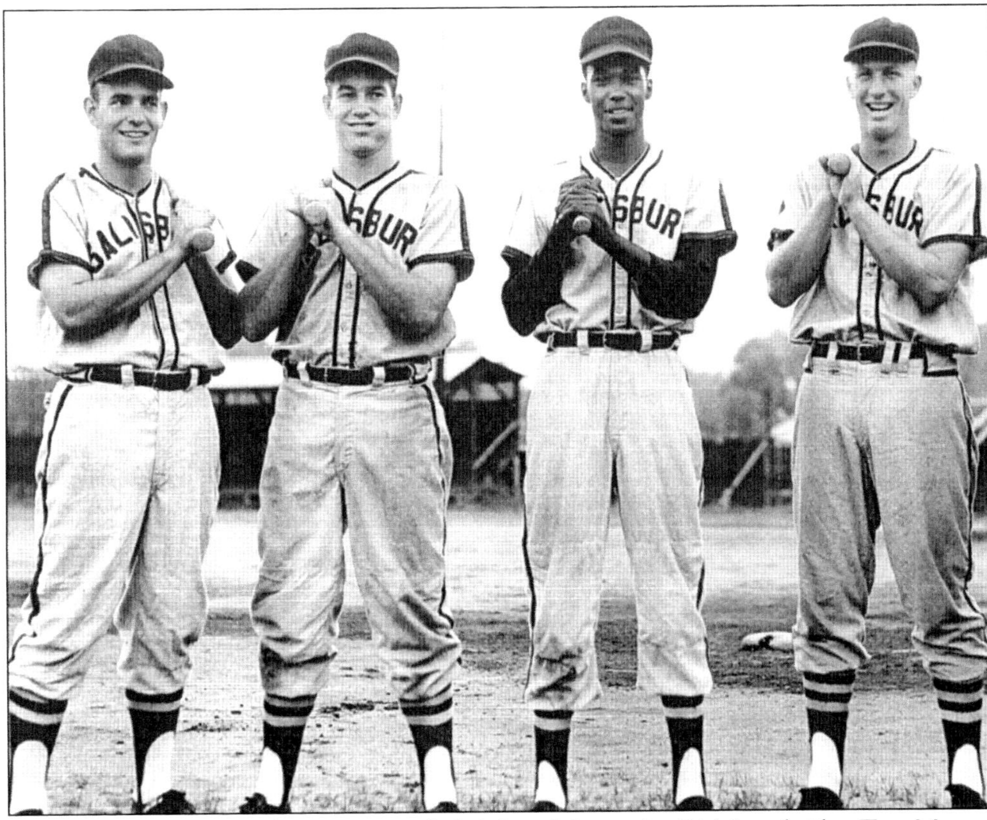

Members of the 1961 Salisbury Braves included, from left to right, Dick Loughridge, Tom Murray, Aaron Pointer, and Fred White. Pointer won the batting title with a .402 average and was named the Western Carolina League's Most Valuable Player. (Courtesy of Alex Cosmidis.)

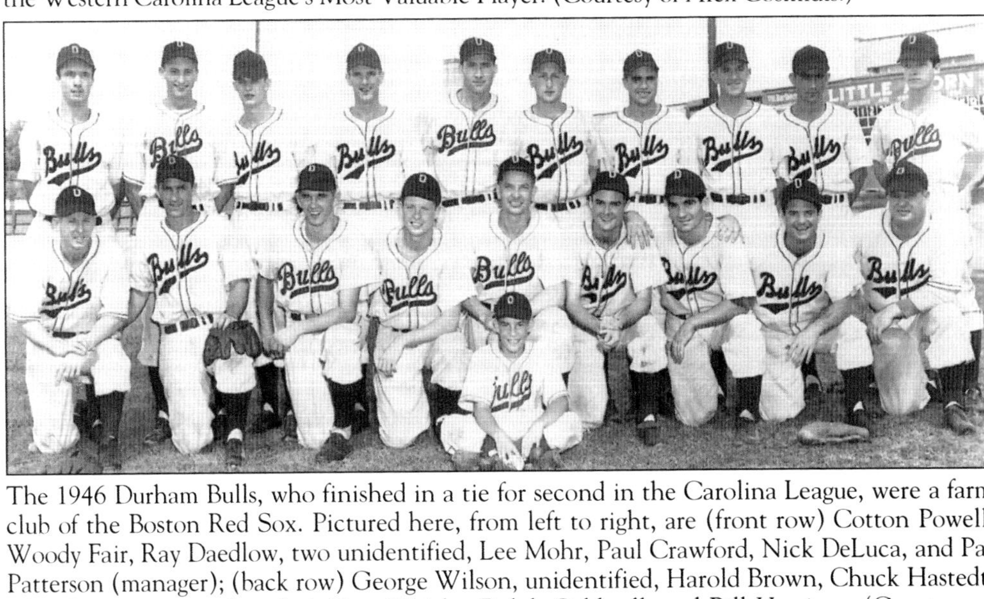

The 1946 Durham Bulls, who finished in a tie for second in the Carolina League, were a farm club of the Boston Red Sox. Pictured here, from left to right, are (front row) Cotton Powell, Woody Fair, Ray Daedlow, two unidentified, Lee Mohr, Paul Crawford, Nick DeLuca, and Pat Patterson (manager); (back row) George Wilson, unidentified, Harold Brown, Chuck Hastedt, John Streza, two unidentified, Tom Wright, Ralph Caldwell, and Bill Harrison. (Courtesy of Cotton Powell.)

Raleigh shortstop Cotton Bagwell is shown here receiving an award for being the Capitals' most popular player in 1946. (Courtesy of Mahlon "Cotton" Bagwell.)

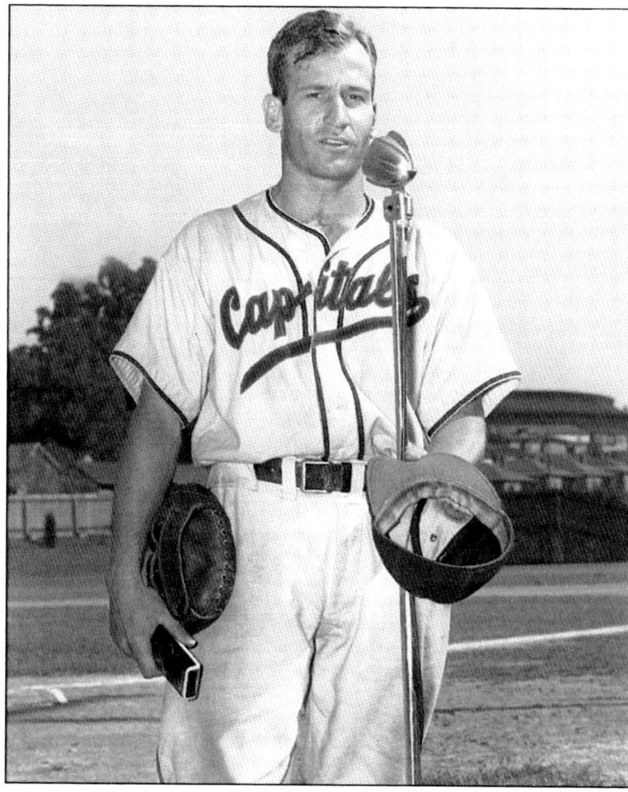

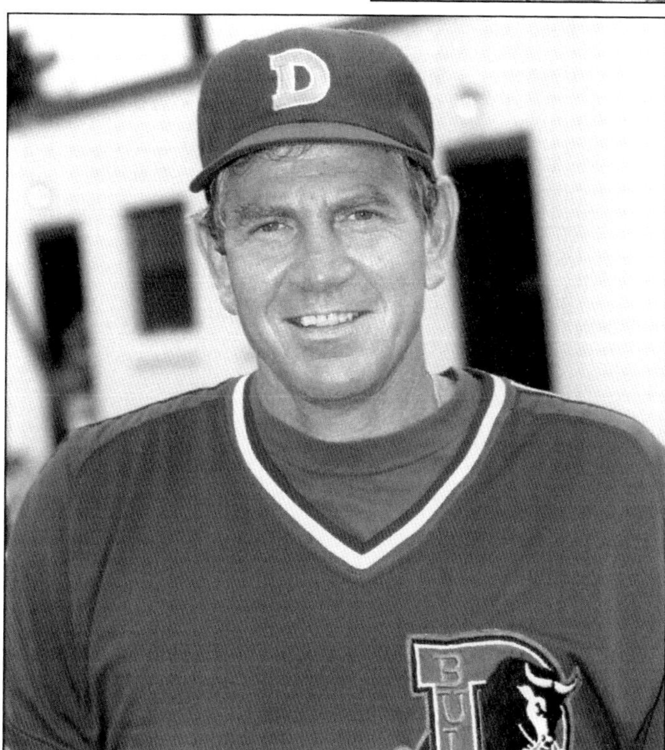

By training and developing young players, Durham pitching coach Bruce Dal Canton passed on some of the skills that helped him spend 11 seasons in the big leagues. He tutored young Bulls pitchers in 1982 (when this photo was taken) and again in 1996. (From the collection of the author.)

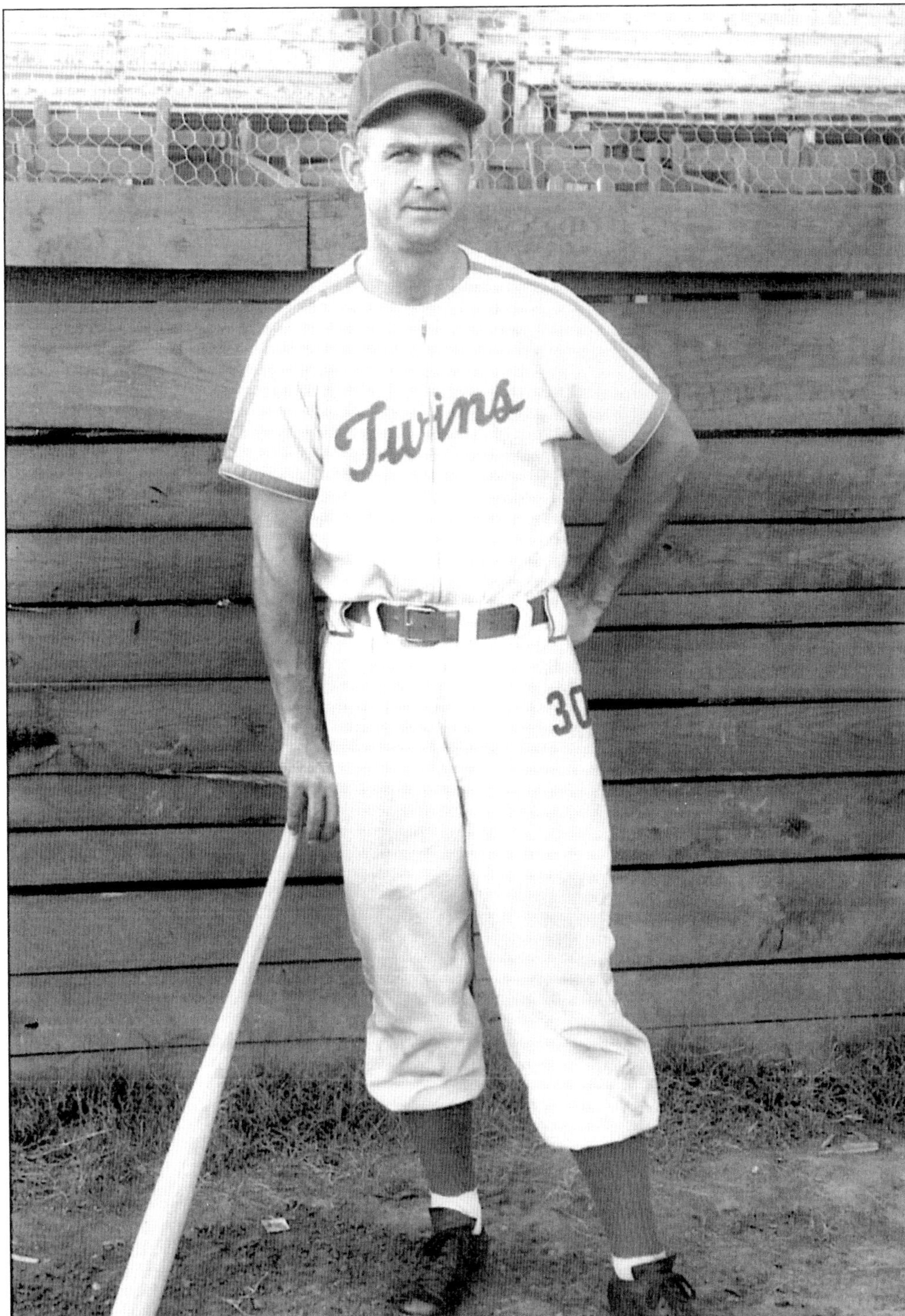

Eddie Yount, a native of Newton who had made brief appearances in the big leagues with the Athletics and the Pirates, served as manager and catcher for the Newton-Conover Twins from 1948 through 1951. (Courtesy of Joe Plick.)

Henry "Flash" Loman played in the minor leagues for a dozen years and his career included stops in Virginia and Ohio as well as the North Carolina towns of Mayodan and Cooleemee. Popular and talented, Loman finished out his career as a playing manager for the North Wilkesboro Flashers, a team that was even named after him. This photo was taken at North Wilkesboro in 1948. (Courtesy of Worth Cuthbertson.)

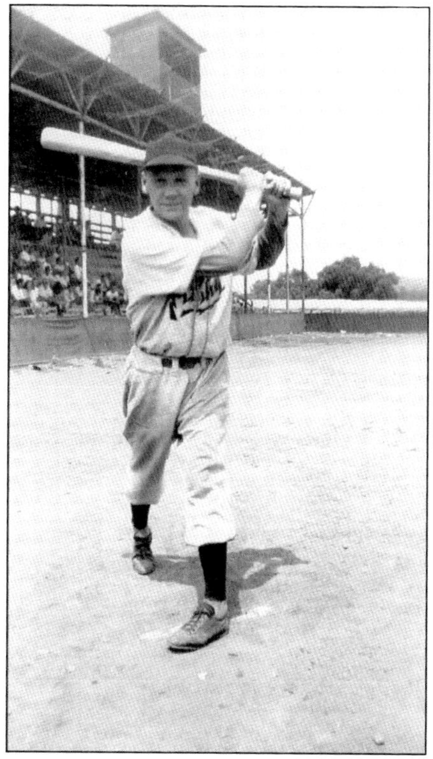

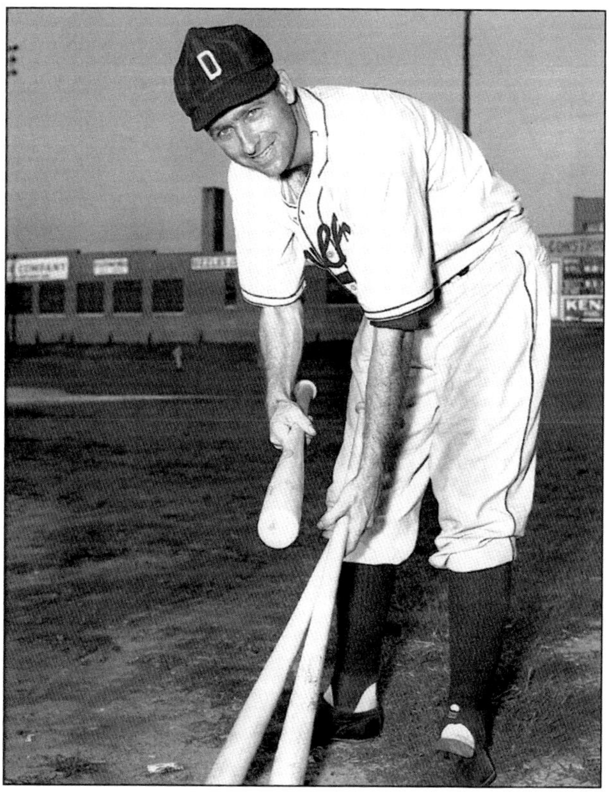

Cecil "Turkey" Tyson worked his way up the baseball ladder and in 1944 made it to the big leagues where he got into one game for the Philadelphia Phillies. Eventually the 6-foot 5-inch first baseman returned to his native North Carolina where he was a star for the Durham Bulls. Tyson spent the 1949 season with Lumberton in the Tobacco State League and in 1950 joined the Rockingham Eagles, where he served as manager. (Courtesy of Cecil "Turkey" Tyson.)

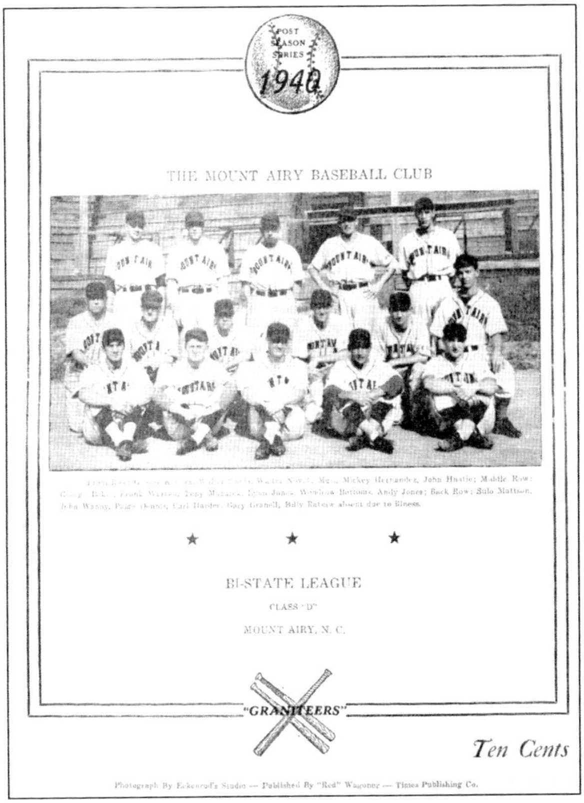

In 1940, the Mount Airy Graniteers, as seen on the cover of this scorecard, finished third in the Bi-State League with a record of 63-56. Made up of teams from both North Carolina and Virginia, the Bi-State League included such towns as Reidsville and Mayodan as well as Martinsville, Virginia. Mount Airy was a member of this league from 1934 through 1941. (From the collection of the author.)

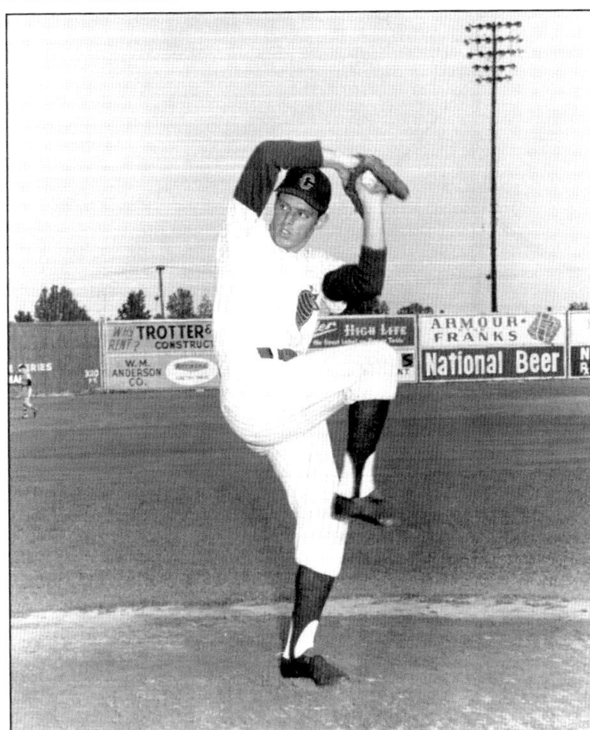

Dick Hoover, a member of the Charlotte Hornets pitching staff, winds up for a pitch in this late 1950s photo. A well-traveled minor league veteran, Hoover even made a brief big league appearance with the Boston Braves in 1952 before coming to Charlotte. (Courtesy of Gene Verble.)

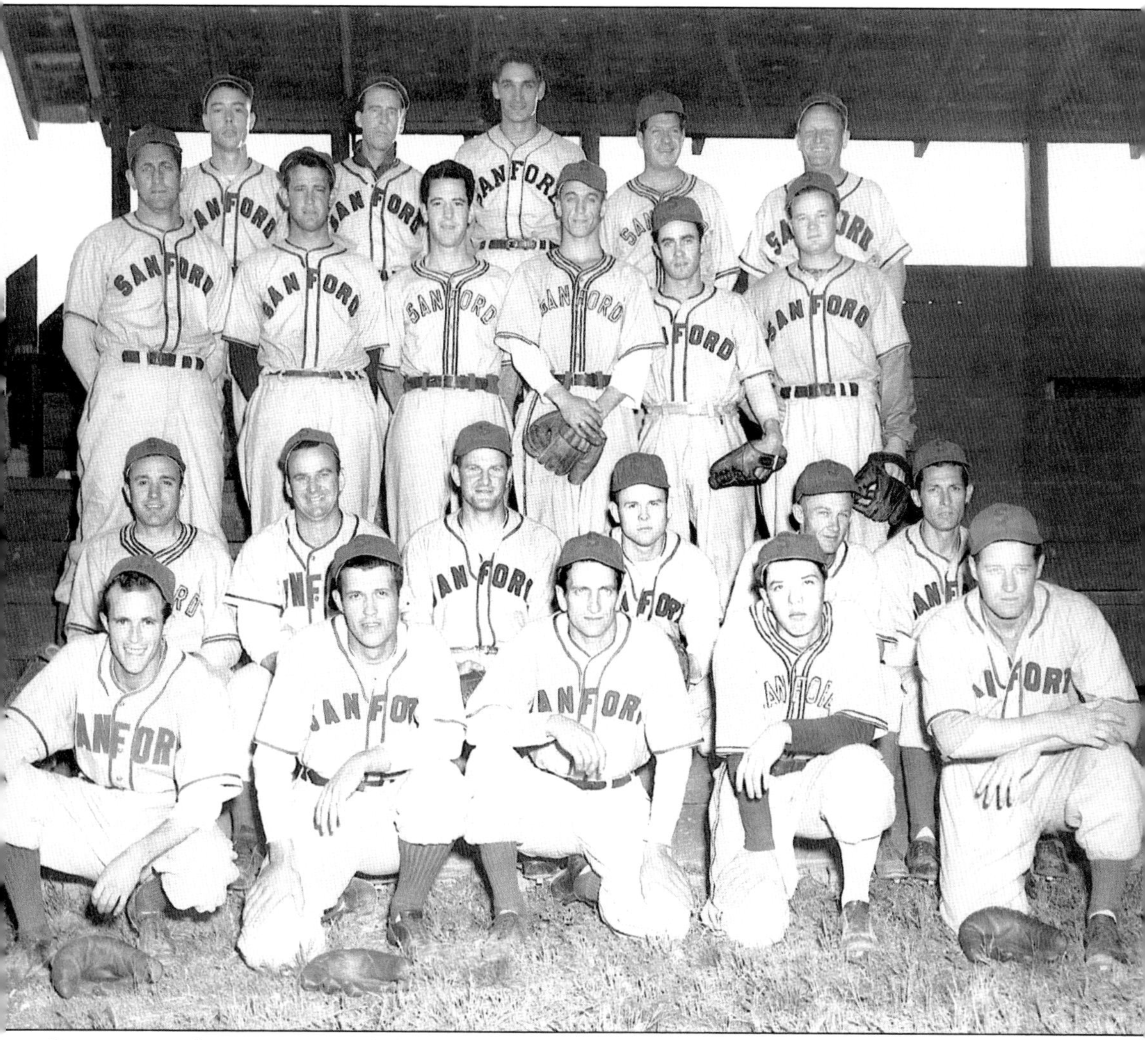

Since minor league rosters of that era generally carried around 15 players, this photo of the 1947 Sanford Spinners was probably taken during spring training before cuts had been made. The Spinners, from right to left, are (first row) unidentified, Guthrie Watson, John McFadden, unidentified, and Robert Pugh; (second row) Phalti Shoffner, Bruce Hedrick, Joe Nessing, Jimmy Wilson, Cecil Cotten, and Jimmy Guinn; (third row) Hank Nesselrode, three unidentified, Hoyt Clegg, and Jim House; (fourth row) unidentified, George Bortz, unidentified, Ned Butcher, and Zeb Harrington (manager). (Courtesy of Zeb "Dan" Harrington.)

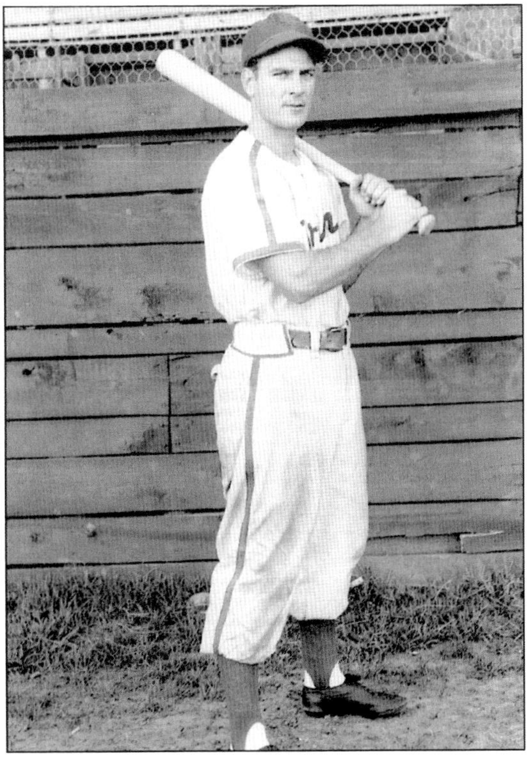

Newton-Conover first baseman Joe Plick was one of the Western Carolina League's better hitters in 1950. (Courtesy of Joe Plick.)

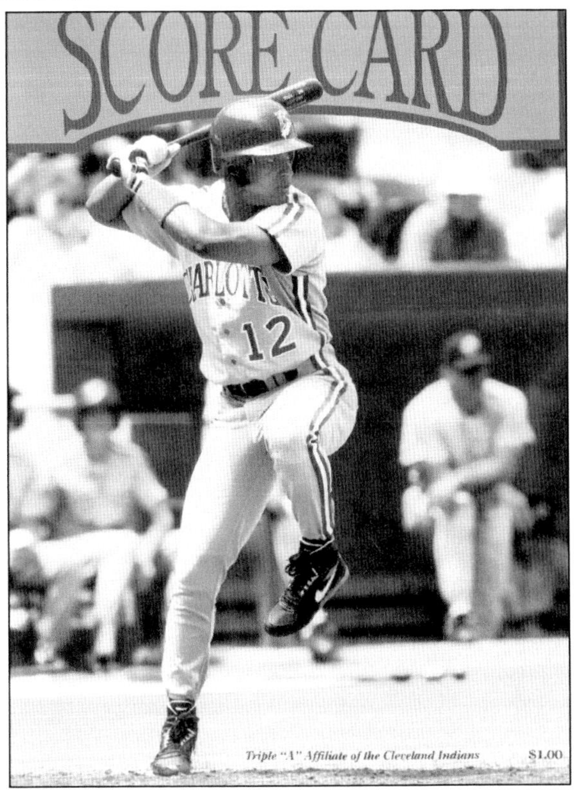

This 1994 Charlotte Knights score card features outfielder Manny Ramirez, who played 40 games for the team the previous season before getting promoted to the Cleveland Indians. Ramirez, who began his pro career at Burlington in 1991, has since gone on to become one of the game's most feared hitters. (From the collection of the author.)

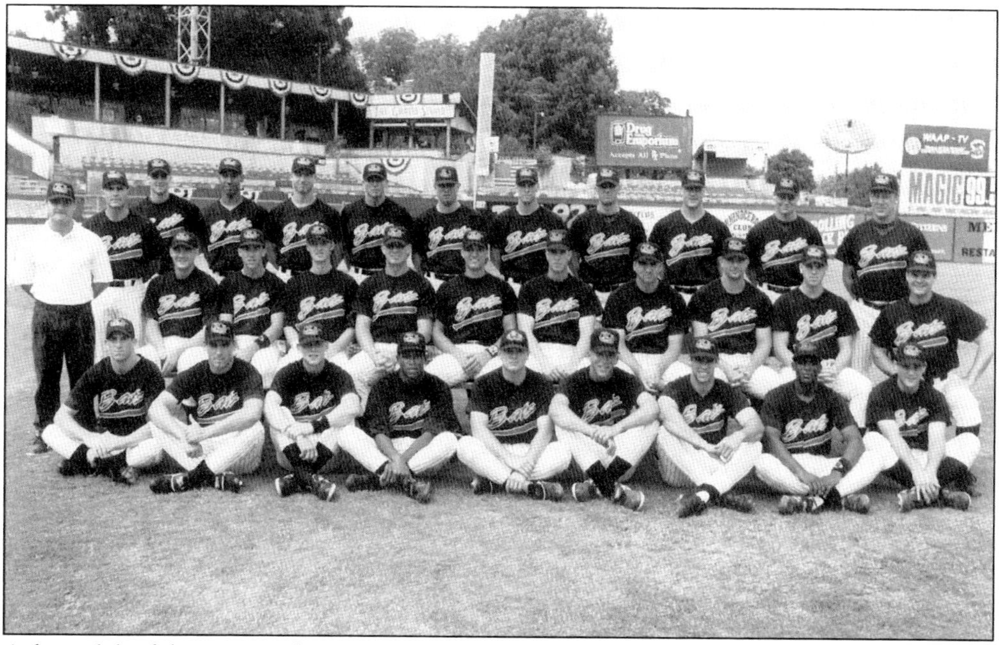

A farm club of the New York Yankees, the Greensboro Bats featured shortstop Derek Jeter (middle row, sixth from right) in 1993. Named to the South Atlantic league's All-Star team that season, he was well on his way to becoming a star in the big leagues. (From the collection of the author.)

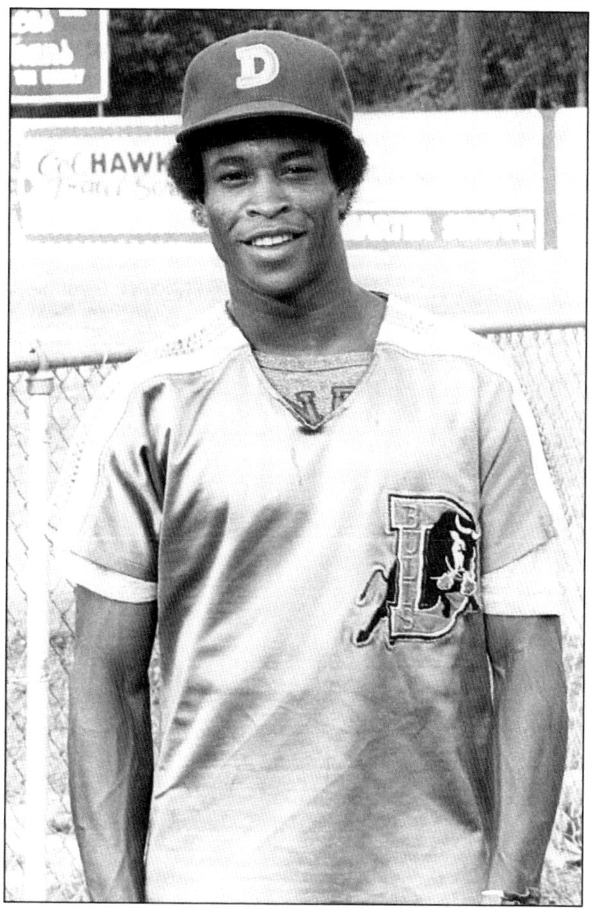

Albert Hall had an outstanding season for the 1980 Durham Bulls, batting .283 and stealing 100 bases. He never equaled that success in the major leagues but did have several good seasons as a back-up outfielder for the Atlanta Braves. (From the collection of the author.)

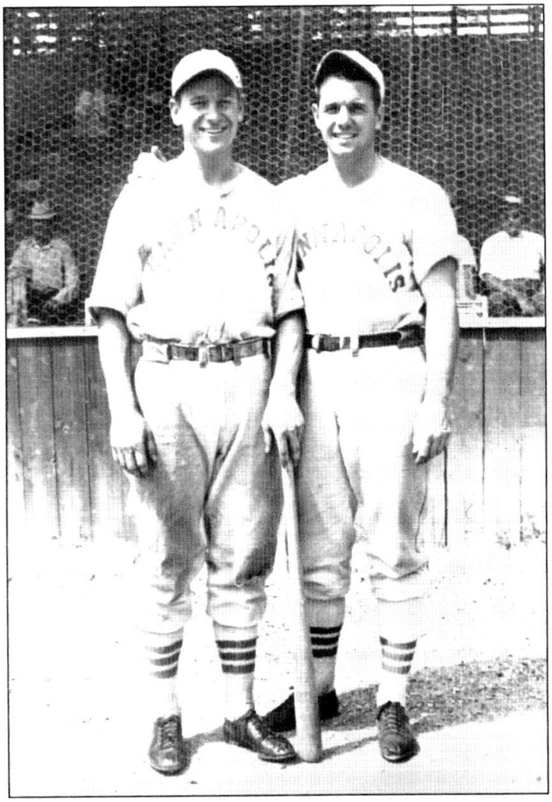

Outfielder Eric Tipton and pitcher Tracey Hart were members of the 1938 Kannapolis Towelers, a team that competed in the independent Carolina League. Tipton was an All-American football and baseball player at Duke University and in 1939 made his big league debut with the Philadelphia Athletics. (Courtesy of Hank Utley.)

The 1956 Charlotte Hornets included third baseman Harmon Killebrew (back row, third from right) and outfielder Bob Allison (middle row, second from left). Killebrew would go on to become one of the big leagues' all-time great power hitters, earning election to the Hall of Fame in 1984. Allison also had a standout career and was a three-time All-Star with the Minnesota Twins. (Courtesy of Gene Verble.)

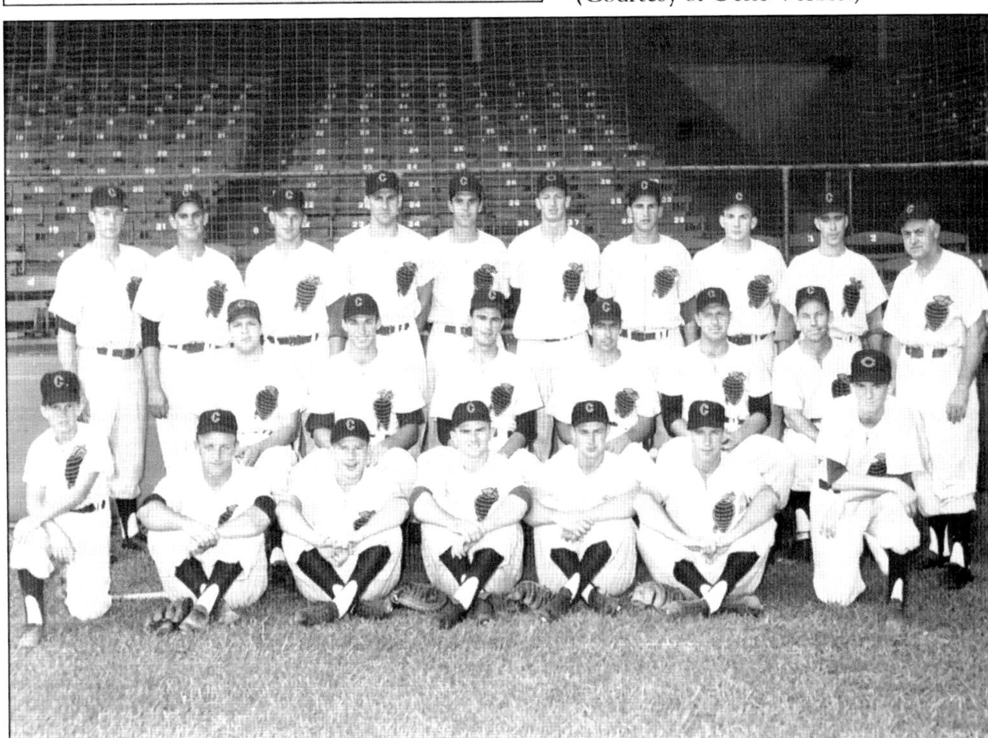

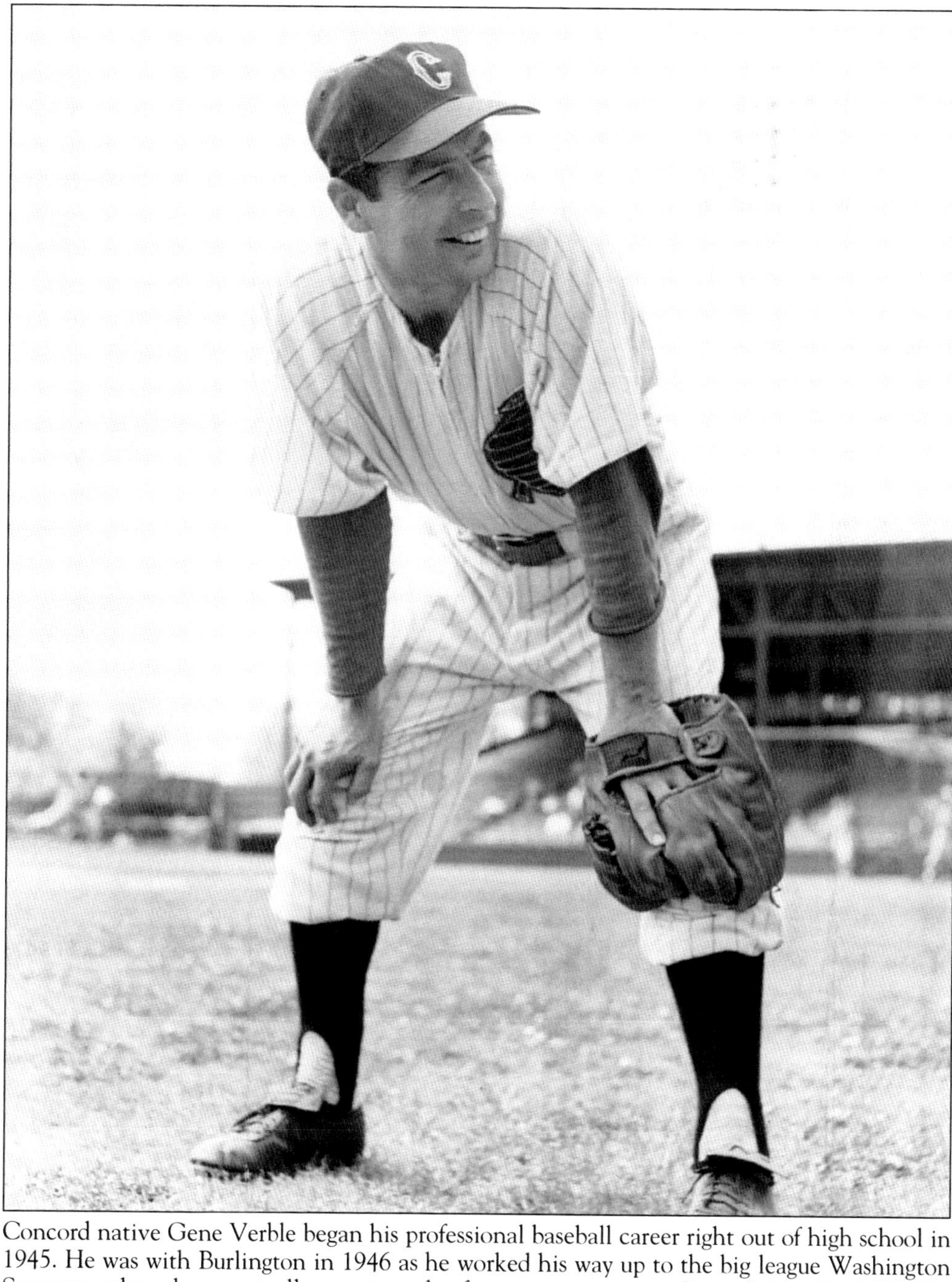

Concord native Gene Verble began his professional baseball career right out of high school in 1945. He was with Burlington in 1946 as he worked his way up to the big league Washington Senators, where he eventually spent much of two seasons as a utility infielder. In 1956, the Senators appointed Verble as playing manager for their Charlotte club in the South Atlantic League. For five seasons he was at the helm of the Hornets. (Courtesy of Gene Verble.)

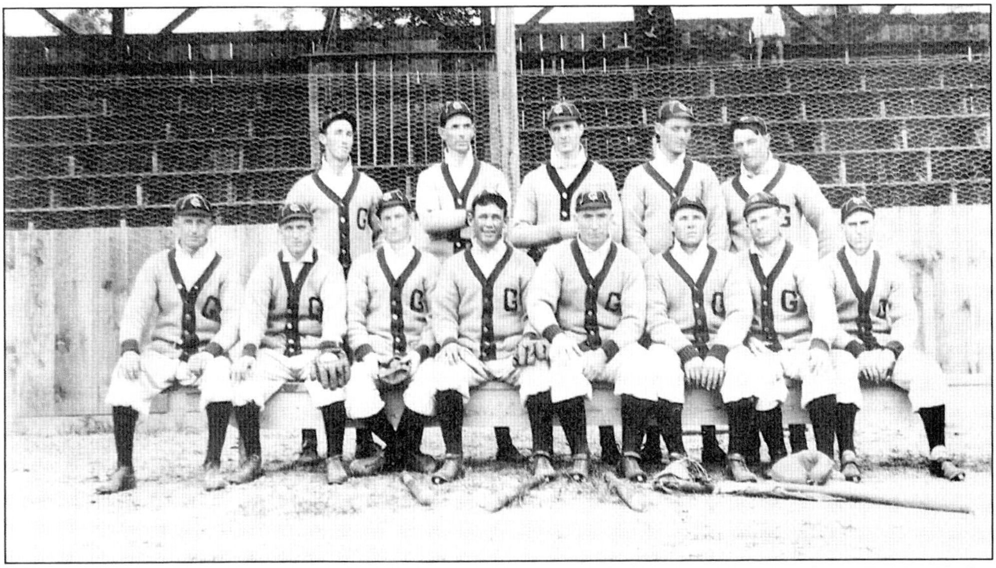

The city of Greensboro fielded its first professional baseball team in 1902 when it joined the brand new North Carolina League. The league failed to survive the entire season as did the next league the city joined, the Virginia-North Carolina League of 1905. In 1908, however, the Carolina Association was formed and proved to be more stable. This team, which represented the city in either 1910 or 1911, competed in that league. (Courtesy of Greensboro Historical Museum Archives.)

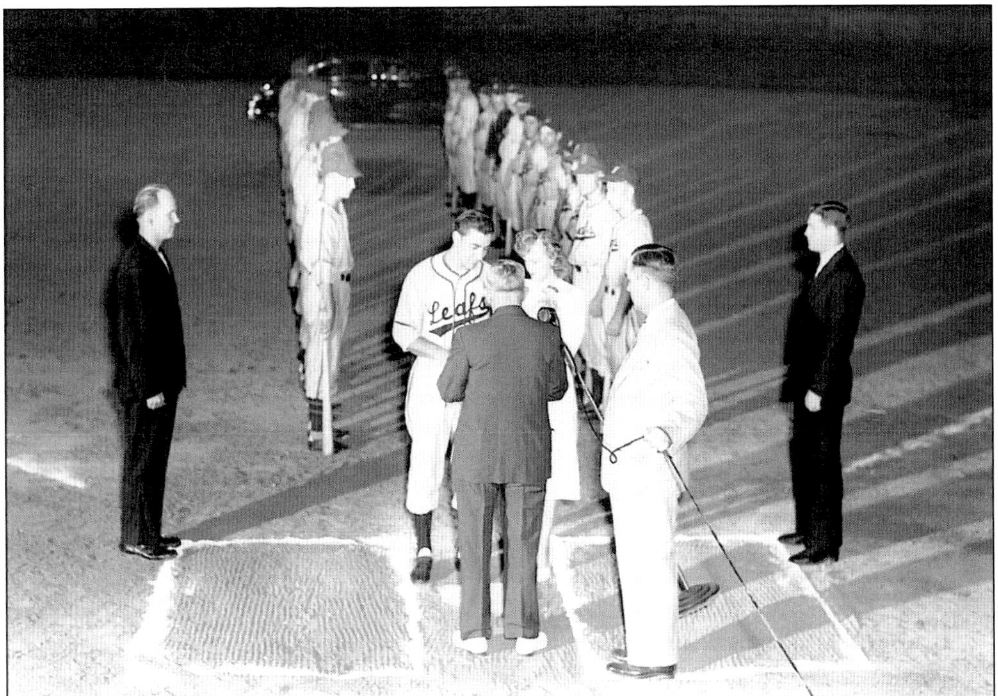

Smithfield-Selma Leafs outfielder Joe Eonta was married at home plate in 1947. Even today, minor league ballplayers will occasionally tie the knot at their team's home park. (Courtesy of Pete Howard.)

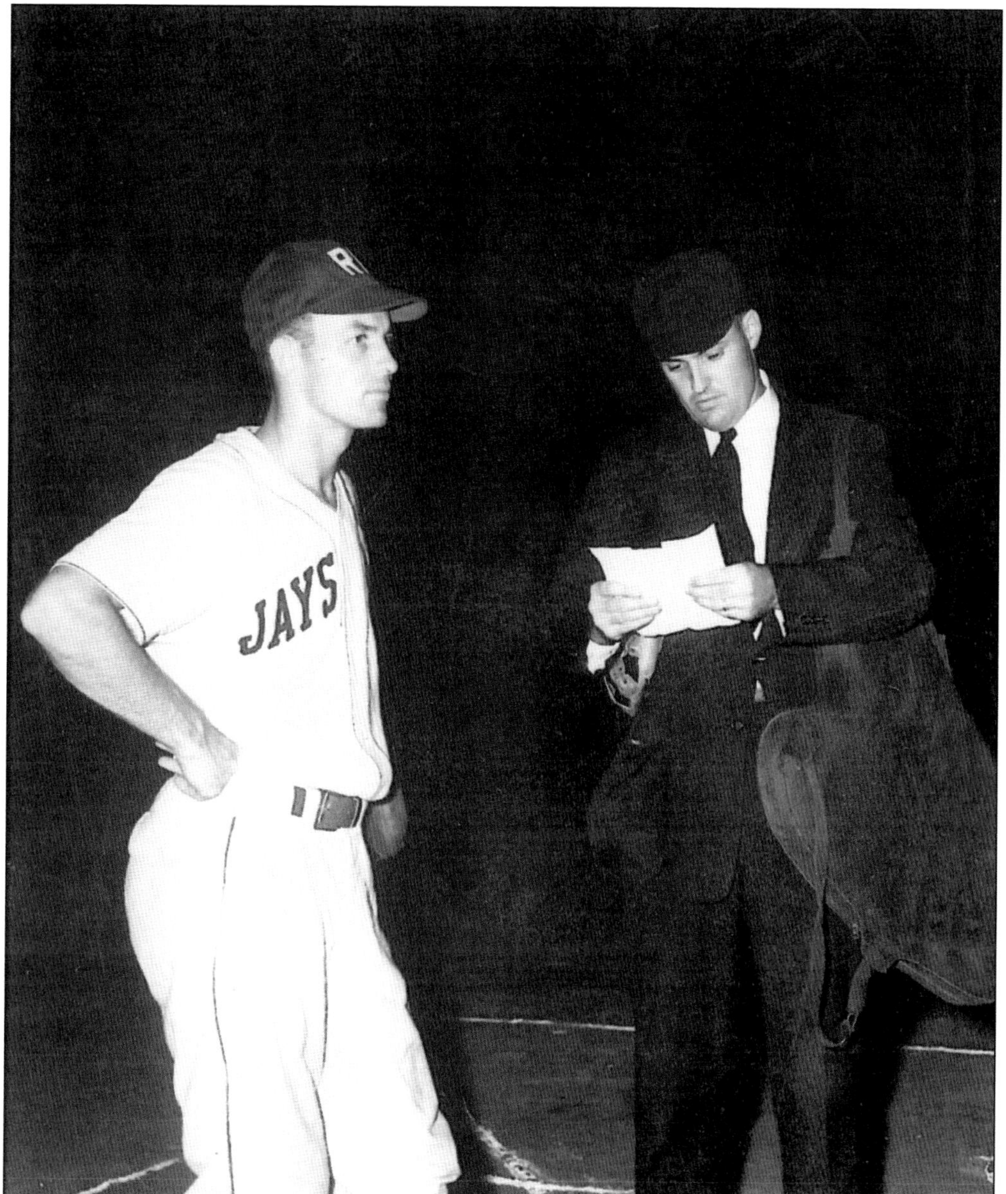

Walt McJunkin, manager and outfielder for the Roanoke Rapids Jays, turns his roster in to the umpire before a game in 1950. The Jays were members of the Coastal Plain League from 1947 to 1952. (Courtesy of Harry Land.)

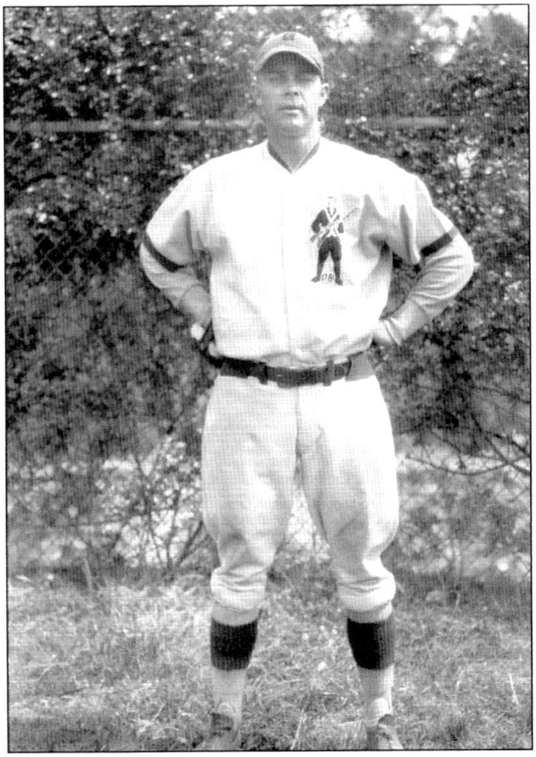

Bill Averette was a pitcher for the 1931 Greensboro Patriots. The Patriots' unique uniforms featured a Revolutionary War soldier and the date 1781, the year in which the city's Battle of Guilford Courthouse was fought. (Courtesy of Greensboro Historical Museum Archives.)

In 1954, the Fayetteville Hilanders posted an 86-51 record and won both the Carolina League pennant and the post-season playoffs. The Hilanders, pictured here from left to right, are (front row) Gus Montalbano, two unidentified, and Bobby Lyons; (middle row) Bill Fowler, Art Raynor, Bucky Jacobs, Harry Helmer, and Jim Pokel; (back row) Claude "Diz" Voiselle, Aaron Robinson, Jim Foxworth, two unidentified, and Jack Hussey. (Courtesy of Bill Fowler.)

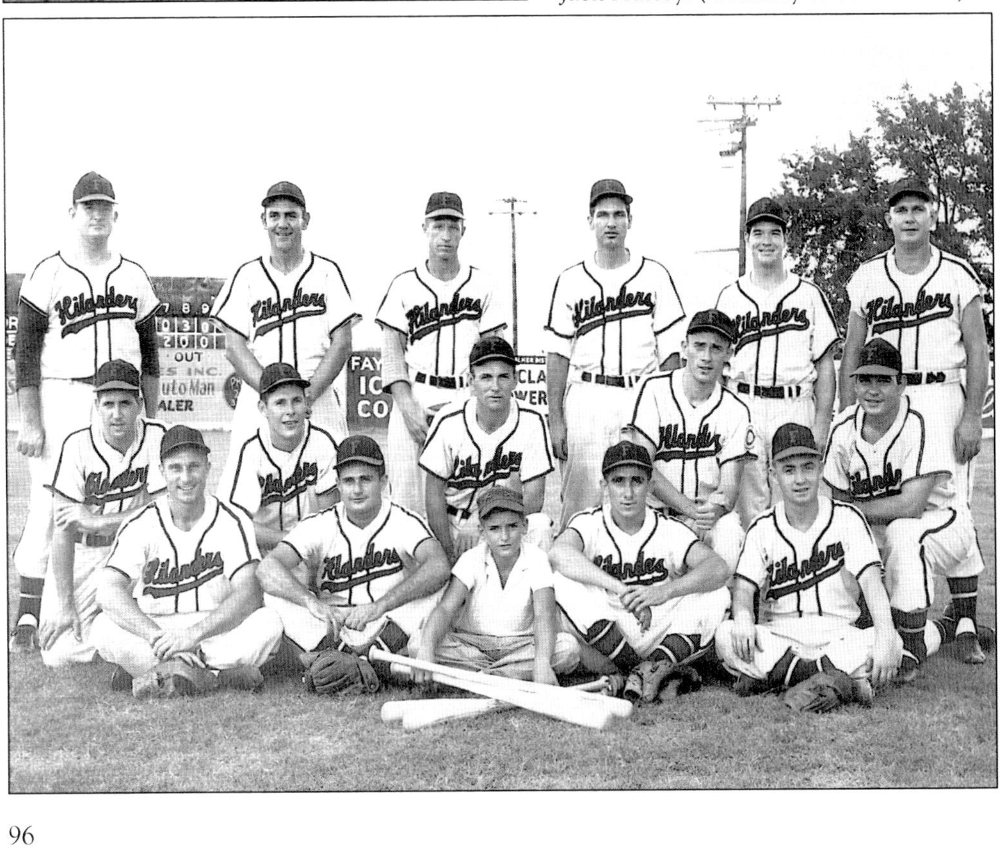

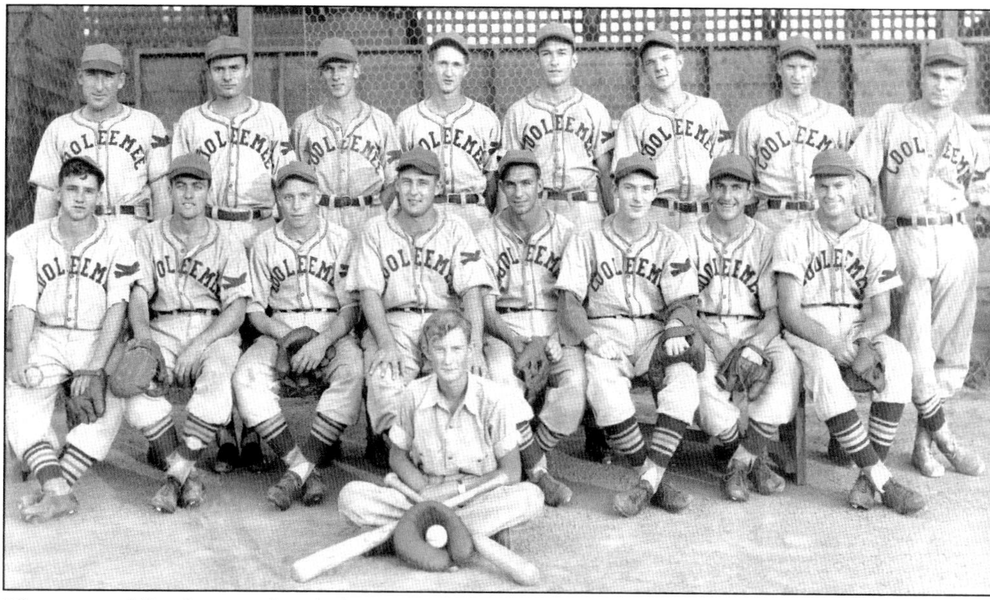

The town of Cooleemee decided to enter professional baseball in 1937 and for five seasons the town fielded a team in the North Carolina State League. This is the 1941 Cooleemee Cardinals, a farm club of the St. Louis Cardinals. They are, from left to right, (front row) Hubert "Thang" Shoaf, Conrad Graff, Charles Skubovious, Forest Rogers, George Marra, William Cost, Larry Pustay, and Grimes "Fat" Parker; (back row) Clanard "Firpo" Creason, Merle Muhl, Harry Hadley, Fred Dickman, George Boerner, Robert Vales, George Jenkins, and Walter Wrona. The batboy is Baxter "Bo" Turner. (Courtesy of Cooleemee Textile Heritage Center Archives.)

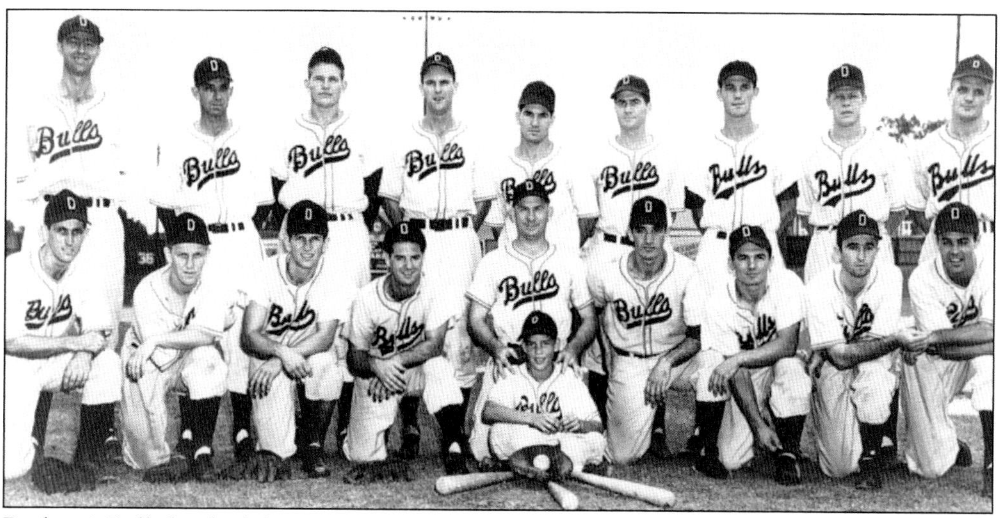

Durham's Bulls finished the 1947 Carolina League season with a record of only 70-71, but it was good enough for fourth place and a spot in the playoffs. In the first round of the postseason they upset Winston-Salem but in the finals they fell to Raleigh. From left to right are the following: (front row) Norman Kramer, Jim McClintock, Del Duckworth, Nick DeLuca, Willie Duke, Frank Strum, Fred Pacitto, Alex Palica, and Bill Sawyer; (back row) Cecil "Turkey" Tyson, Claude "Buck" Weaver, Larry Hartley, Charles Hastedt, Paul Crawford, Mickey McPadden, unidentified, Charles Ferrell, and Adolph Honeycutt. (Courtesy of Miles Wolff.)

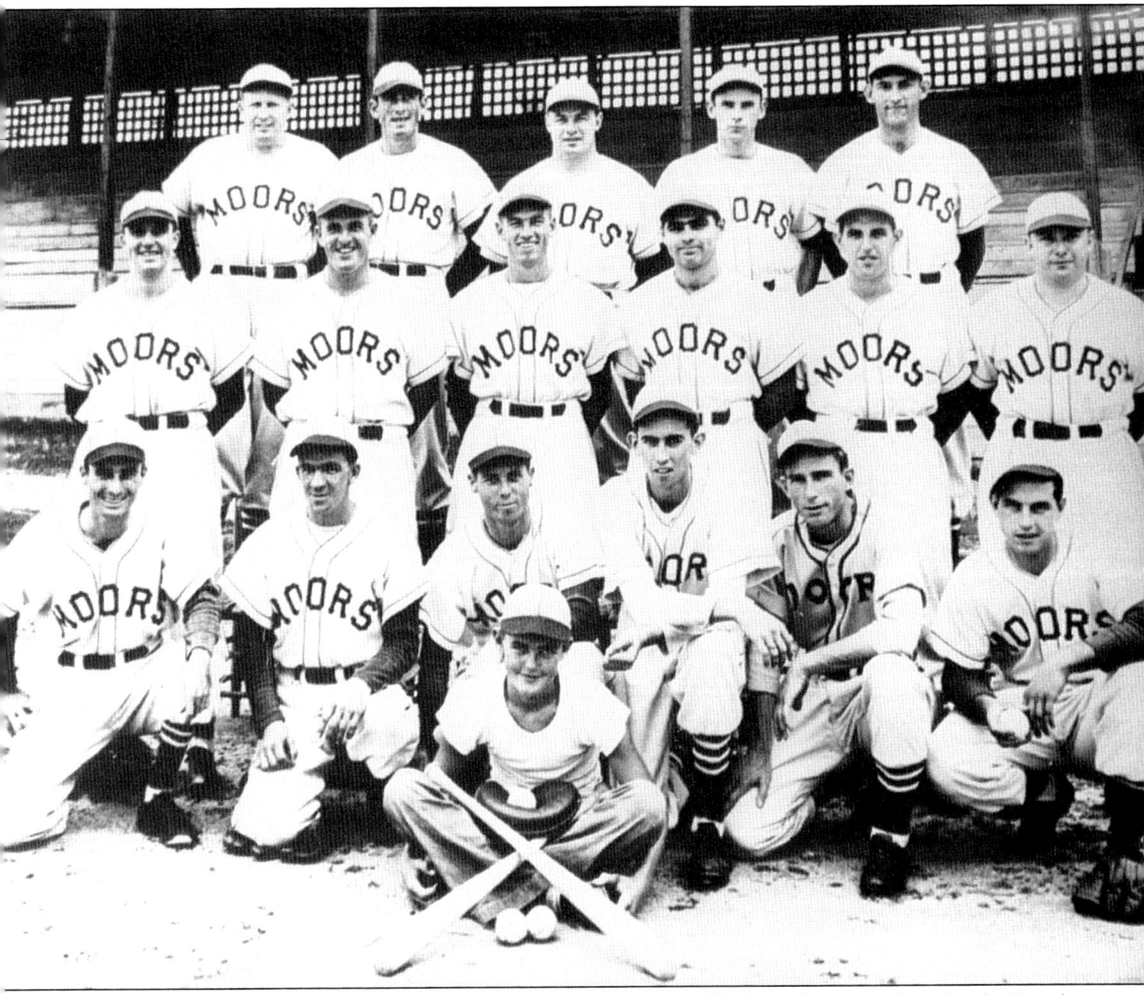

The 1947 Mooresville Moors featured pitcher Hoyt Wilhelm, who was the North Carolina State League's best that season with 20 wins. By 1952 he had worked his way up to the big leagues and for 21 seasons—thanks to a nearly unhittable knuckleball—he would be one of the most effective relief pitchers in the history of the game. He was elected to the Hall of Fame in 1985. Pitcher Dave Jolley, a native of Stony Point, North Carolina, played two seasons for the Moors and also made it to the big leagues. For five seasons, beginning in 1953, he was one of the Milwaukee Braves' most frequently used relievers. Pictured here, from left to right, are (front row) Lefty Jetum, Tom McCall, Dave Jolley, Earl Sorrels, Dewey Hoyt, and Hoyt Wilhelm; (middle row) Martin Pollio, Eddie Walczak, Brooks Harrington, Buddy Milito, Ray Walczak, and Gene Deal; (back row) Wilmer "Red" Lane, Harvey "Ike" Isenhour, Norman Small, Carl Wray, and Ross Morrow. (Courtesy of Norman Small.)

Outfielder Dan Morejon, the Carolina League's batting champion and Most Valuable Player in 1955, helped lead the High Point-Thomasville Hi-Toms to the pennant. (Courtesy of High Point Museum Archives.)

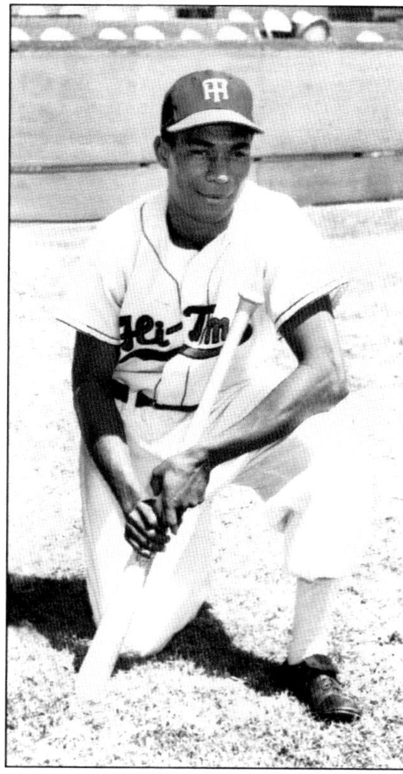

Veteran first baseman Cecil "Turkey" Tyson gives instruction to fellow infielders Frank Sturm, Jim McClintock, and Nick DeLuca at Durham Bulls spring training in 1947. (Courtesy of Cecil Tyson.)

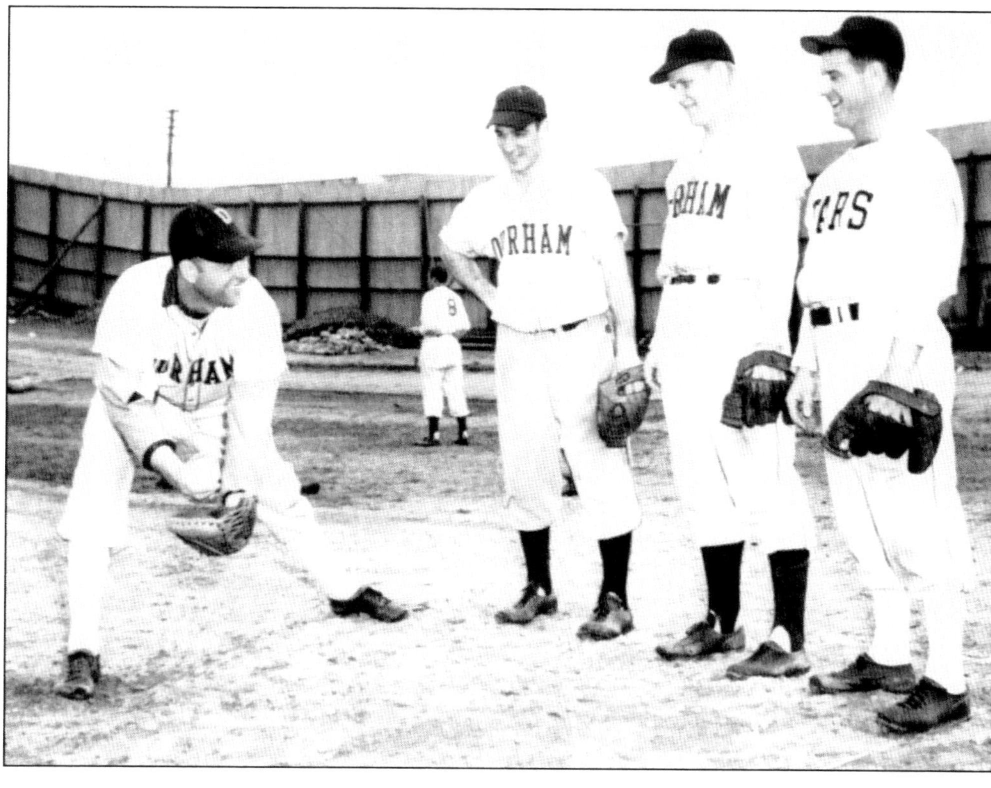

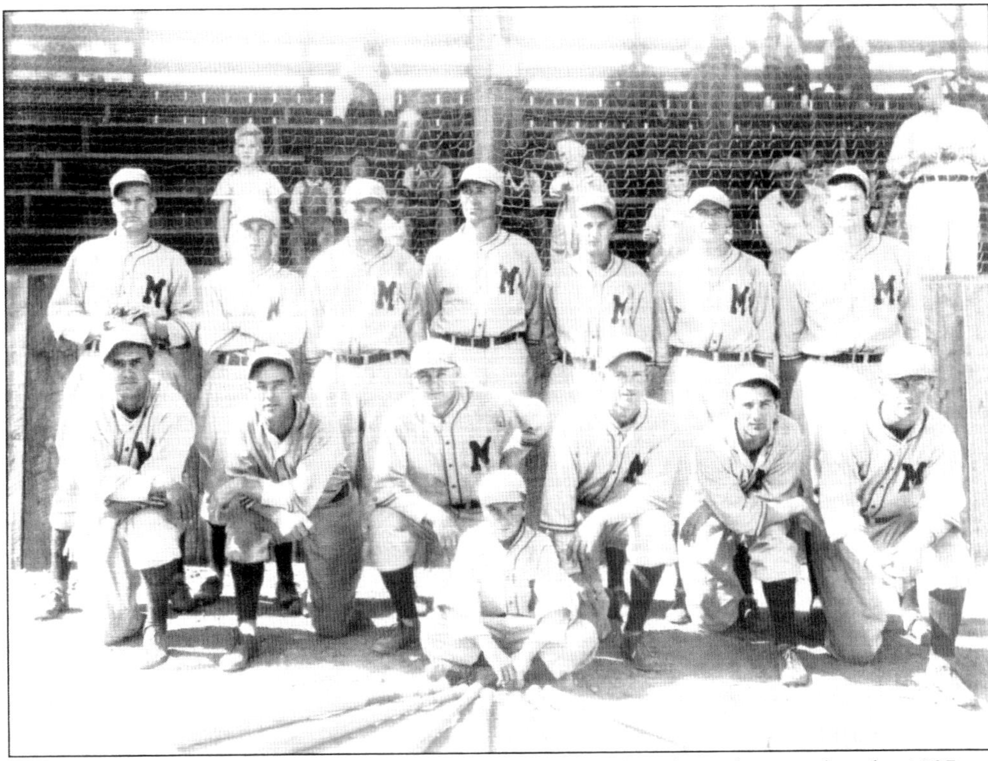

This photo shows either the 1937 or 1938 Mayodan Millers of the Bi-State League. In each of those seasons, the Millers, managed by Harry Daughtry, finished second to the Bassett Furniture Makers. (Courtesy of Buddy Payne.)

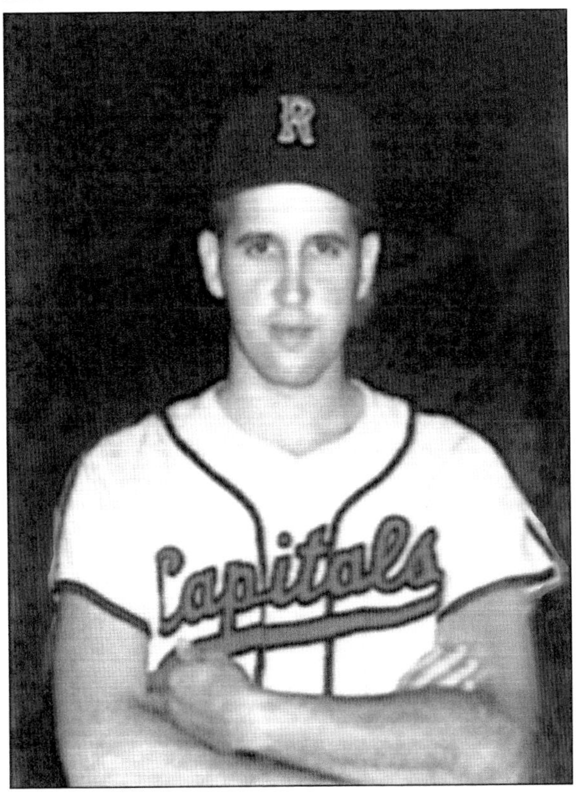

A star baseball player at Charlotte High School in the early 1940s, Bill Fowler had offers to turn pro after graduation but he decided to accept a scholarship to play for North Carolina State University instead. After college Fowler did enter the pro ranks and spent several successful years in the minor leagues with clubs including Raleigh and Fayetteville before turning to a career in education. (Courtesy of Bill Fowler.)

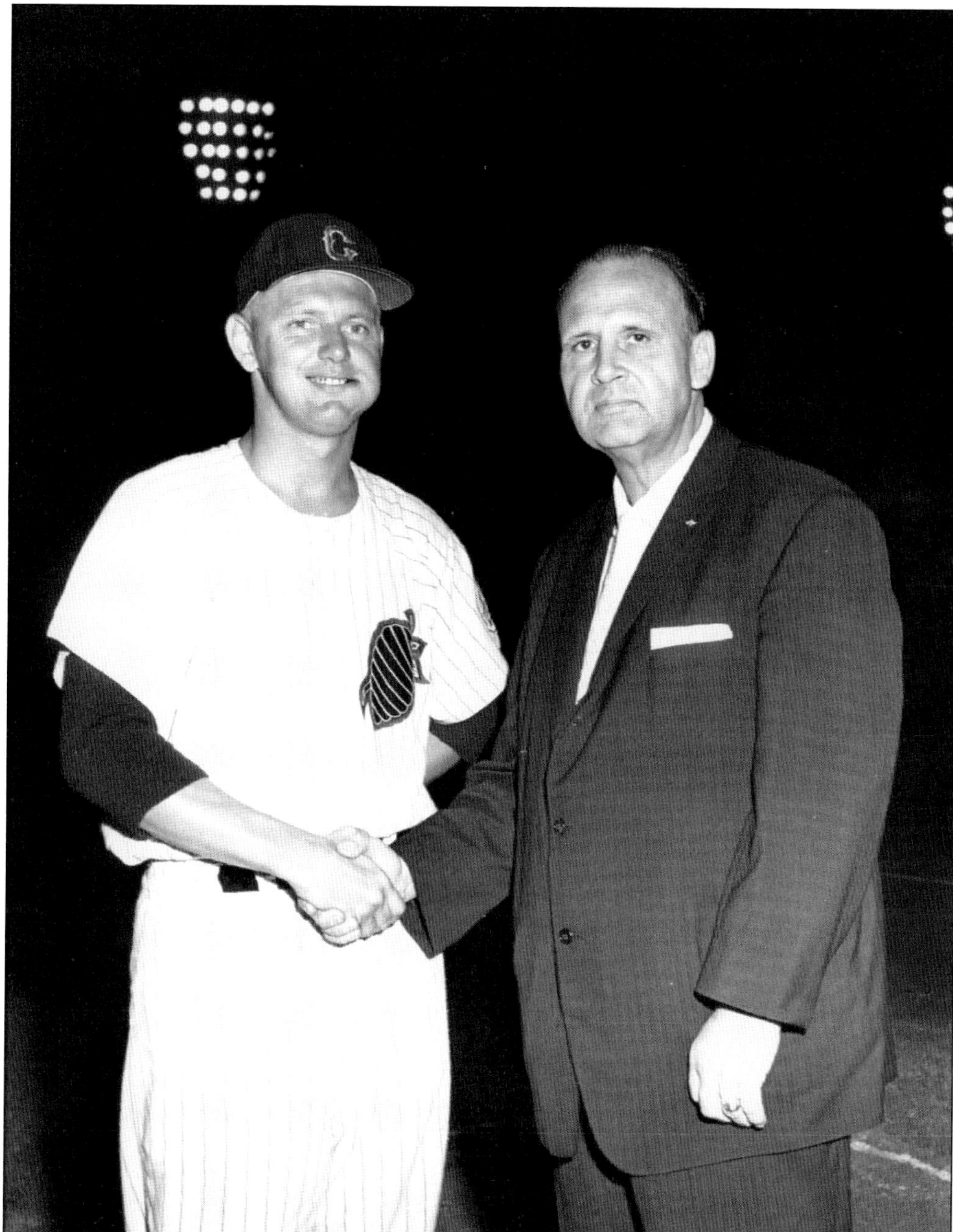

Charlotte Hornets player Bill Felker poses with team president Phil Howser in this c. 1960 photo. The Griffith family, who also owned the Washington Senators, appointed Howser to run their Charlotte ballclub in the late 1930s. He would eventually spend 30 years running the Hornets' front office. In 1962, Howser was honored by minor league baseball's governing body for his years of service as the King of Baseball at the annual National Association convention and in 1968 the Sporting News named him Class AA Executive of the Year. (Courtesy of Gene Verble.)

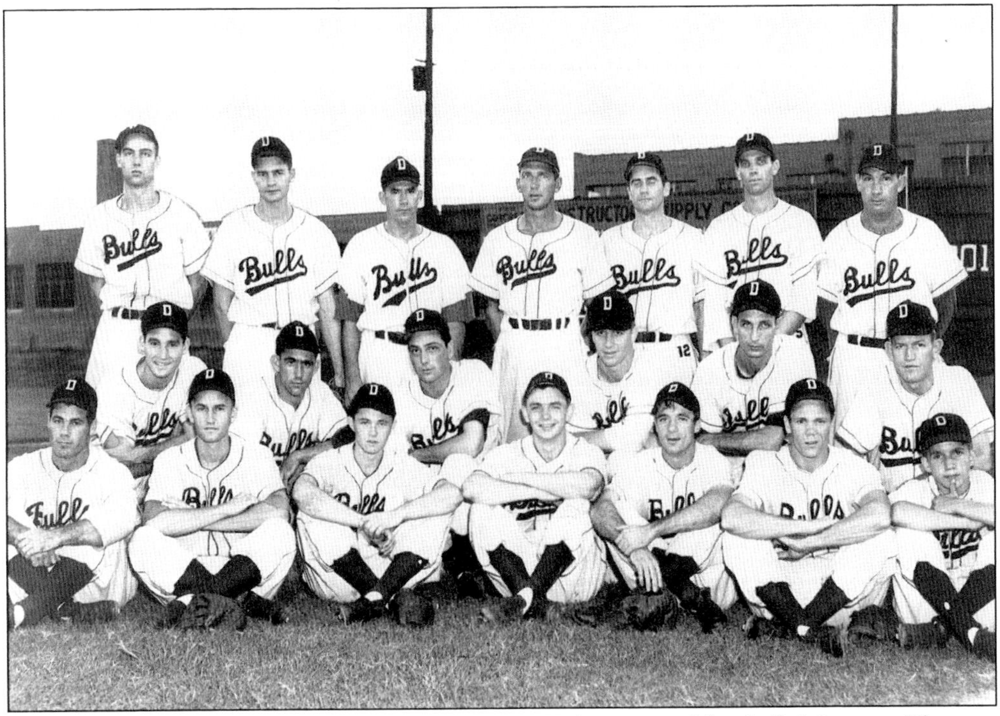

The 1949 Durham Bulls had quite a connection to the game of football. Manager Clarence "Ace" Parker (back row, far right), a former All-American football player at Duke, had a standout career in the NFL and is now in the Hall of Fame. Speedy outfielder Pat Haggerty (front row, third from right) would go on to become one of the most respected referees in the National Football League. In a career that lasted more than 20 years he officiated three Super Bowls. (Courtesy of Miles Wolff.)

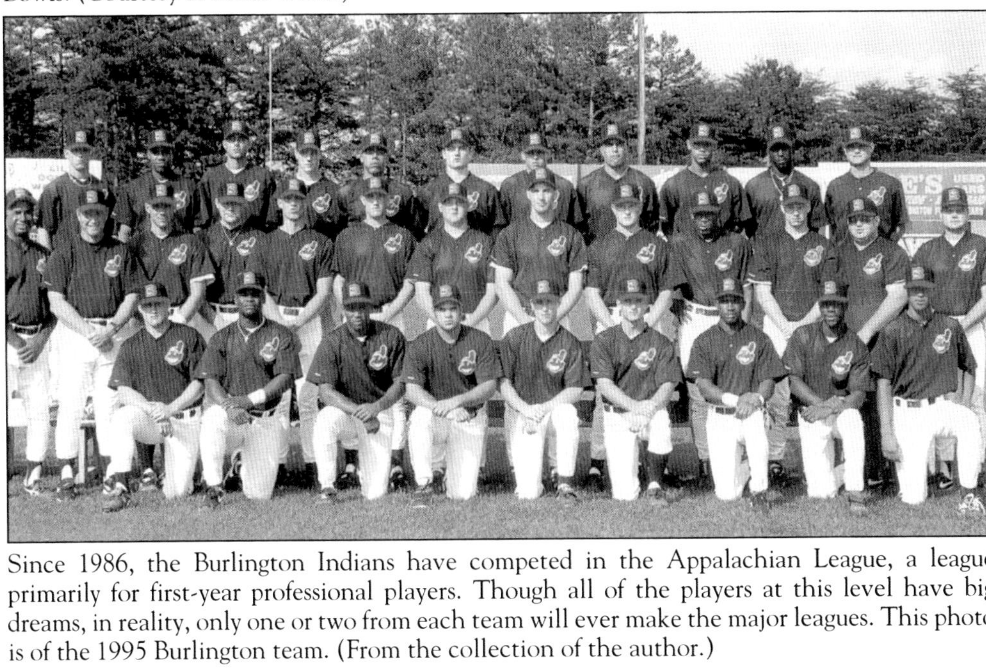

Since 1986, the Burlington Indians have competed in the Appalachian League, a league primarily for first-year professional players. Though all of the players at this level have big dreams, in reality, only one or two from each team will ever make the major leagues. This photo is of the 1995 Burlington team. (From the collection of the author.)

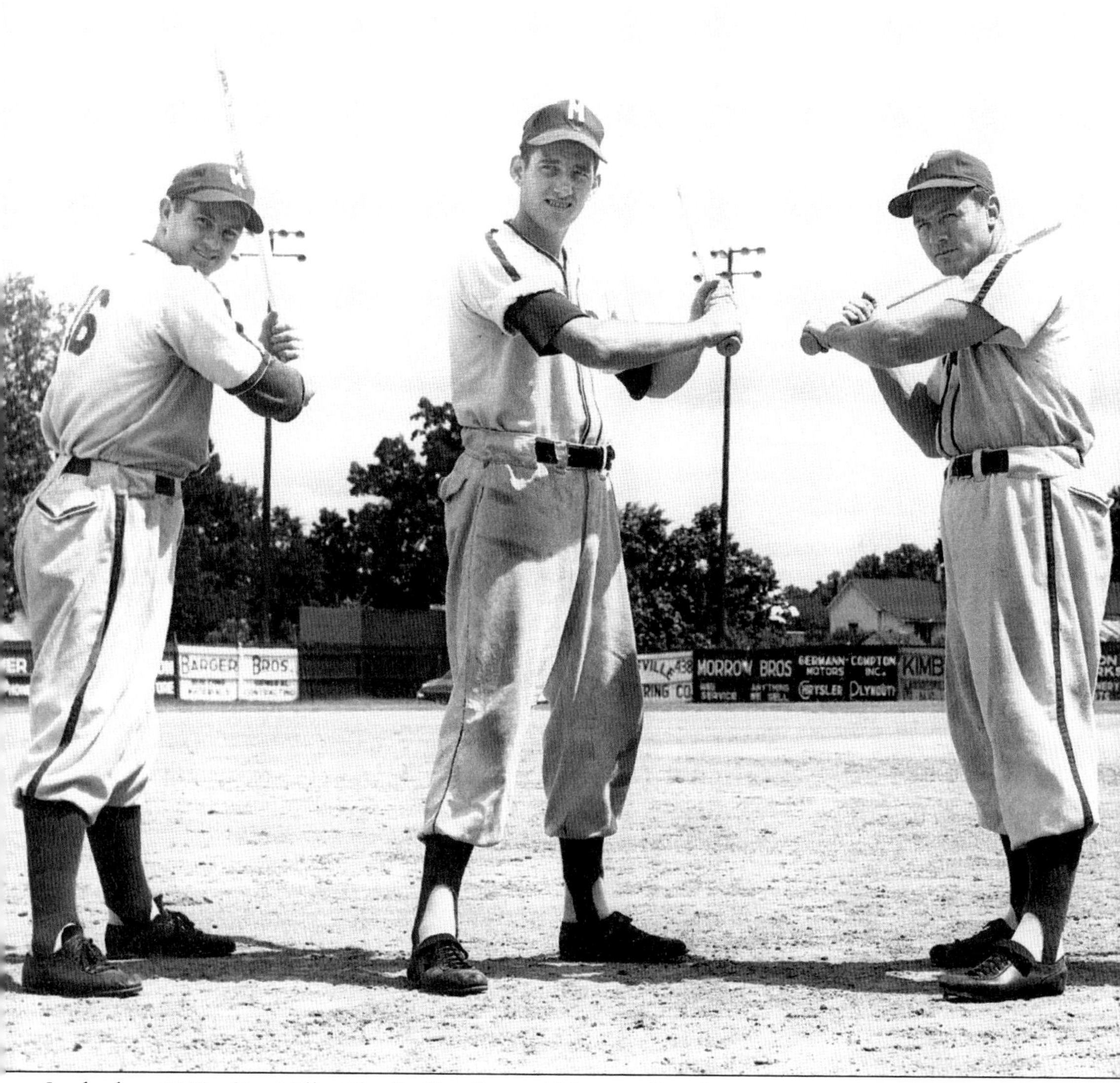

In the late 1940s, Jim Mills, Charlie Knight, and Norman Small were among three of the most feared hitters in the North Carolina State League and they helped make the Mooresville Moors perennial pennant contenders. Mills, who played third base and was manager of the team, and first baseman Knight hit for average and got on base while slugging outfielder Small provided the power to drive them home. (From the collection of the author.)

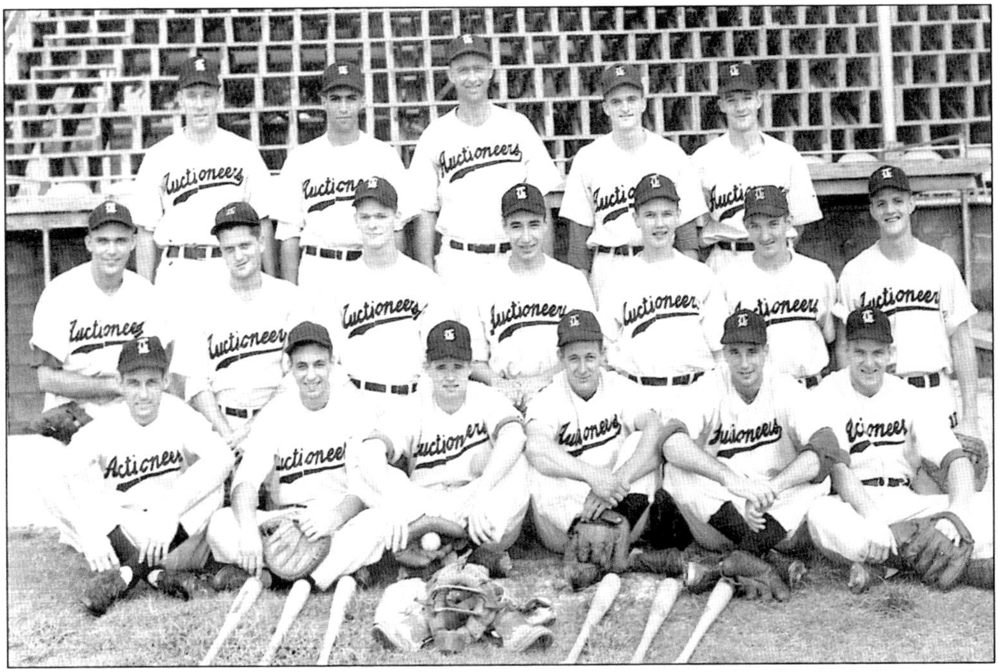

The 1949 Lumberton Auctioneers, a farm club of the Chicago Cubs, finished third in the Tobacco State League with a record of 75-61. The Robeson County town of Lumberton fielded a professional team for four seasons, from 1947 through 1950 when the Tobacco State League folded. (Courtesy of Cecil Tyson.)

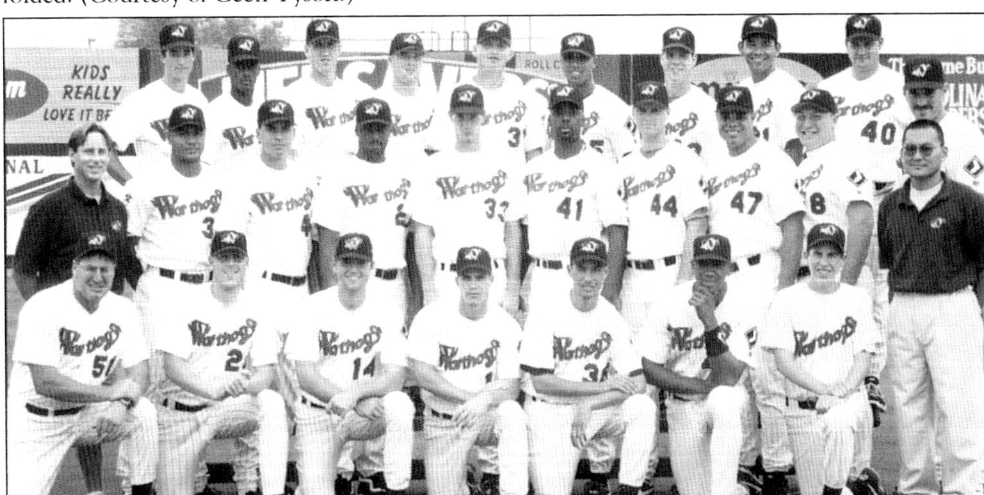

The 1997 Winston-Salem Warthogs were the Carolina League affiliate of the Chicago White Sox. From left to right are the following: (front row) Mark Haley (manager), Brian Schmack, Jason Secoda, Kevin Connacher, Jim Parque, Ramon Gomez, Chris Huebner (batboy), and Scott Takao (trainer); (middle row) Coach Don Toddings, Carlos Lees, Luis Garcia, Robert Theodile, John Ambrose, Kendrick Mitchell, Chad Bradford, Juan Thomas, Pete Pryor, and Coach Curt Hasler; (back row) Darren Baugh, Rashad Albert, Mark Roberts, Mark Johnson, Jim Dixon, Jerry Whittaker, Jon Hunt, Wil Polidor, and Brian Downs. (From the collection of the author.)

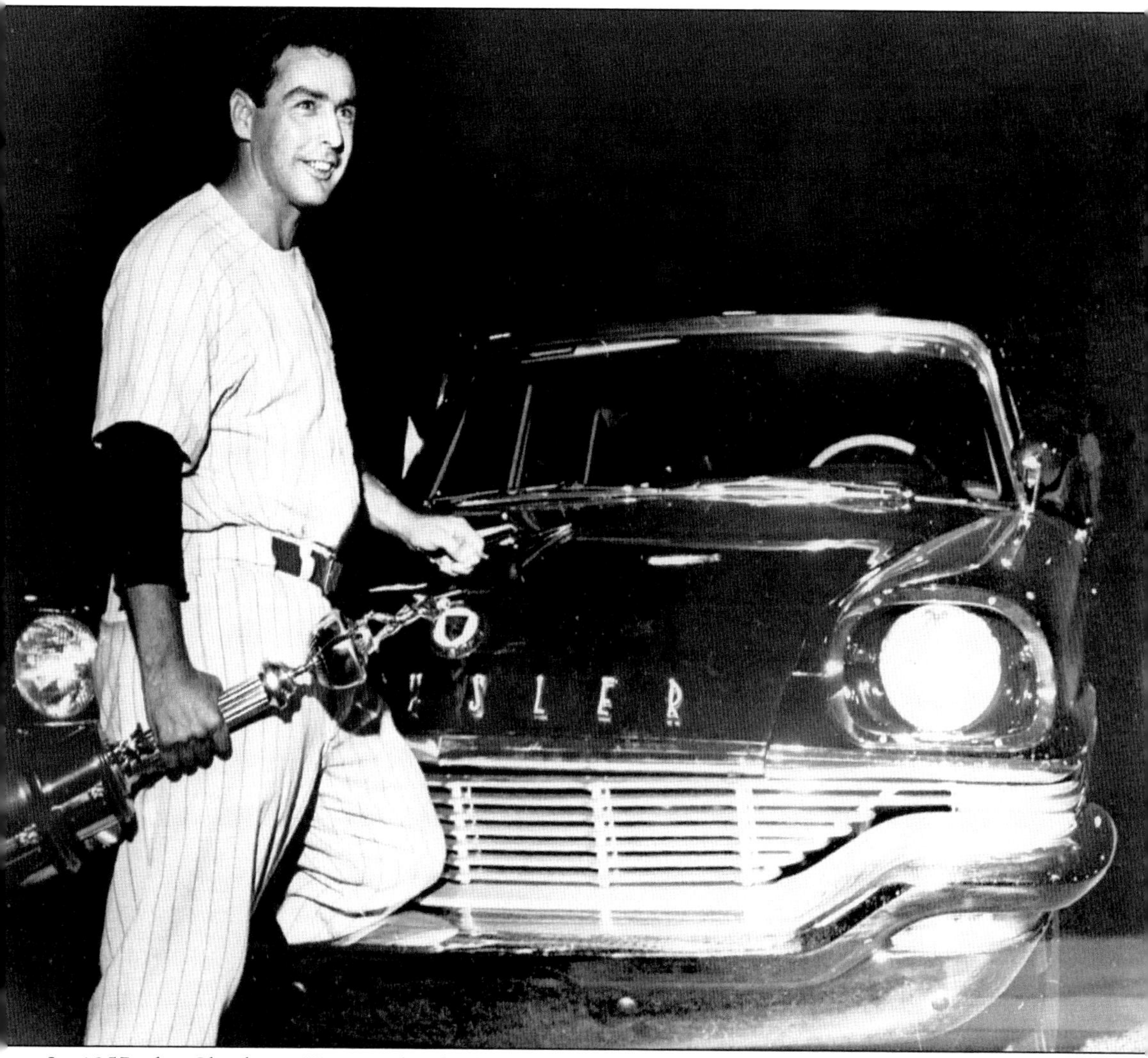

In 1957, the Charlotte Hornets finished the regular season in second place with a record of 86-67. Advancing to the playoffs they swept Knoxville in the first round and then defeated Augusta, two games to one, for the title. For his efforts, manager and second baseman Gene Verble was presented a new Chrysler automobile by the team. (Courtesy of Gene Verble.)

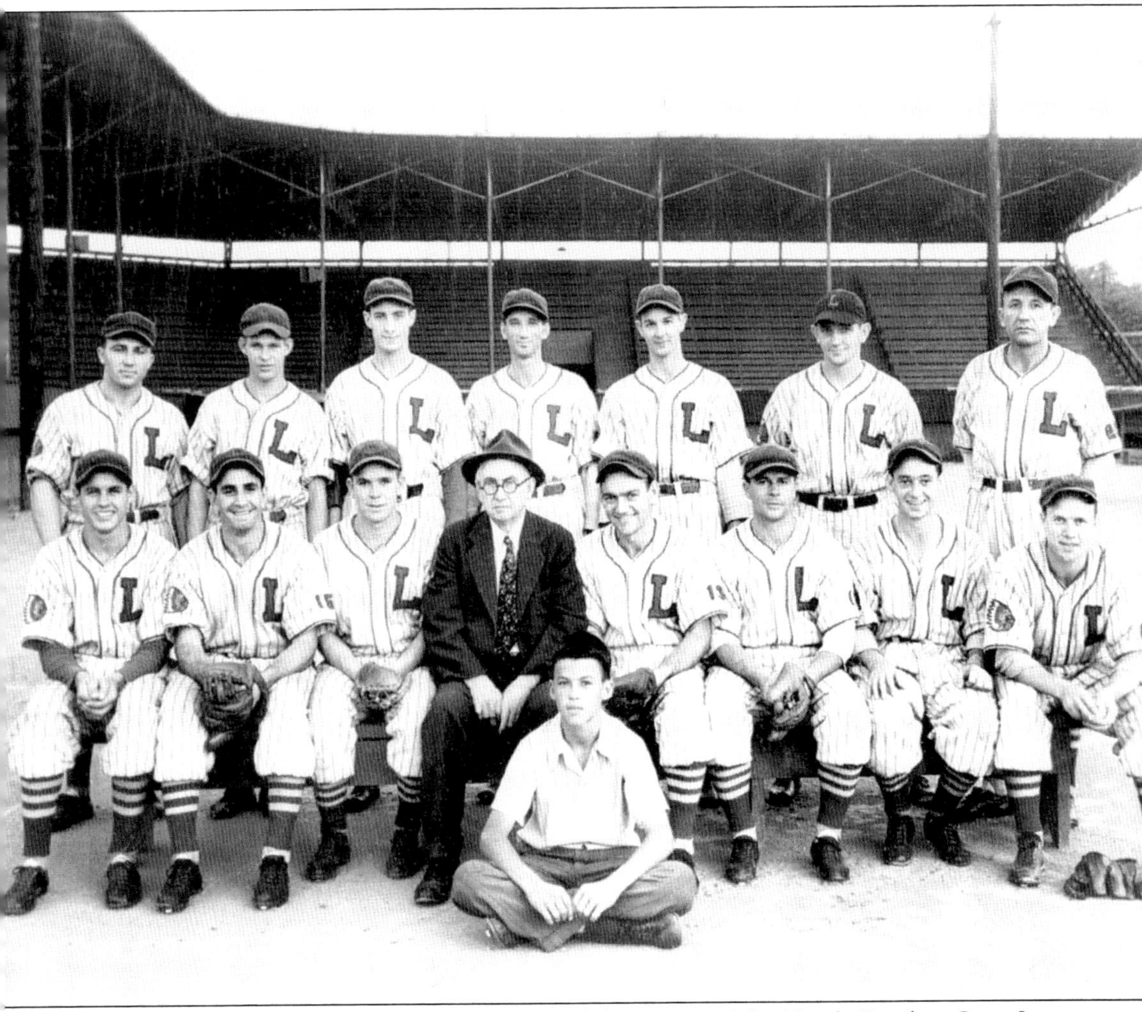

The 1940 Lexington Indians were the playoff champions of the North Carolina State League. Here they pose in front of the grandstand at Holt-Moffitt Field. From left to right are (front row) Paul Gassoway, George Saab, Robert "Buck" Glover, A.C. Fite (owner), Lester Smith (manager), Stan Hoyniski, Walter Posey, and Borden "Goose" Helms; (back row) L.C. "Buck" Kelly, Roy Pinkston, Ray Ross, Reid Gowan, Fremont Connor, Wilbur Reeser, and Ramon Couto. (Courtesy of Betty Fite.)

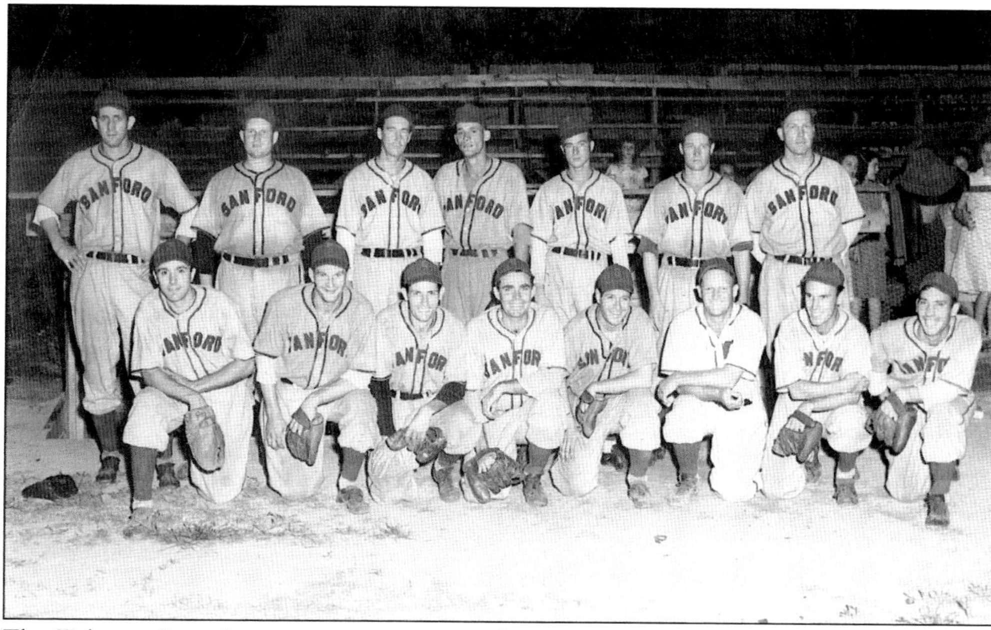

The Tobacco State League was in existence from 1946 to 1950 and the Sanford Spinners, shown here, were the league's first pennant winners. The members, from left to right, are (front row) Phalti Shoffner, Joe Nessing, Jimmy Guinn, Jim Gales, Ned Butcher, Zeb Harrington (manager), Carl Powell, and Joe Trentalange; (back row) Hank Nesselrode, Dave Odom, George Bortz, Howard Auman, Bill Stone, Bob Pugh, and Bob Wicker. (Courtesy of Zeb "Dan" Harrington.)

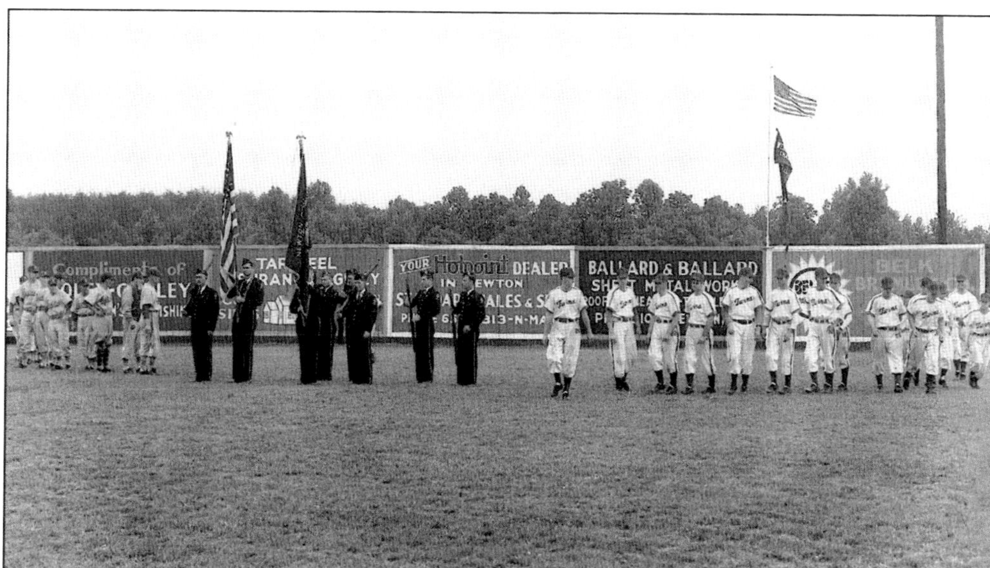

Members of the color guard prepare to march off the field after the playing of the National Anthem before a Western Carolina League game between the Newton-Conover Twins (right) and the Morganton Aggies (left) in 1950. Newton-Conover's pennant for winning the league title in 1949 can be seen flying beneath the American flag. (Courtesy of Joe Plick.)

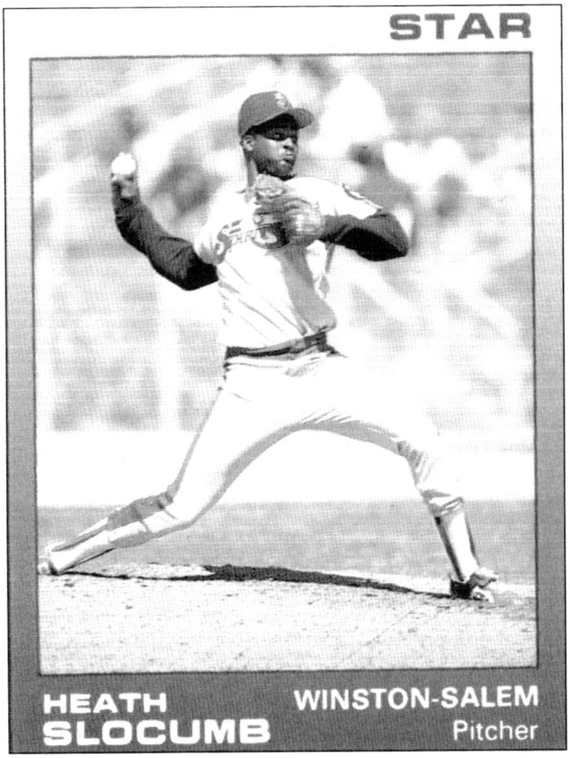

Heath Slocumb pitched for the Winston-Salem Spirits in 1987 and 1988. After making his big league debut with the Cubs in 1991, Slocumb went on to a long career as a relief pitcher and was named to the All-Star team in 1995. (From the collection of the author.)

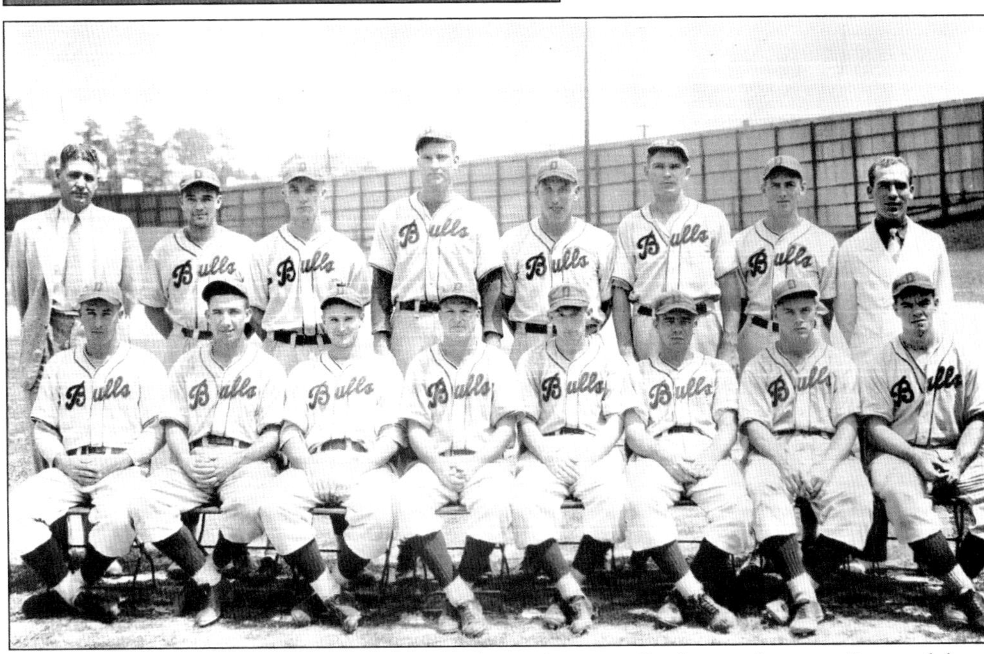

The 1937 Durham Bulls finished fifth in the eight-team Piedmont League. Pictured here, from left to right, are (front row) unidentified, Al Hunt, unidentified, Gene Handley, Paul "Red" O'Malley (manager), Hal Blackstock, Norman Small, and unidentified; (back row) Paul Florence (president), Joe Bestudik, unidentified, John O'Flynn, Paul Gehrman, unidentified, Jesse Cole, and unidentified (business manager). (Courtesy of Norman Small.)

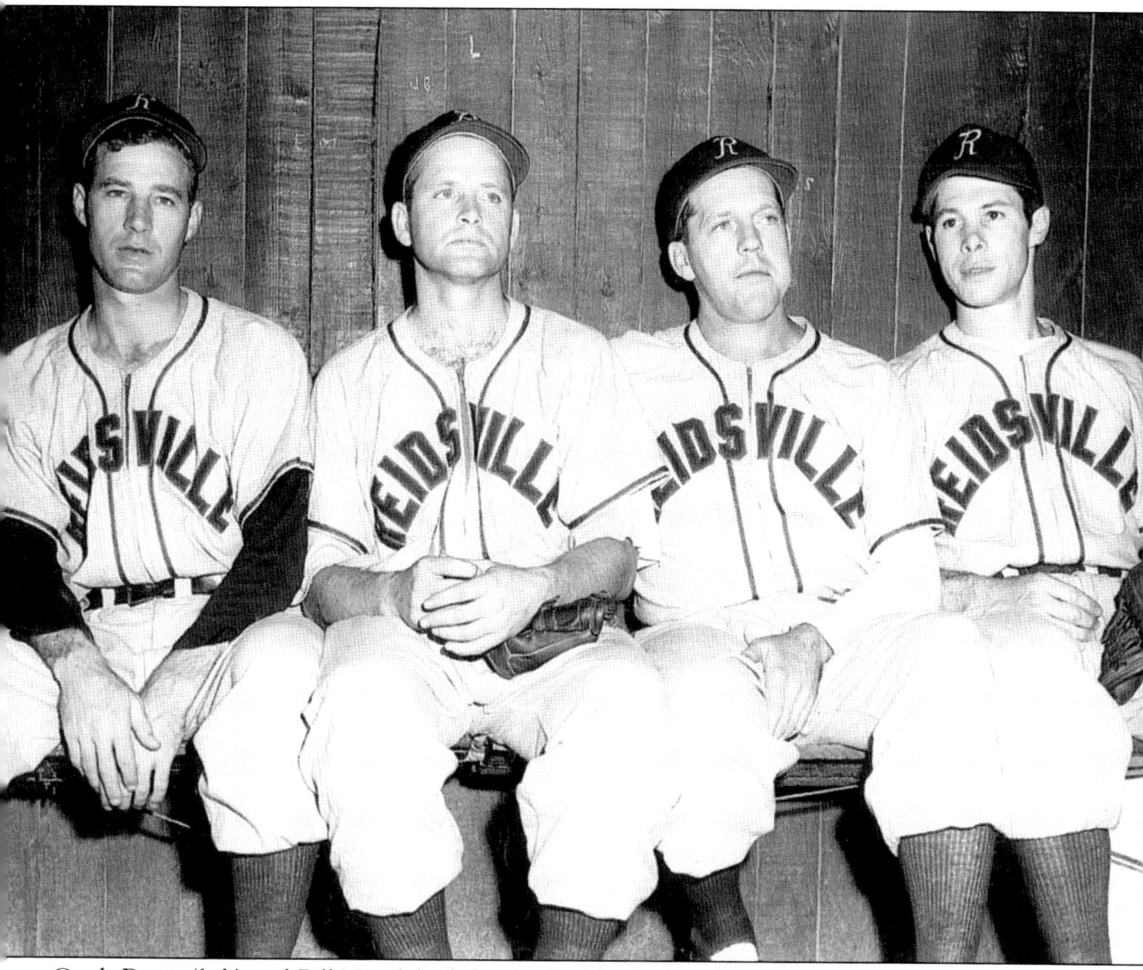

Crash Davis (left) and Bill Nagel (right), who had both played for the Philadelphia Athletics in the years right before the war, sit between two unidentified teammates in the dugout of the 1950 Reidsville Luckies. Like many other players who had their baseball careers interrupted by World War II, Davis and Nagel found their jobs taken by younger players upon return from military service. Instead, they both spent several successful seasons in the high minor leagues. (Courtesy of Lawrence "Crash" Davis.)

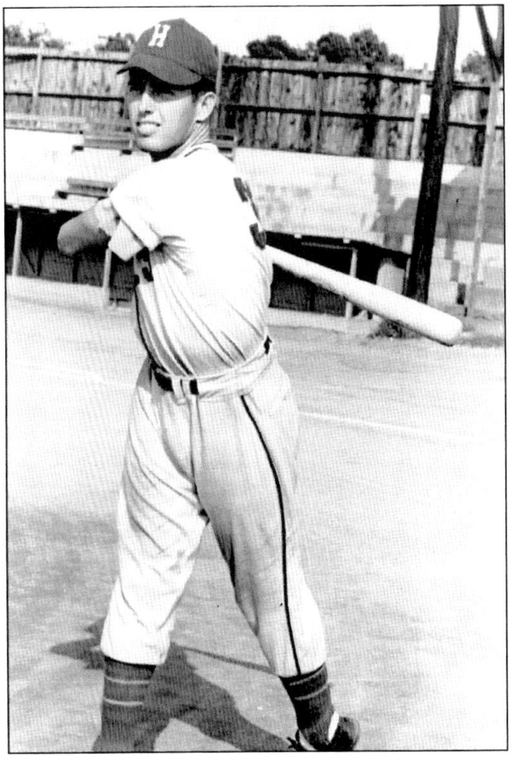

With 32 homeruns and 105 runs batted in, Hickory outfielder Otis Stephens was one of the top sluggers in the Western Carolina League in 1948. A native of Roxboro, Stephens began his pro career as a teenager with Angier in 1946 and appeared to be on his way to the big leagues until injuries cut his career short in the early 1950s. (Courtesy of Otis Stephens.)

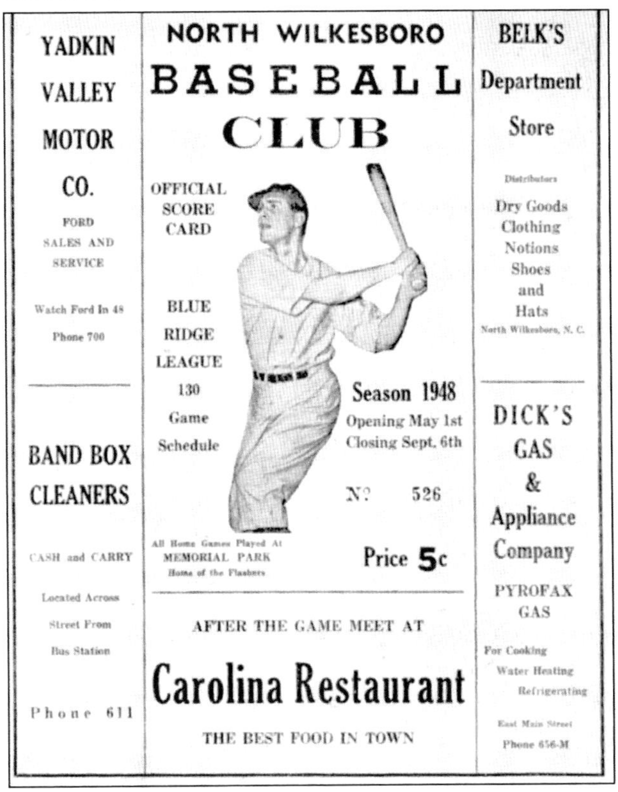

Fans of the North Wilkesboro Flashers would have used this scorecard in 1948. Members of the Blue Ridge League, the Flashers took second place that season. North Wilkesboro's foray into professional baseball lasted three seasons, from 1948 through 1950. (Courtesy of Worth Cuthbertson.)

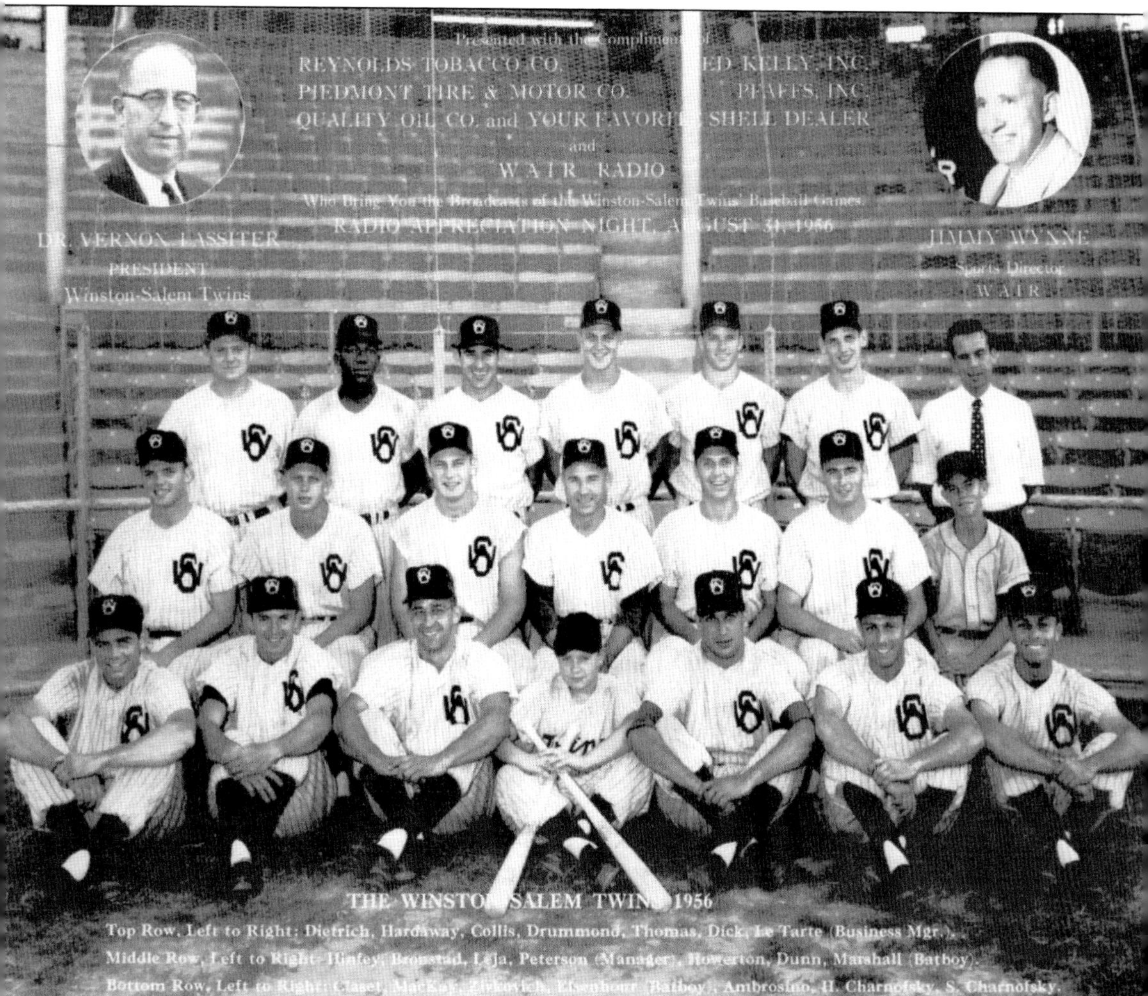

Though their big league affiliate, the New York Yankees, won the World Series that season, the 1956 Winston-Salem Twins were not so fortunate and finished in the Carolina League cellar. From left to right are (front row) Claset, MacKay, Zivkovich, Eisenhour (batboy), Ambrosino, H. Charnofsky, and S. Charnofsky; (middle row) Hinfey, Bronstad, Leja, Peterson (manager), Howerton, Dunn, and Marshall (batboy); (back row) Dietrich, Hardaway, Collis, Drummond, Thomas, Dick, and LeTarte (business manager); (insets) Dr. Vernon Lassiter (team president) and Jimmy Wynne (sports director at WAIR). (From the collection of the author.)

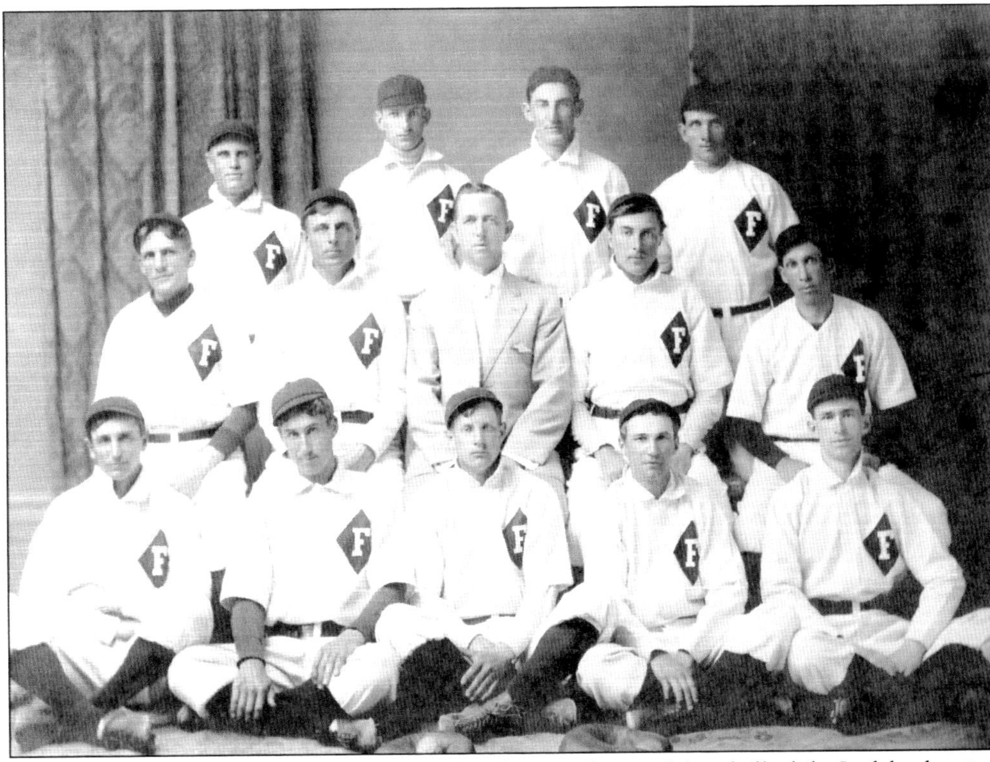

The Highlanders of 1909 were Fayetteville's first professional baseball club. Led by batting champ Bill Schumaker, the team finished third in the Eastern Carolina League standings with a 49-41 record. (From the collection of the author.)

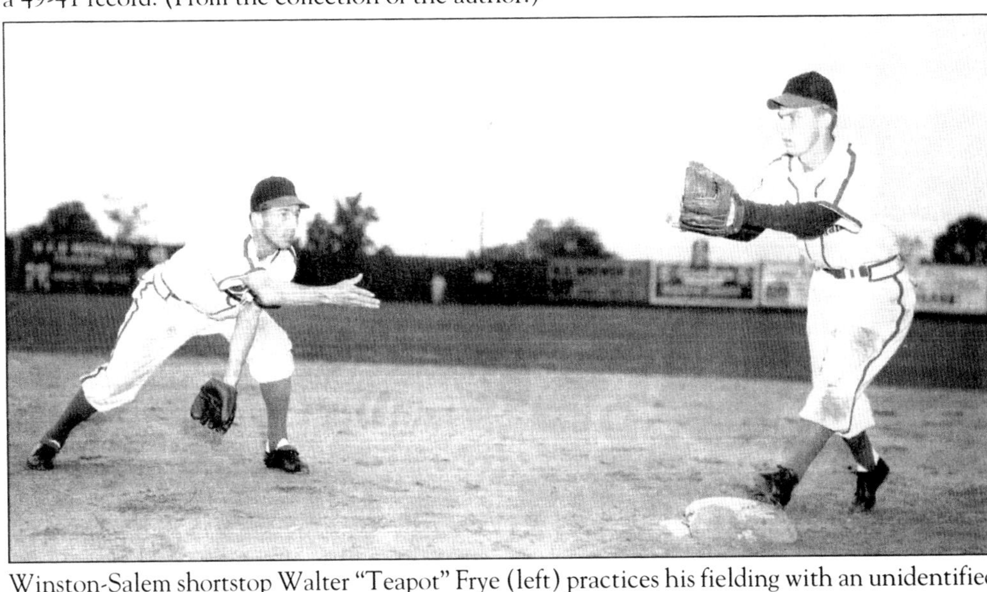

Winston-Salem shortstop Walter "Teapot" Frye (left) practices his fielding with an unidentified teammate in this 1947 photo. Frye played in a record 953 Carolina League games over seven seasons with Leaksville, Reidsville, and Winston-Salem. The slick-fielding Stoneville native retired from the playing field in 1953 and went on to have a long career as the baseball coach at Oak Ridge Military Institute near Greensboro. (Courtesy of Buddy Payne.)

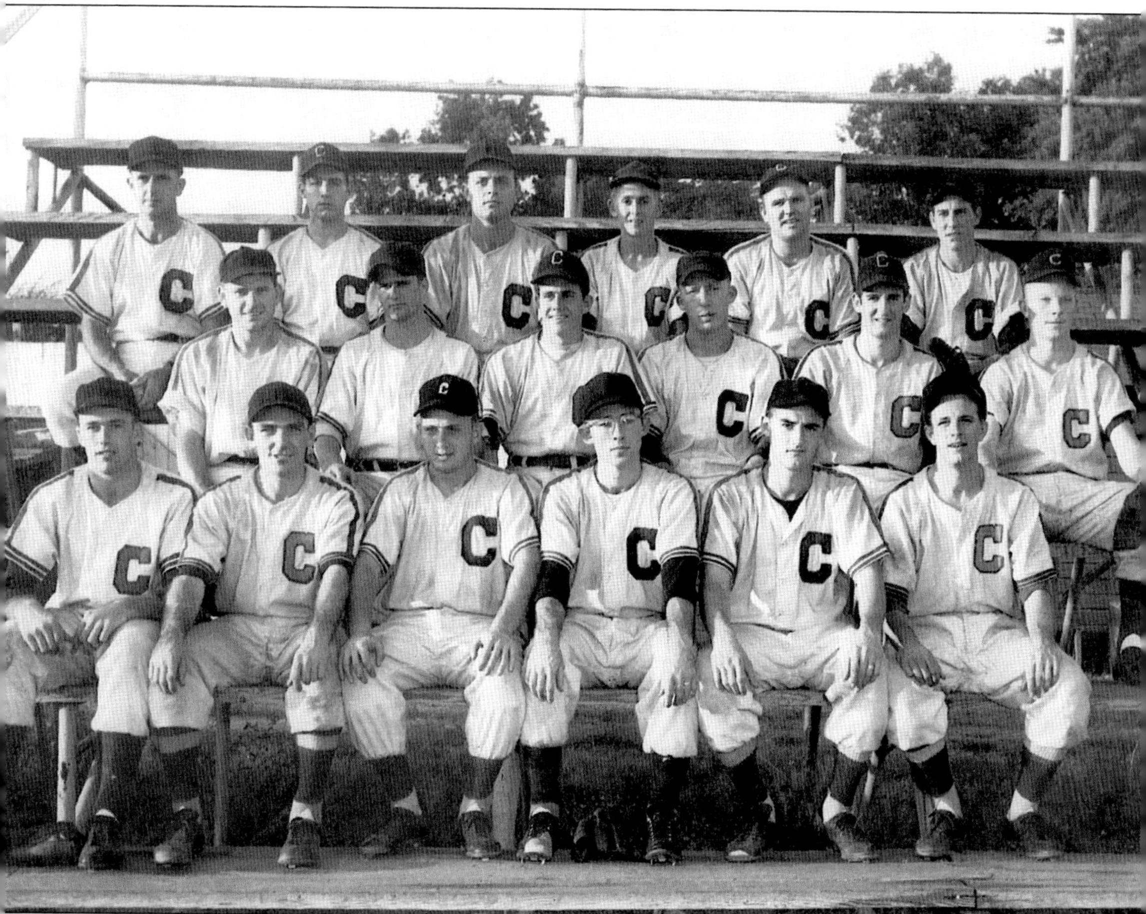

The 1950 Concord Nationals, a Washington Senators farm club, finished only seventh in the North Carolina State League but pitcher Dick Hyde did go on to spend much of six seasons in the big leagues. The Nationals, from left to right, are (front row) Steve Colley, Tom Hockenbury, Marty Cribbins, Dick Hyde, Levi "Buck" Fleshman, and unidentified; (middle row) two unidentified, Ray Nesbit, Paul Baldigowski, and two unidentified; (back row) Herman "Ginger" Watts (manager), unidentified, Paul Petrea, two unidentified, Len Cross, and unidentified. (Courtesy of Hank Utley.)

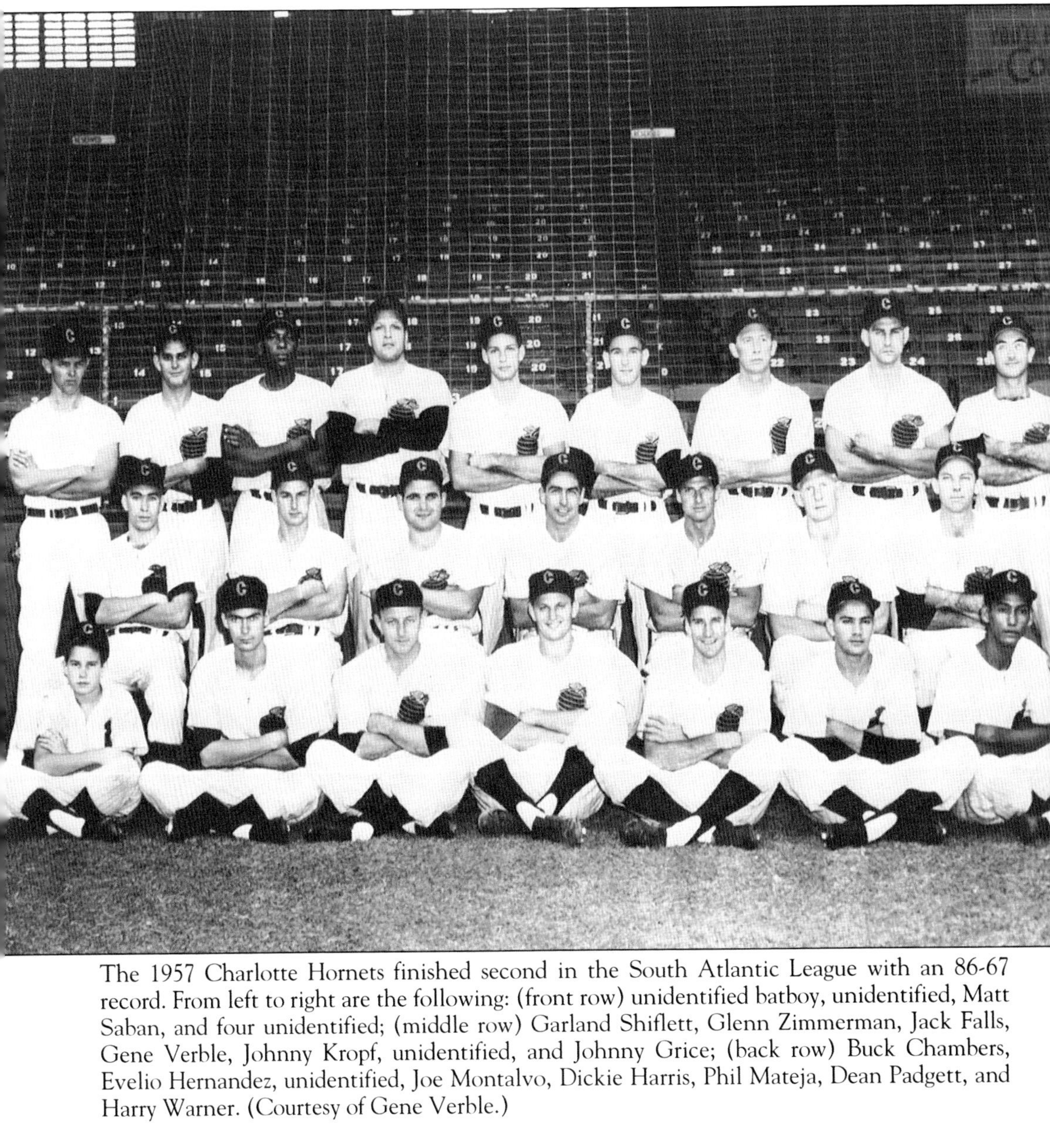

The 1957 Charlotte Hornets finished second in the South Atlantic League with an 86-67 record. From left to right are the following: (front row) unidentified batboy, unidentified, Matt Saban, and four unidentified; (middle row) Garland Shiflett, Glenn Zimmerman, Jack Falls, Gene Verble, Johnny Kropf, unidentified, and Johnny Grice; (back row) Buck Chambers, Evelio Hernandez, unidentified, Joe Montalvo, Dickie Harris, Phil Mateja, Dean Padgett, and Harry Warner. (Courtesy of Gene Verble.)

Five

BALLPARKS

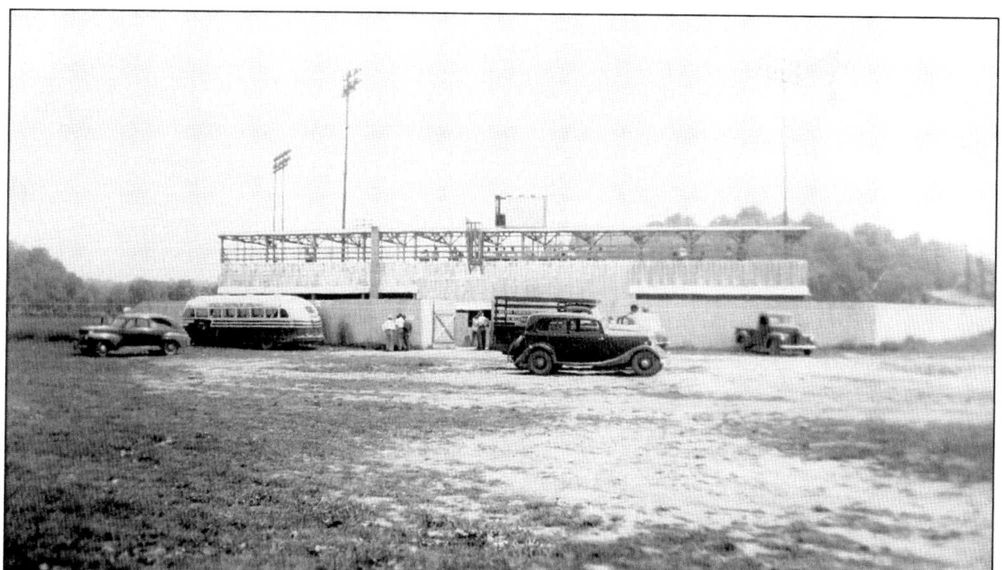

North Wilkesboro's Memorial Park was typical of the size ballpark that could be found in many Piedmont towns during the middle part of the 20th century. This park was home to the minor league North Wilkesboro Flashers from 1948 to 1950. (Courtesy of Worth Cuthbertson.)

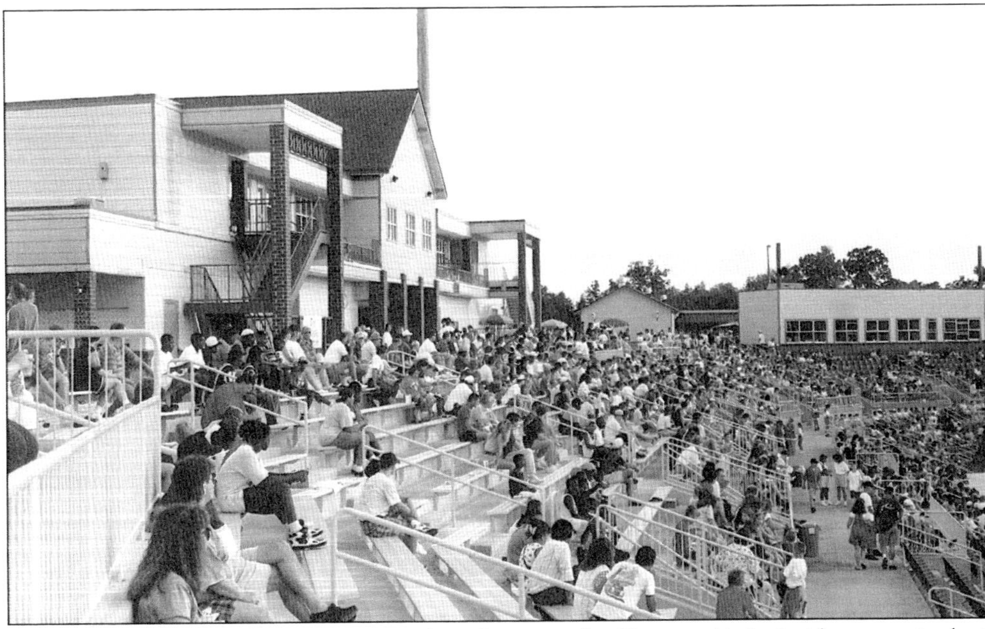

Fieldcrest-Cannon Stadium in Kannapolis is home to the Kannapolis Intimidators, a single-A affiliate of the Chicago White Sox in the South Atlantic League. Built in 1995, the 4,700-seat facility features many of the accommodations common at today's minor league ballparks including luxury suites, picnic areas, large concession stands, a playground for children and a souvenir store. (Photo by the author.)

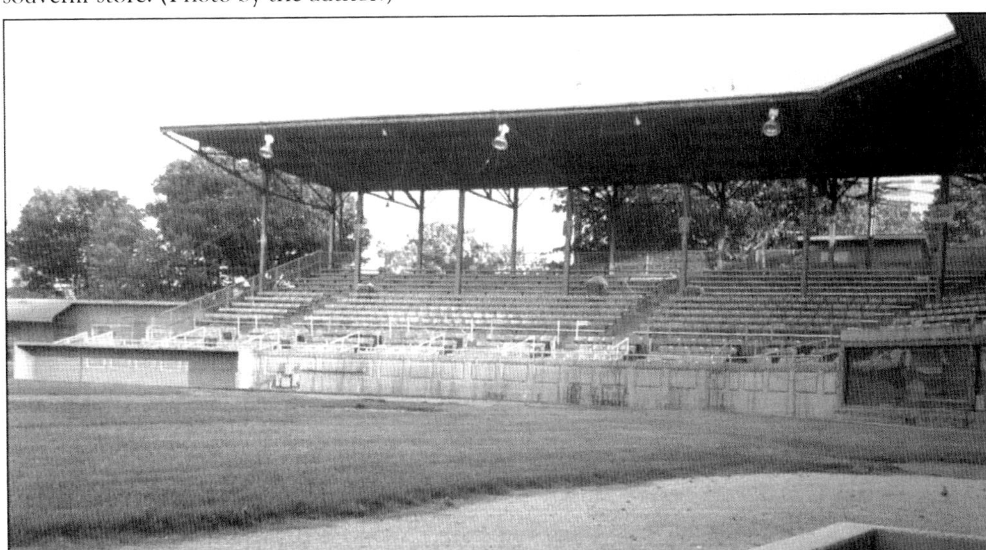

Durham Athletic Park, as seen from the visitors' dugout, was built in 1939 and is probably one of the most well-known minor league ballparks in the country. The Durham Bulls moved to a newer and bigger facility after the 1994 season but the venerable old park is still used by the Durham Braves, a team that plays collegiate summer baseball in the Coastal Plain League. (Photo by the author.)

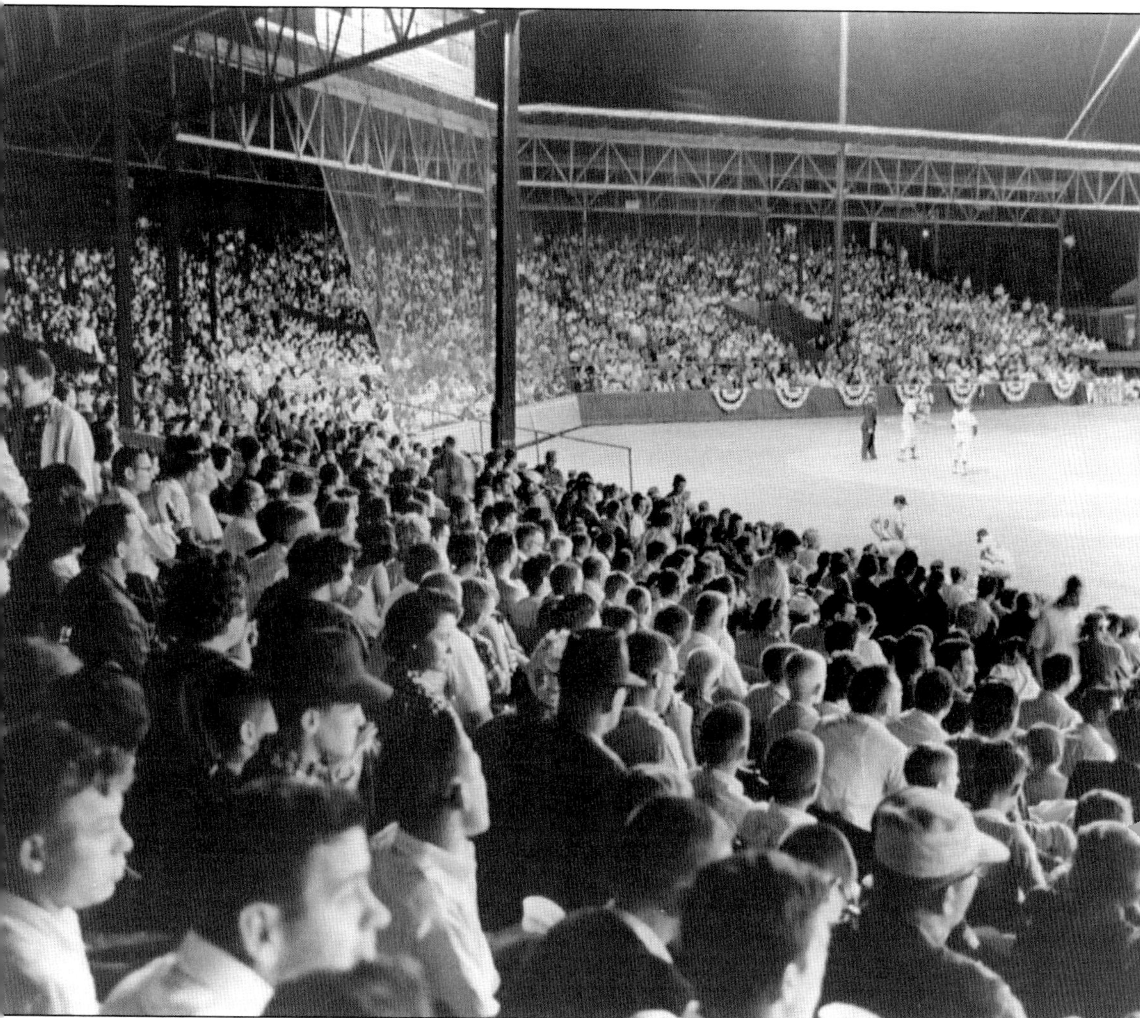

This photo shows the packed grandstand at Charlotte's Griffith Park, *c.* 1950. With a few exceptions, Charlotte's teams always drew well during their years as a Washington farm club and the Hornets even led the Tri-State League in attendance in 1951 and 1952. (Courtesy of Gene Verble.)

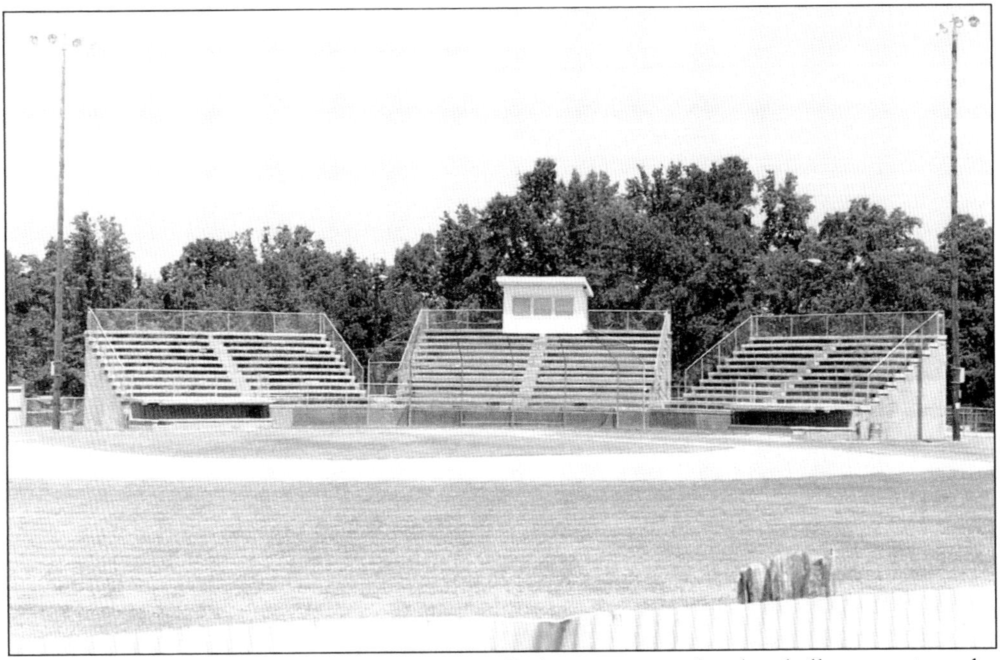

Finch Field on National Highway in Thomasville has seen countless baseball games since the late 1930s. Once the home of the professional High Point Thomasville Hi-Toms, the park is now used by Thomasville High School, the High Point Adult Men's League, and a new Hi-Toms team that plays in a summer league for top college players called the Coastal Plain League. The park has been upgraded somewhat since this photo was taken in the mid-1990s. (Photo by the author.)

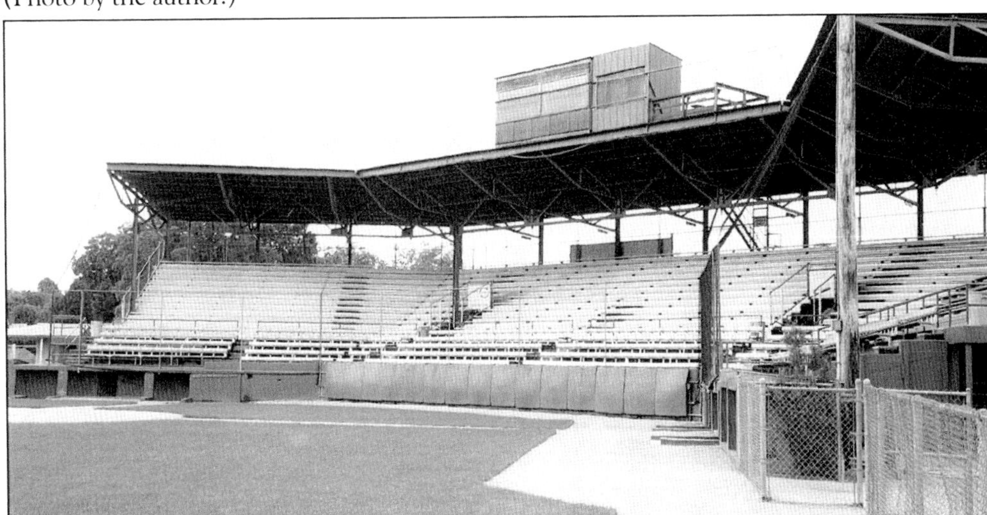

The home of the Appalachian League's Burlington Indians, Burlington Athletic Stadium has an interesting history. The grandstand was originally erected in Danville, Virginia but after several years of use the company that owned the land on which the ballpark sat wanted to develop it for other purposes. The city of Burlington, in need of a new ballpark, purchased the grandstand for $5,000, disassembled it, and relocated it to Burlington where it was rebuilt at Fairchild Park. (Photo by the author.)

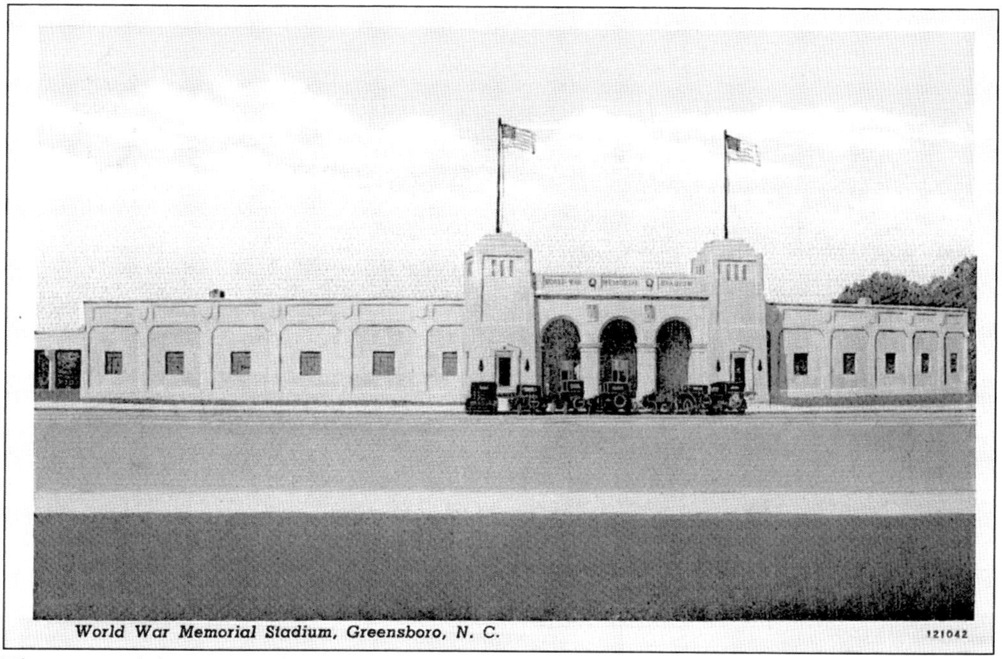

This postcard shows an early view of Greensboro's War Memorial Stadium. Built in 1926 at the corner of Yanceyville and Lindsay Streets in Greensboro, its original purpose was to serve as a football and track stadium but in the 1930s baseball began to be played there as well. Home to the Greensboro Bats of the South Atlantic League, the War Memorial is one of the oldest minor league ballparks still in use. (From the collection of the author.)

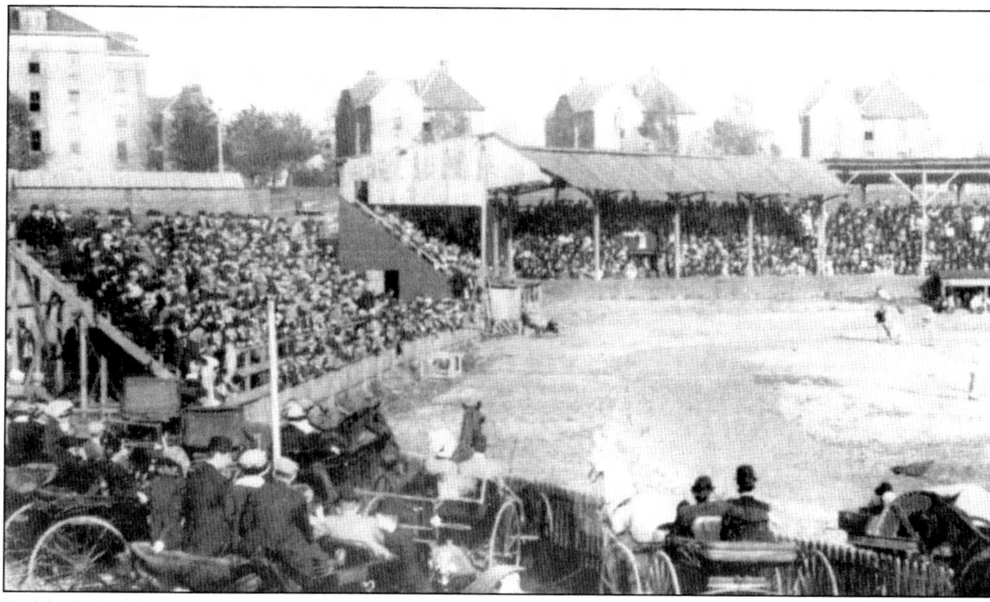

Riddick Field was used for both football and baseball in the early years of North Carolina A&M College (now North Carolina State University). This 1912 photo shows a packed house as fans turned out to watch the school's annual Easter Monday baseball game against Wake Forest College. The three identical buildings in the background are the first dormitories built on the campus. (Courtesy of the University Archives, North Carolina State University Libraries.)

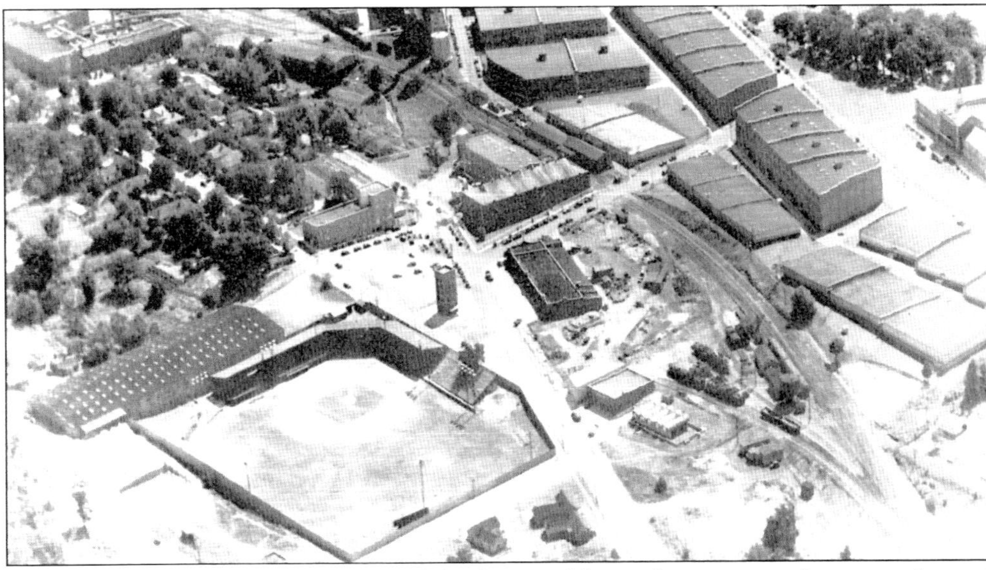

This aerial view of Durham's El Toro Park (and some of the city's numerous tobacco warehouses) was taken in the 1930s. The grandstand burned during the 1939 season but was rebuilt on the same site and renamed Durham Athletic Park. (Courtesy of Miles Wolff.)

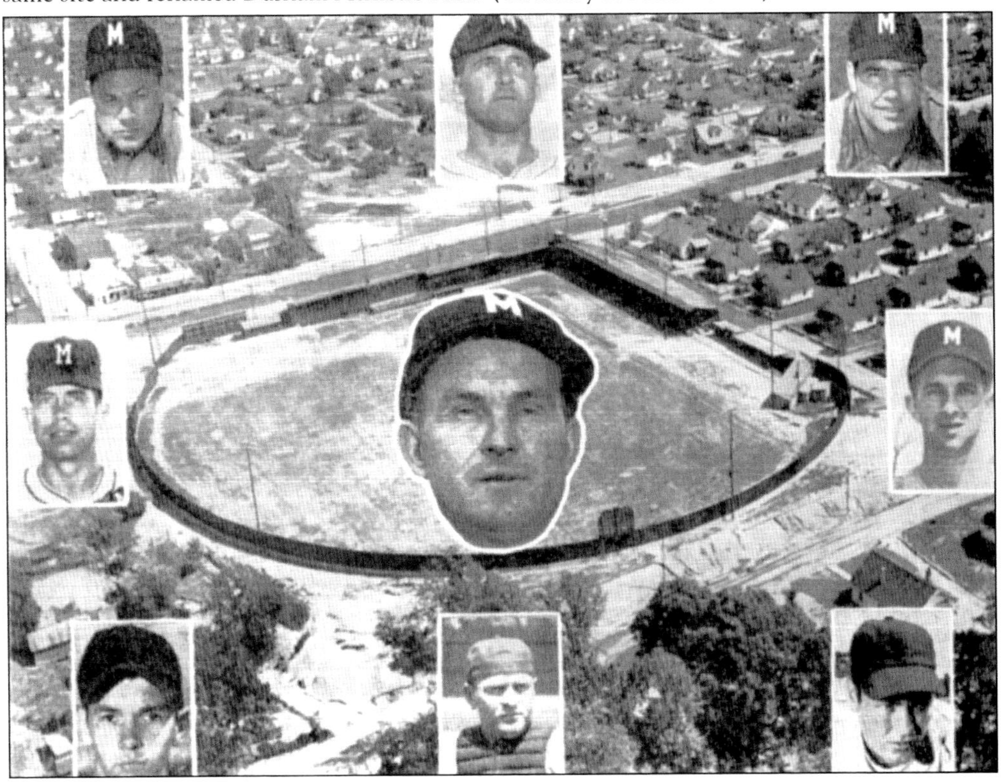

Moors Park, originally built and maintained by the local textile mill, was the home to the minor league Mooresville Moors from the mid-1930s through 1953. The site is still used today for baseball and softball but the grandstand no longer exists. This photo from the late 1940s features insets of manager Jim Mills and some of his top players. (Courtesy of Mac Lackey.)

Smithfield-Selma shortstop Pete Howard poses in the batter's box in front of the grandstand at Smithfield's Legion Park. The park, which had a reported seating capacity of 4,000, was used for high school and American Legion baseball before and after Smithfield's brief foray into professional baseball from 1946 to 1950. (Courtesy of Pete Howard.)

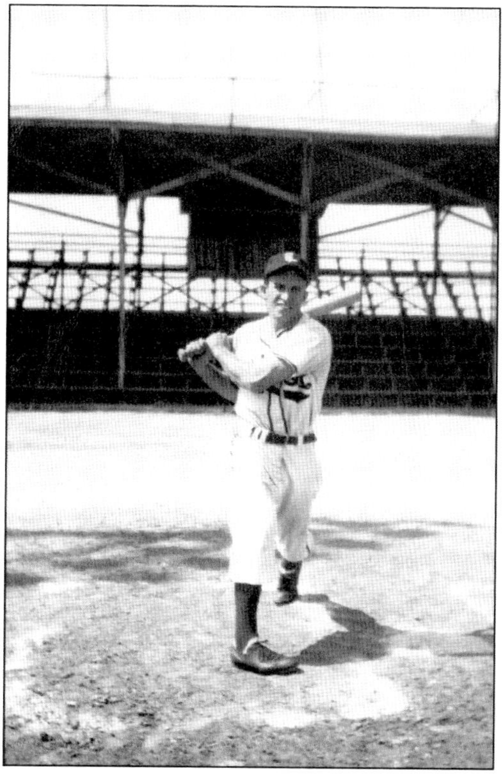

Unidentified scorekeepers and an announcer sit inside the press box at Finch Field, home of the High Point-Thomasville Hi-Toms, in this early 1950s photo. Built before World War II, Finch Field was the only home the Hi-Toms ever knew. The original grandstand burned in the 1980s but it was replaced with a smaller one and amateur play continues at the field to this day. (Courtesy of High Point Museum Archives.)

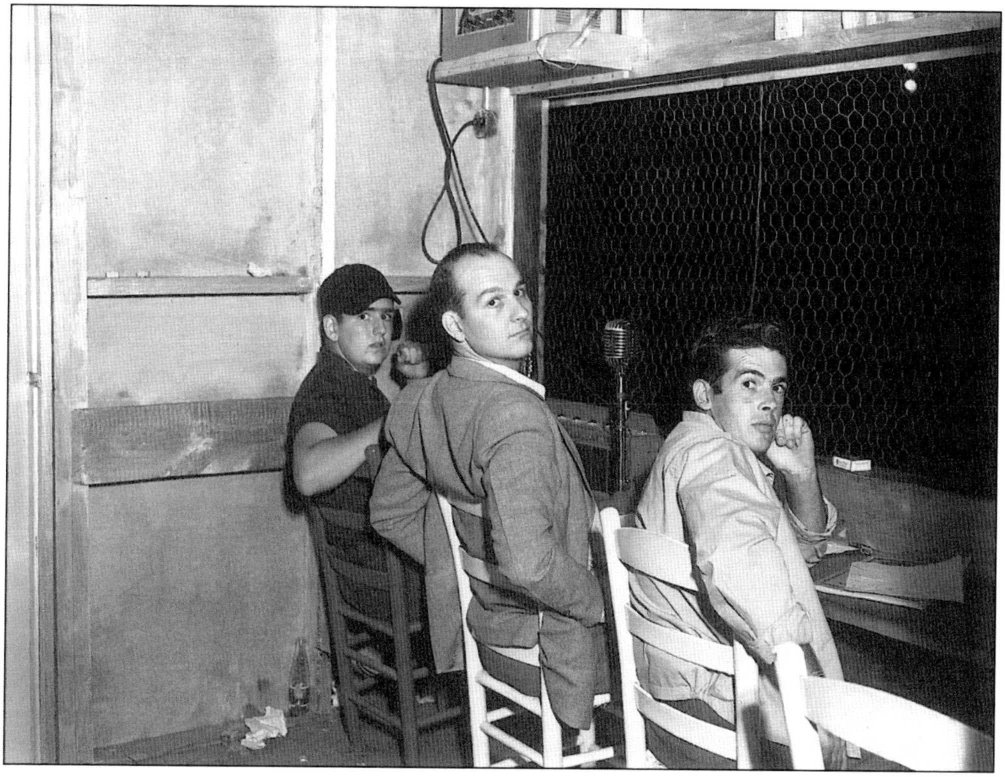

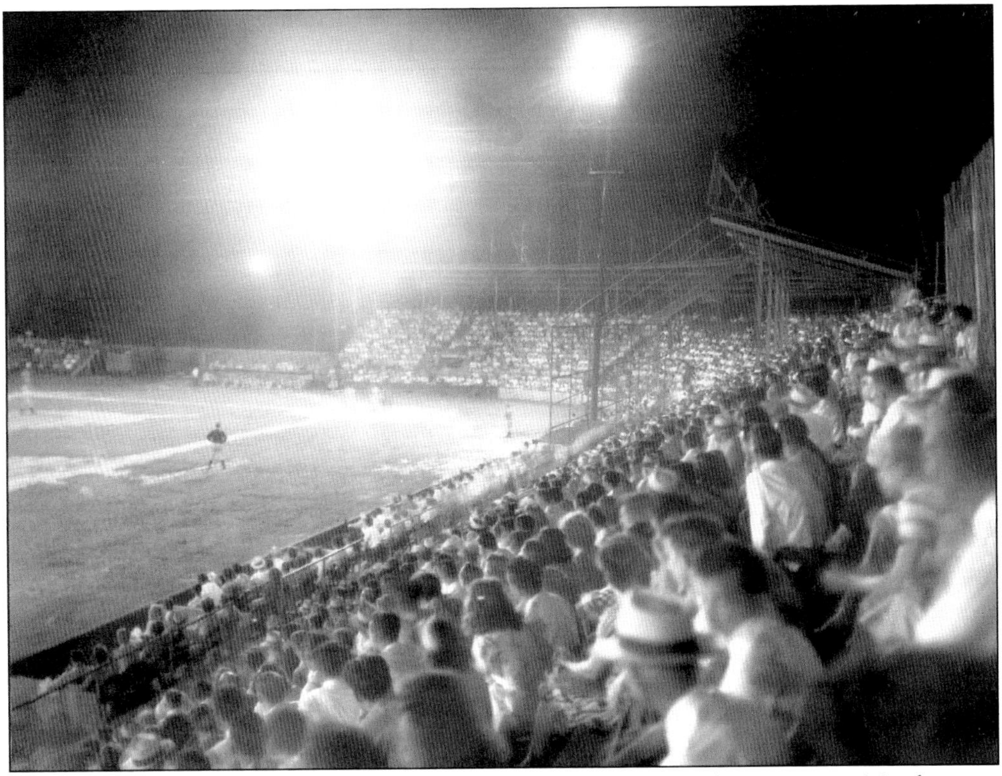

Built in 1939 with Works Progress Administration money, Raleigh's Devereux Meadow was home to the city's professional teams until minor league baseball left the city in the early 1970s. It was also used for countless amateur games and often those of North Carolina State University's baseball team. The park with the idyllic name came to a rather inglorious end as it was razed in the 1970s to make way for a parking lot to house the city's garbage truck fleet. (Courtesy of the North Carolina Department of Archives and History.)

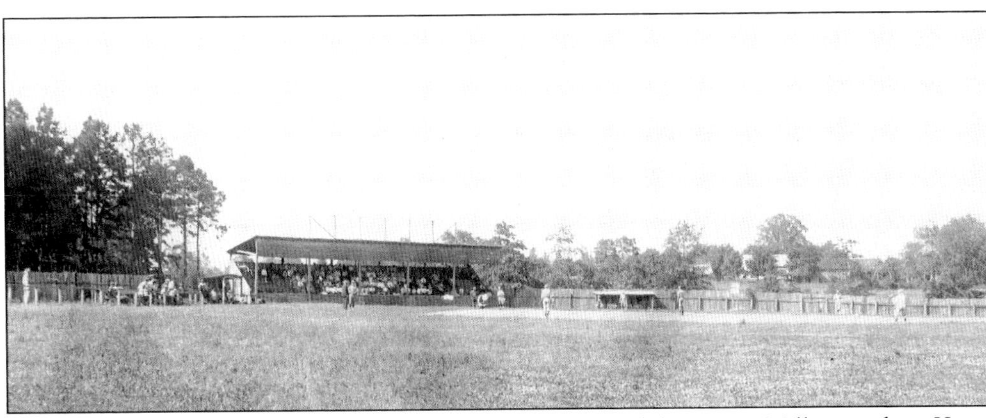

K.P. Lewis Ball Park in the town of Cooleemee was named for Erwin Mills president Kemp Plumber Lewis following renovations after the 1934 General Textile Strike. Lewis promised the mill workers that the ballpark would be improved if they would not go on strike and the workers agreed. An elementary school now sits on the site. (Courtesy of Cooleemee Textile Heritage Center Archives.)

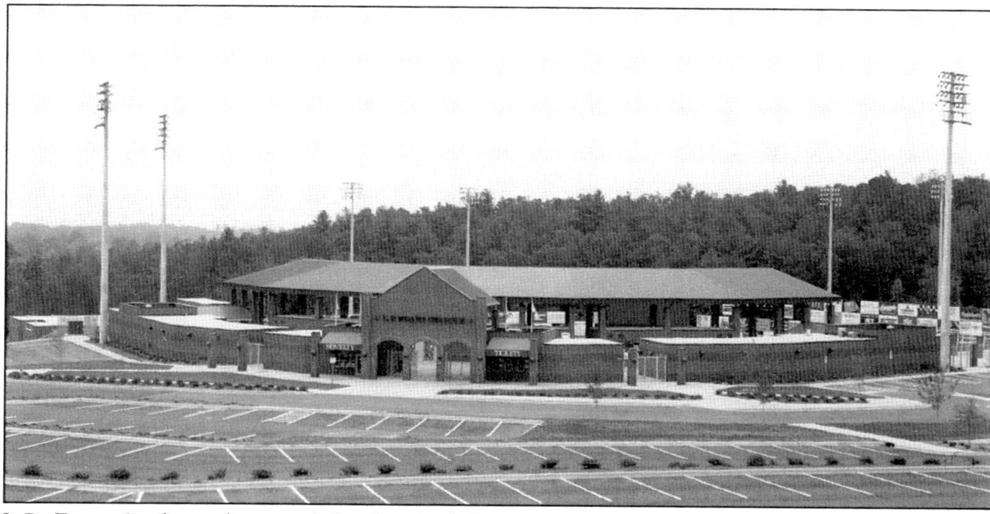

L.P. Frans Stadium, home of the South Atlantic League's Hickory Crawdads, has a seating capacity of 5,062. Named after the local Pepsi-Cola bottler who partially funded its construction, the ballpark opened in 1993. (Photo by the author.)

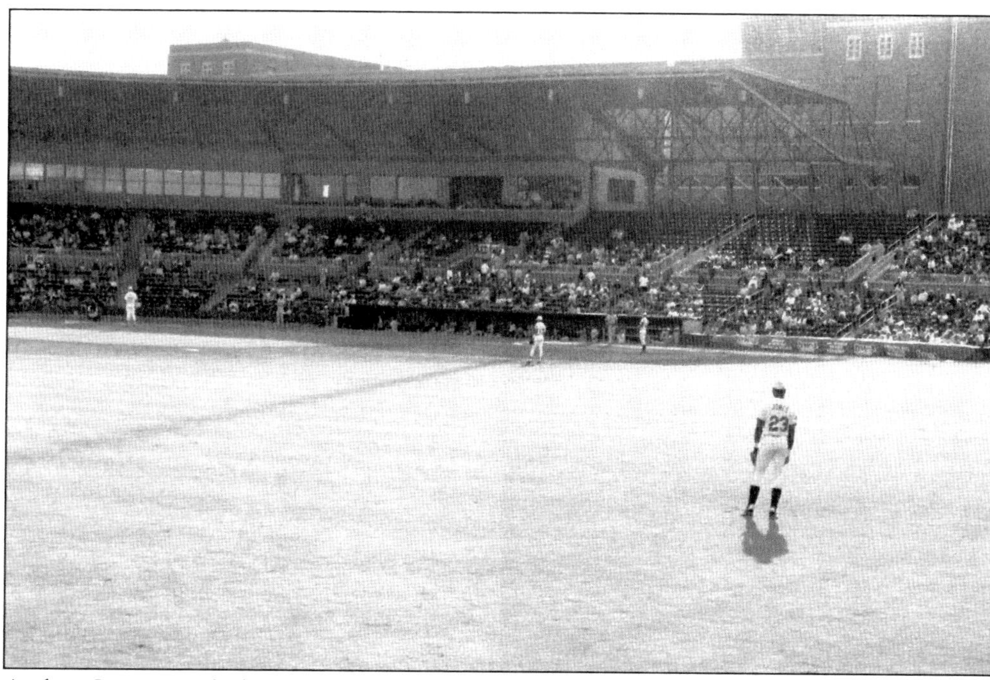

Andruw Jones patrols the outfield at Durham Bulls Athletic Park in this 1996 photo. When the Bulls outgrew their old home on the other side of downtown, they built this new $16-million, state-of-the-art park that opened in 1995. It was expanded to 10,000 seats in 1998 when the Bulls began playing in the AAA International League. (Photo by the author.)

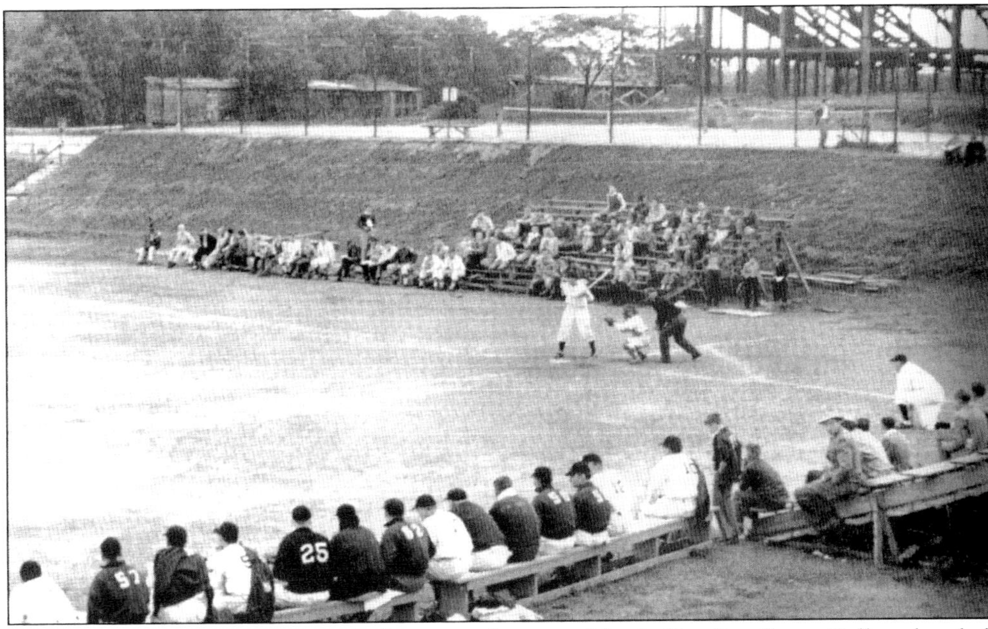

Doak Field, shown here in a 1946 photo, was home to North Carolina State College baseball for many seasons. Construction on Reynolds Coliseum, which can be seen in the background, had begun before the war but had been halted due to material shortages. The site of the baseball field is now a parking deck. (Courtesy of the University Archives, North Carolina State University Libraries.)

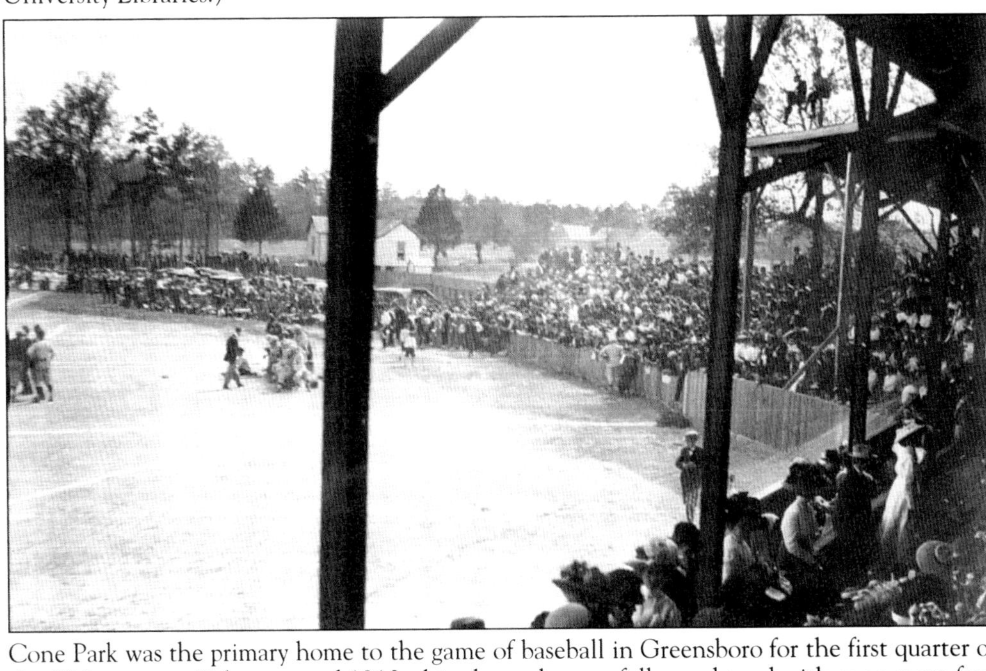

Cone Park was the primary home to the game of baseball in Greensboro for the first quarter of the 20th century. Taken around 1910, this photo shows a full grandstand with even more fans watching from their horse-drawn buggies down the right-field line. Greensboro's professional team moved out around 1930 but Cone Park remained in use for amateur baseball until it was torn down in the 1950s. (Courtesy of Greensboro Historical Museum Archives.)

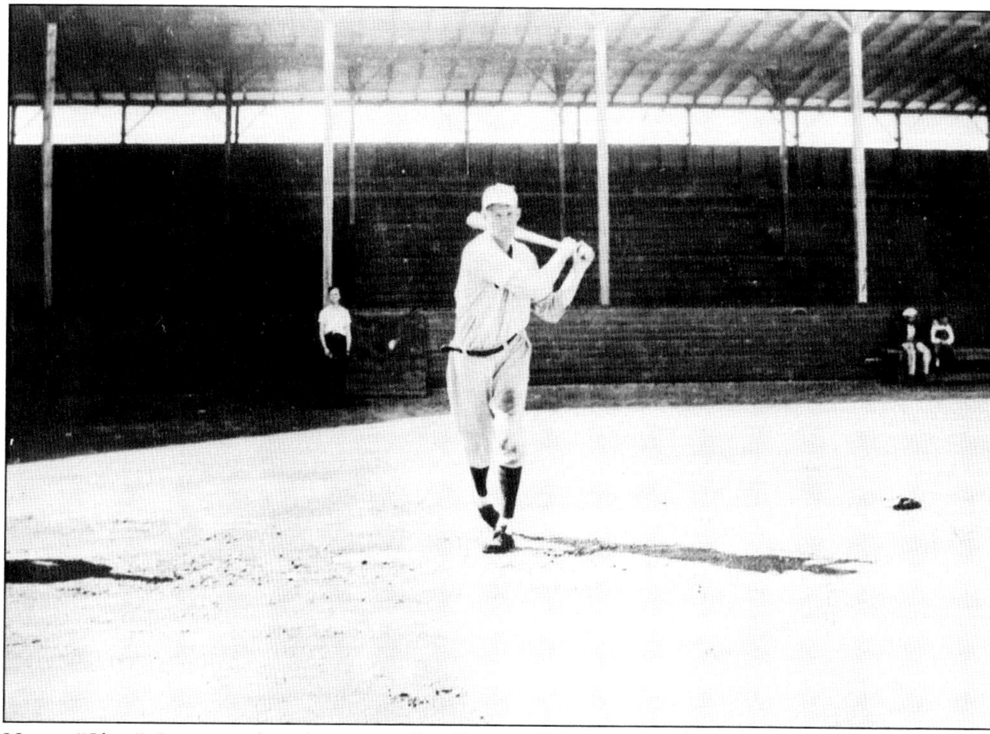

Harry "Slim" Ingram, first baseman for Concord's entry in the Carolina Textile League, practices his swing at Webb Field in 1935. The 1,200-seat grandstand was built behind Concord High School during the Depression with federal emergency relief money. (Courtesy of Hank Utley.)

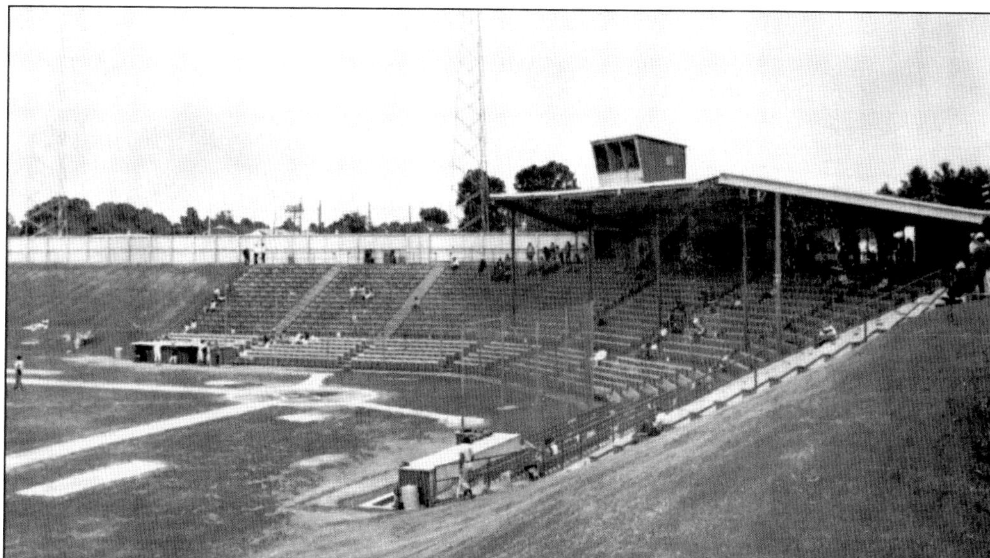

Winston-Salem's Ernie Shore Field opened in 1956 and was christened after the former Red Sox pitcher and area native of the same name. Parts of the ballpark, which is home to the Winston-Salem Warthogs of the Carolina League, were renovated in 1993 and the seating capacity is now 6,200. (Postcard from the collection of the author.)

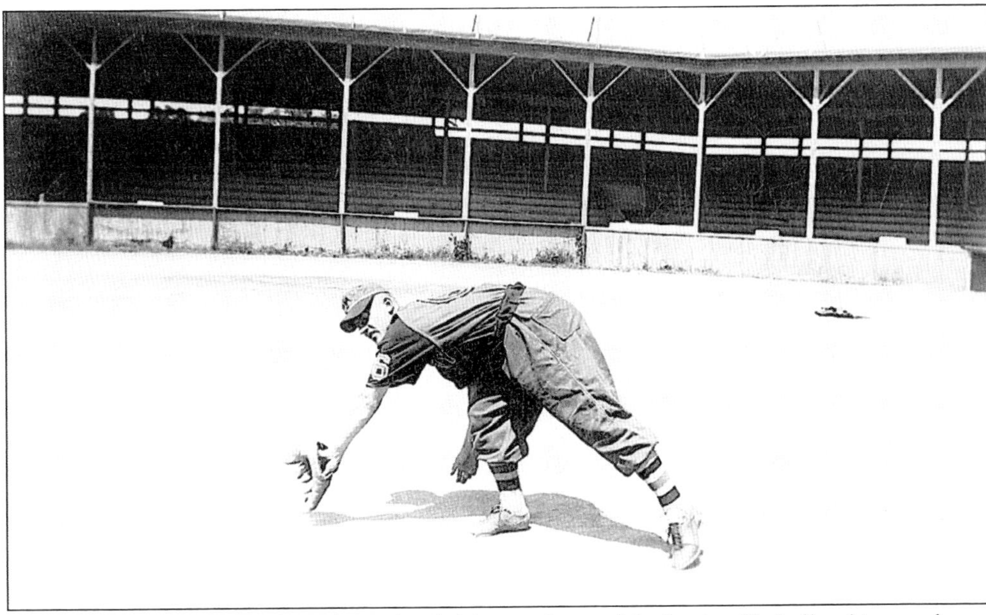

Second baseman Al Letrick works on his fielding in front of the Leaksville ballpark's grandstand in 1941. A very nice park when it was originally built in the 1930s, it probably had seating for around 1,500 fans. (Courtesy of Cotton Powell.)

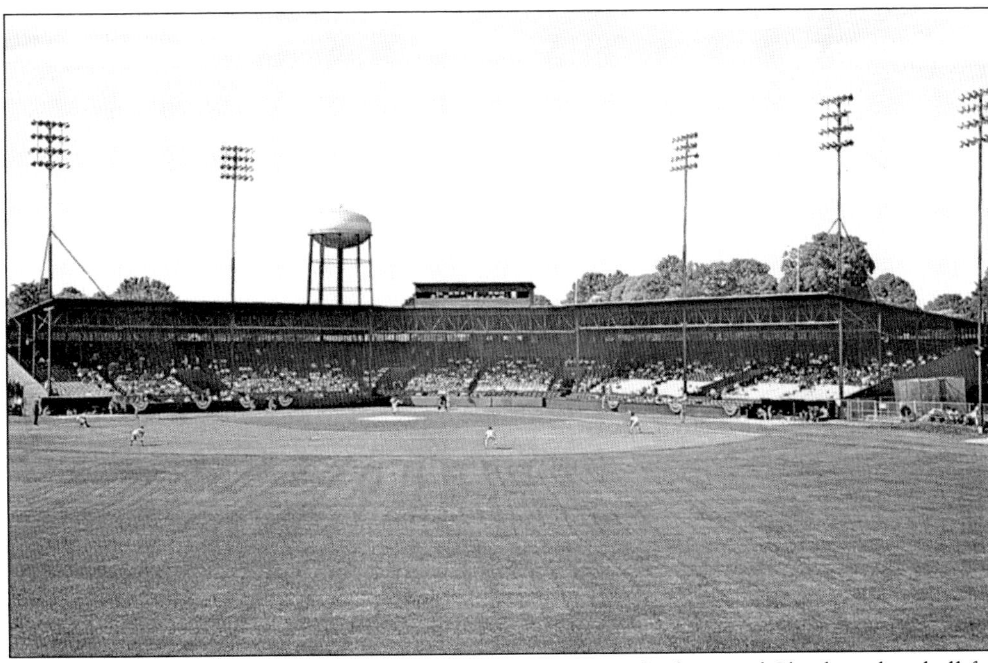

Griffith Park, which was located on Magnolia Avenue, was the home of Charlotte baseball for half a century. Built in 1940 by Clark Griffith, owner of the Washington Senators as well as the Charlotte Hornets, its construction cost $70,000. Renamed Crockett Park, it remained in use—despite a 1985 arson fire—until the late 1980s when Charlotte's team, then called the Knights, moved to the new 10,000-seat Knight's Castle. (Postcard from the collection of the author.)

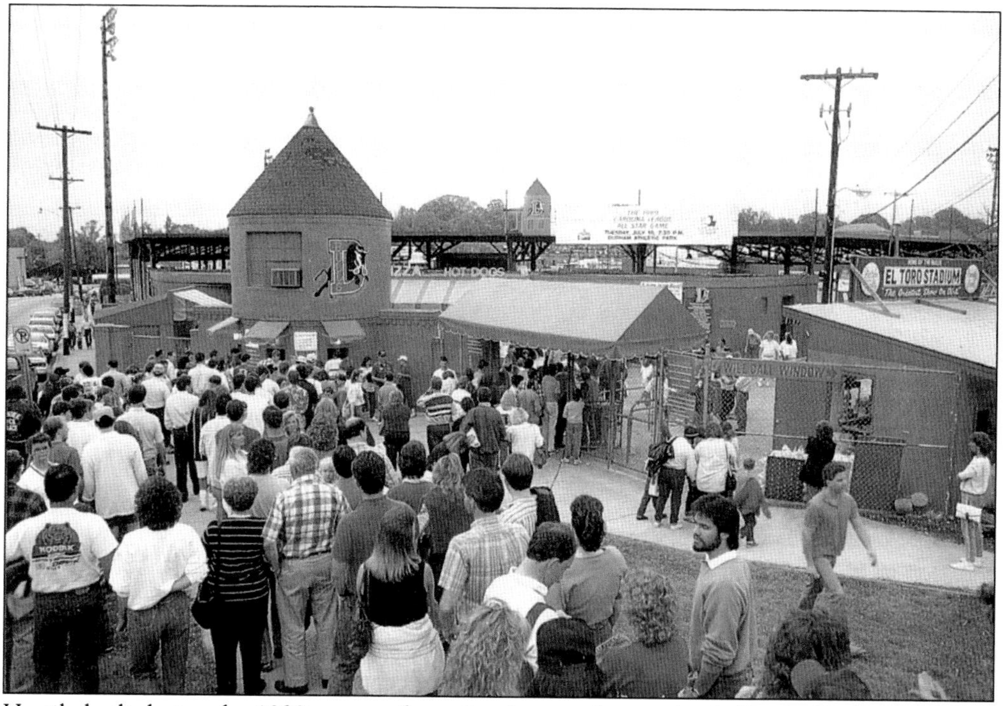

Hastily built during the 1939 season after a fire destroyed an earlier ballpark, Durham Athletic Park was home to the Bulls until 1994. After sitting empty for a few years the park was renovated in 1980 when a new Bulls team was formed and it was soon filled with record crowds. By the early 1990s, however, the park was outdated and did not have room to expand, so a new stadium was built on the other side of downtown Durham. (Postcard from the collection of the author.)

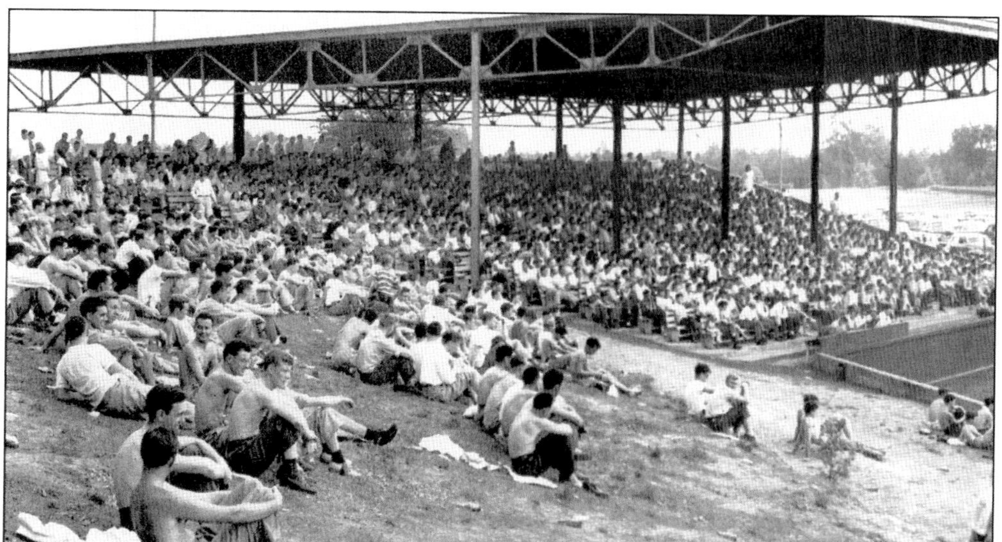

Jack Coombs Stadium has been home to Duke University baseball since it opened in 1931. Originally called Duke Park, the name was later changed to honor longtime Duke baseball coach Jack Coombs. This photo was taken in the late 1940s. (From the collection of the author.)

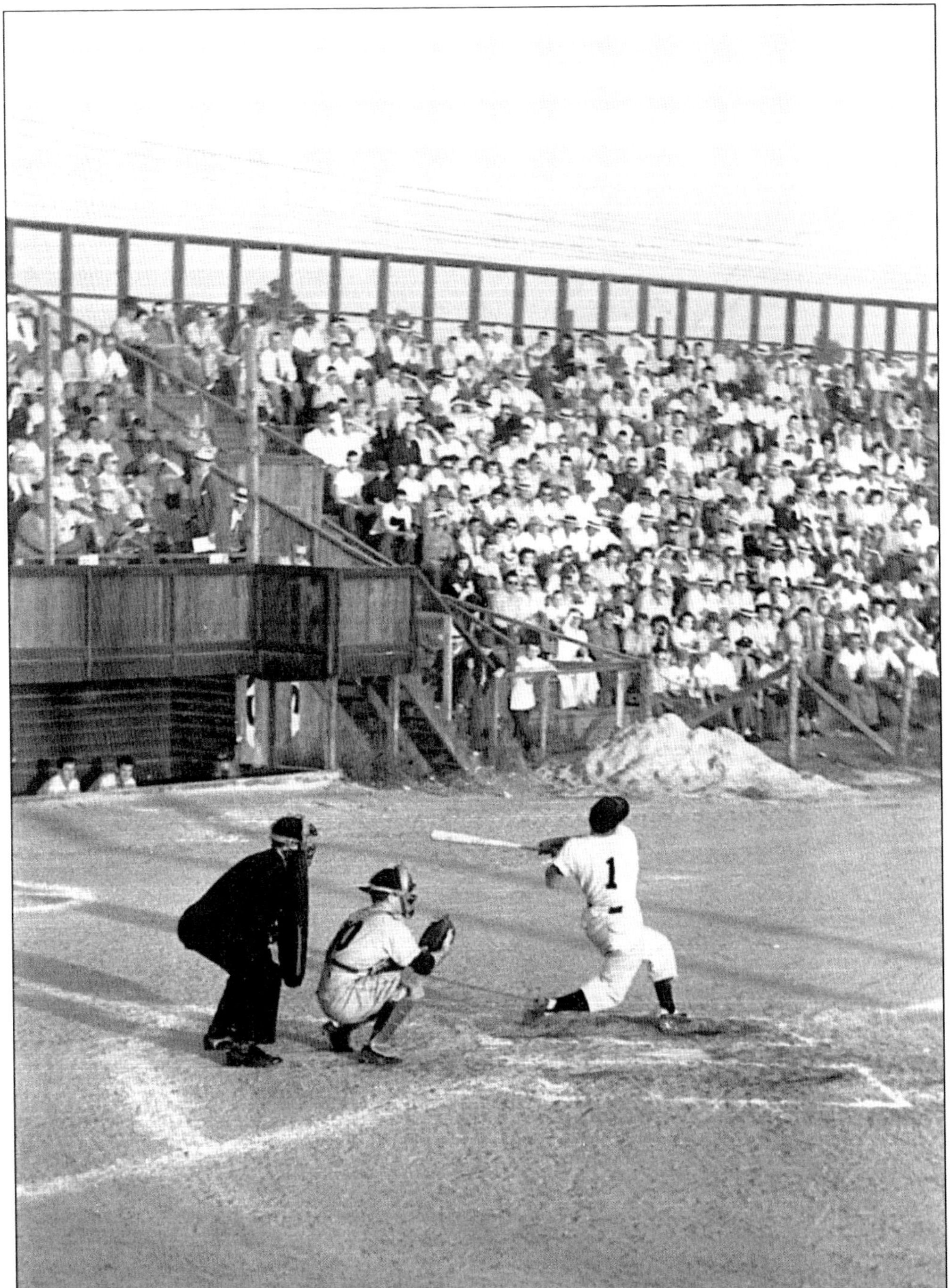

The Burlington Bees once used Elon College's ballpark as their home. This is Burlington shortstop Pete Howard batting before a sold out crowd in 1949. (Courtesy of Pete Howard.)